I0820232

THE AVIATOR

THE AVIATOR

A Biography of James R. McConnell, Lafayette Escadrille Fighter Pilot

Schiffer Military History
4880 Lower Valley Road
Atglen, PA 19310

Other Schiffer books on related subjects
The 147th Aero Squadron in World War I: A Training and Combat History of the "Who Said Rats" Squadron
Jack Ballard
978-0-7643-4400-8

British and American Aces of World War I: The Pictorial Record
Norman Franks
978-0-7643-2341-6

Library of Congress Control Number: 2025930654

Designed by Jack Chappell
Cover design by Danielle Farmer
Type set in Abril/Elza/Baskerville

ISBN: 978-0-7643-7030-4
ePub: 978-1-5073-0585-0

Printed in India
10 9 8 7 6 5 4 3 2 1

Published by Schiffer Publishing, Ltd.
4880 Lower Valley Road
Atglen, PA 19310
Phone: (610) 593-1777; Fax: (610) 593-2002
Email: Info@schifferbooks.com
Web: www.schifferbooks.com

CONTENTS

INTRODUCTION

The Aviator

On the campus of the University of Virginia (UVA) stands a 12-foot-high bronze statue of a winged Icarus, leaping into the sky. The inscription reads "Soaring like an eagle into new heavens of valor and devotion." Many of the students who walk past this statue have no idea that it honors a former UVA student, James Rogers McConnell. A few may know that McConnell was "some sort of a World War I hero." When Jim was a student at UVA, he would have been better known, but his fellow students would have been astonished to learn that Jim would become a hero. He was well liked, a good student, and a member of numerous clubs and fraternities, but a hero? The "Lord High Executioner" of the New York Club? The guy who marched around campus wearing a kilt and playing bagpipes? The "King of the Hot Foot Society," a club renowned for hijinks and beer parties? Jim's reputation around campus was such that when he dropped out of school in 1910, a rumor started that he was expelled for placing a bedpan on the head of a soon-to-be-unveiled statue of Thomas Jefferson. It seemed highly unlikely that this man would become a hero. His transformation from practical joker to hero would not begin until five years later.

At the beginning of 1915, war had been raging in Europe for five months. America would not enter that war for another two years. Many Americans sympathized with France and her allies, but they weren't willing to go to war. Some Americans sided with Germany and her allies, but they weren't willing to go to war either. People were slowly beginning to realize that this was not a "glorious" war, where thundering cavalry charges and cheering infantry chased a fast-fleeing enemy. Generals still dreamed of breaking through the enemy lines, but the war had become a stalemate, where soldiers huddled in muddy trenches while machine guns and artillery killed or maimed thousands each day. In five months, the war had already killed more soldiers than had died during all four years of the American Civil War, and there was no reason to think it would end soon. President Wilson urged Americans to be impartial in thought as well as in action. Most felt this was sound advice. Jim McConnell thought otherwise.

In January 1915, Jim sailed to France to join the American Ambulance Field Service. He was assigned to Pont-à-Mousson, a town that was within range of German rifles and was frequently bombarded by German artillery. He risked his life driving a rickety ambulance to first-aid stations immediately behind the front lines, picking up wounded soldiers and rushing them to the nearest field hospital. During the day he drove through sections of road that were actively shelled by the enemy. At night he had to drive without lights, picking his way past the marching soldiers and supply convoys that used the cover of darkness to hide the logistical lifeline that supported the war. They all prayed the Germans wouldn't choose that moment to blindly open fire on the road, hoping to catch one of the nighttime convoys.

When the Germans shelled Pont-à-Mousson, the American ambulance drivers had an additional job. Picking up dead and wounded civilians and carrying them to a hospital or to the morgue. French civilians idolized the American volunteers. French soldiers thanked them profusely for their services. Jim earned the Croix de Guerre (Cross of War) for his bravery in picking up wounded civilians under heavy shellfire. But still, he felt he was not doing enough. He clearly saw the horrors of modern warfare, but as he watched the French soldiers march bravely into battle, and as he hauled their mangled bodies to the hospital afterward, he felt he should be doing more. He enlisted in the French Foreign Legion and became a fighter pilot.

Jim's move to the Air Service coincided with the birth of combat aviation. As a rookie, he was thrown into the Battle of Verdun, a monstrous battle that saw the first use of massed airpower. For the first time, fighter planes flew together in squadrons, trying to shoot down the enemy's observation and bombing planes. To succeed, they had to battle squadrons of the enemy's fighter planes. The air war was intense, deadly, and, in the days of highly flammable airplanes and no parachutes, terrifying. Jim flew with a group of volunteer American pilots known as the Lafayette Escadrille, a group that achieved worldwide fame and set the stage for the Flying Tigers of World War II. Amazingly, Jim survived his baptism of fire at Verdun and lived to fly over the Battle of the Somme and other major conflicts.

Jim was also an exceptionally talented author. Although writing is not normally considered a heroic endeavor (present company excepted), the articles and the book he published during the war had a significant impact on America's attitude toward the conflict. Jim's articles about his experience as an ambulance driver were published in some of the most widely read magazines of the day. One article was so popular that former president Teddy Roosevelt wrote a foreword, praising Jim and his fellow volunteers. By the time the US entered the war, over 3,500 Americans had followed Jim's example and volunteered to drive ambulances.[1] His articles and his bestselling book *Flying for France* also grabbed the attention of thousands of Americans. His book went to press shortly before the US entered the war. There's no way to tell how many of the thousands of Americans who volunteered for the US Air Service were influenced by his book, but the book and the articles that preceded it certainly excited a public already entranced by the air war. The book went into its second printing within a year and is still considered a classic today. (As a sidenote, it's surprising how many World War 1 ambulance drivers went on to become famous writers. E. E. Cummings, John Dos Passos, Archibald McLeish, Charles Nordhoff, and of course Ernest Hemingway. Hemingway may have gained more fame as a writer than McConnell, but McConnell was a better ambulance driver.)

With all this in Jim's favor, why then was it unlikely he would become a hero? To begin with, he showed no signs of greatness before the war. The son of a prominent Chicago lawyer and business tycoon, Jim grew up in the shadow of his father. He had a privileged childhood. He attended private schools, spent summers touring France with his mother, and was given a new car when he was fourteen. His reputation at the University of Virginia has already been described. While the rumor that he was expelled is probably untrue, the "Hot Foot Society" was permanently banned from the university the year after McConnell left.[2]

When World War I began in August 1914, several Americans immediately volunteered to fight for France. Kiffin Rockwell, who would later become one of Jim's friends and fellow pilots, announced his intention to fight for France the day *before* war was declared. He caught the first available ship to Europe and joined the French Foreign Legion upon arrival. There he met other Americans who shared his conviction that this was not just a war between European countries; it was a battle to save all humanity. Jim McConnell had no such conviction, at least not at that time. He was working in a small town in North Carolina when the war broke out, writing pamphlets for the local board of trade and handling publicity for a tiny railroad. Jim's decision to go to France and drive an ambulance was based more on a quest for adventure and on boredom in his current job than on a dedication to a cause. These are not the earmarks of a hero.

Driving an ambulance changed Jim. His dedication to France grew as he saw the ordeals endured by her soldiers, and the destruction suffered by her civilians. His decision to become a pilot was based on his growing commitment to France, not on a desire for adventure. Flying definitely was an adventure at that time, since it was something most people had never experienced. It was the newest, most technically advanced form of warfare, and the sight of airplanes battling in the clear blue sky stood in sharp contrast to the grim horrors of trench warfare. However, Jim's letters make it clear that he was motivated by a desire to take a more active role in the defense of France. The romance of flying undoubtedly influenced his decision, but it wasn't the main reason he enlisted. In one of his letters, he worried that flying would become "monotonous once the novelty wears off."[3]

There has always been a tendency to romanticize World War I aviation. In the popular imagination, a World War I pilot is always a fighter pilot, and probably an ace as well. He is a carefree, cocksure "knight of the air," jousting with a chivalrous opponent against a background of fluffy white clouds. And, of course, the pilots we visualize are always victorious. We forget that for every ace, there were at least five pilots who weren't so fortunate.

In reality, World War I aerial combat was a deadly occupation that subjected pilots to enormous physical and emotional strain. By the time Jim entered the war, much of the flying was done at altitudes above 12,000 feet, where the cold was debilitating and pilots struggled to get enough oxygen to breathe. Posttraumatic stress disorder was not recognized as a medical condition at the time, but the nightmares, personality changes, and aged appearance of pilots after a few months of air combat were commonly observed. Historian Steve Ruffin wrote an insightful series of articles about the physical and mental effects of early combat flying.[4] His articles were aptly subtitled "Rx for Misery."

One of McConnell's fellow pilots in the Lafayette Escadrille, Ted Parsons, was unusually candid in his memoirs. He freely admitted to being scared during patrols. He described leaning against his plane after he landed, trying to look casual, so people wouldn't see that his legs were too wobbly for him to walk. He described the predicament of the Lafayette pilots this way:

> None of us had any real idea of what we were getting into. We had hold of the bear's tail and no one to help us let go. With few exceptions, I believe most of us would have welcomed an opportunity to bow out gracefully. In fact, some, after they'd awakened to what they'd let themselves in for, stole away on silent feet before they'd heard any guns fired in anger, perhaps not so gracefully or honorably, but most wisely. While there was some slight criticism at the time, it may well be they were the smart ones after all.[5]

Two hundred sixty-nine Americans volunteered to fly for France. Many were disqualified medically or failed to qualify as aviators, but 179 of them actually made it to the front.[6] This was far more than could serve in the Lafayette Escadrille, a single squadron, so most flew with regular French units and were referred to as the "Lafayette Flying Corps." All of them faced great danger. Of the 179 who made it to the front, fifty-one were killed in combat, six died in accidents, five died of illness, fifteen were taken prisoner, and nineteen were wounded in combat.[7] That's more than a 50 percent casualty rate. One way some pilots coped with these odds was to convince themselves that it couldn't happen to them. They were too good, or too lucky, to get shot down. Talismans and routines to ensure luck were common, but so was the conviction that, one on one, they could dominate any enemy they encountered. I once asked a pilot who flew F-4 Phantoms in Vietnam about the stereotype of a fighter pilot ego. He told me, "When you're facing the odds those guys faced, you've got to have gonads the size of basketballs or you'd never climb into the cockpit."

Jim McConnell was different. He had no illusion that it couldn't happen to him. He commented on several occasions that he didn't think he was an outstanding pilot. He was obviously a very good pilot, or he never could have survived in the skies over Verdun, but he didn't have the cocksure ego that said it couldn't happen to him. When he wrote about flying, there was no bravado. He freely admitted to making mistakes, and he knew he was damned lucky to have survived them.

One of the bravest things he ever did, and on the basis of Ted Parsons's quote one of the most *unlikely* things, was to keep flying. Unlike his fellow pilots, Jim McConnell had more than one opportunity to bow out gracefully. No one would have criticized him, and no one would have thought less of him if he had stopped flying, but he didn't.

My father-in-law, who survived multiple amphibious landings in the Pacific during World War II, once told me that in the heat of combat, you're not fighting for your country. You're not fighting for your family. You're fighting for your buddies. You don't want to let your buddies down. Jim McConnell didn't let his buddies down. He kept flying. He was committed to France, and he wanted to drive the Germans back to their own soil, but I firmly believe that the main reason he didn't quit was because he didn't want to desert his buddies. And that makes him a hero in my book.

Thomas Carlyle said, "No one should try to write a biography who cannot put himself into the skull of the subject and see the world as the other saw it." I have tried to put myself "into the skull" of Jim McConnell as I wrote this book. I think it is also important for readers of this book to try to see the world as Jim saw it. With the benefit of hindsight, it's easy to look at World War I as a senseless waste of human life. A pointless struggle that only succeeded in setting the stage for an even-bigger war. That's not the way Jim and his fellow volunteers saw it. They saw the atrocities in Belgium, the shelling of historic cathedrals in France, and the torpedoing of unarmed passenger ships as proof that they were fighting the greatest evil the world had ever known. They felt they truly were fighting "for all humanity." They had no way of knowing that the politicians would bungle the victory they won with their sacrifices.

Novelist and fellow ambulance driver Henry Sydnor Harrison summed up Jim's wartime experiences as follows:

> If he had begun, like most of the young volunteers, largely in the sense of adventurousness, he was more and more recruited to the idea of a cause. He came to feel first a genuine devotion; then, presently, a summons. . . . McConnell, I should say, was the last man in the world to ever think of himself in large terms. But I make no apology for saying here that, for what he and his fellows have done, their country is their debtor.[8]

ONE

Son of a Judge

Jim was not the first McConnell to voluntarily go to war. His MacConnell ancestors backed Bonnie Prince Charles when the prince decided to invade England from Scotland in 1745. The invasion was not a rousing success. Some of Jim's ancestors fled to Ireland, becoming McConnells after the invasion, as British forces chased the supporters of Prince Charles. Jim's great-great-grandfather was one who was caught, sold into indentured servitude, and sent to America. During the Revolutionary War, he made gunpowder for the Americans to use against the British forces, a task that no doubt gave him great satisfaction.[1]

Jim's grandfather John R. McConnell was a lawyer in Springfield, Illinois, who knew Abraham Lincoln personally. When the Civil War erupted, he joined the 3rd Illinois Volunteer Cavalry as a captain. By the end of the war, he had been promoted to brigadier general.[2]

Jim was born on March 14, 1887.[3] His mother was Sarah Rogers McConnell, and his father was Samuel Parsons McConnell. At the time, he had a sister, Julia, who was ten years older than he was, and a brother, Rogers, who was nine years older.

His father was a lawyer who would soon be elected the circuit judge for Cook County, Illinois. He was an imposing man who was active in Illinois politics and business as well as in the legal profession. Although he served on the bench for only six years, he would be referred to as "Judge" McConnell for the rest of his life. The McConnell family life clearly revolved around Judge McConnell's activities, and it would be fair to say that Jim McConnell grew up in his father's shadow.

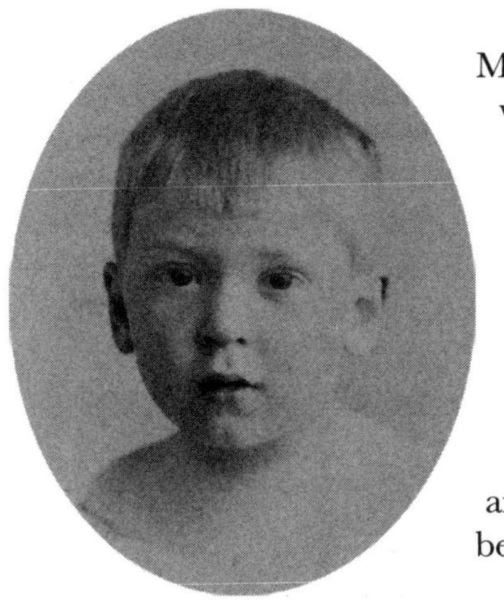

Jim McConnell baby photo. *NASM*

Judge Samuel P. McConnell. *Successful American*

One of the many cases that thrust Judge McConnell into the public limelight was his work to obtain pardons for men convicted of the deaths of seven policemen in the Chicago Haymarket Square "riot." Police responded to a false report that violence had broken out at a labor rally being held in Haymarket Square. Someone threw a bomb into the responding police squadron. The bomb thrower was never identified or caught. Eight men were arrested and charged with inciting the killing because they had written articles or given speeches that denounced capitalism, condemned the current structure of society, and vilified the police. Only one of the men was known to have even attended the rally that sparked the incident, and there was no evidence linking any of them to the bombing. At the trial, the presiding judge said that anarchy itself was on trial, and he instructed the jurors that it was not necessary to prove there was any connection between the accused and the unknown bomber. Newspapers of the day strongly supported that view, publishing stories about the dire threat posed by anarchists. The term "disinformation" was not in vogue at the time, but the men were essentially charged for providing disinformation that was harmful to society and encouraged the bomber. All eight men were found guilty. Seven were sentenced to be hanged, and one received a thirty-five-year prison sentence.[4]

Judge McConnell had no official involvement in this trial, but he was outraged by the actions of the presiding judge and the resulting miscarriage of justice. He persuaded the Illinois governor to pardon the men, but not before four of the men had been hanged and one committed suicide in prison. The pardon was controversial at the time, since there was still widespread fear of anarchists. The pardon was still being condemned several years later by Theodore Roosevelt, then a candidate for vice president, who said the governor's hands were "dyed in blood."

Jim, age eleven. *NASM*

In 1880, Eleanor McConnell was born, giving Jim a younger sister. Then tragedy struck. Jim's older brother, Rogers, died of a fever. Their mother, Sarah, was overcome with grief. For a while she became a "nervous invalid," leaving the care of Jim and Eleanor to their older sister, Julia.[5] Julia was thirteen at the time. Jim was three.

Sarah eventually recovered her health, but as often happens after the death of a child, the death of Rogers created a rift in her marriage. The McConnells did not immediately divorce, but their marriage was never the same. Sarah remained close to her surviving children and took them on extended trips to France. Jim learned to speak French during these trips, and he learned to admire the French people.[6]

During this same period, Jim developed what was then called "muscular rheumatism." This was an indefinite term for chronic muscle or joint pain and inflammation. This diagnosis could refer to arthritis, bursitis, fibromyalgia, ankylosing spondylitis, or other conditions causing chronic pain. Ankylosing spondylitis is a relatively rare condition, but it's a lifelong problem that can begin in childhood and flare up again in adults. Jim suffered back problems later in life, which he attributed to a recurrence of his rheumatism.[7]

In October 1894, Judge McConnell announced he was leaving the bench, effective immediately.[8] The reason he gave for resigning was that he wanted the greater freedom and remuneration he could enjoy as a private attorney. The most important client he represented in this role was George Fuller.

George Fuller was an architect and an early proponent of using steel in building construction, a practice that was considered controversial at the time. In 1882 he formed the George A. Fuller Company to put his ideas into practice. The company was more than just an architectural firm; it handled all aspects of construction, making it one of the first general contractors. In 1889 the company built the Tacoma Building in Chicago, the first modern skyscraper. The concept of using a steel framework to support the weight of the building proved its worth, and George Fuller soon became a multimillionaire.

Mr. Fuller must have been impressed with Judge McConnell, since he asked him to take charge of the New York City office of the company. He had opened the office in 1896, after New York City updated its building codes to allow steel-framework buildings, and there seemed to be an unlimited opportunity to build skyscrapers in New York. In May 1900, the McConnells announced they would leave Chicago and take up residence in New York.[9] Mrs. McConnell and her two daughters spent the fall and winter in France. Jim McConnell, now thirteen, was sent to the private Morristown School (now Morristown Beard School) in Morristown, New Jersey.

Judge McConnell barely had time to get settled in his new job before the job changed dramatically. George A. Fuller, his mentor and the president of the company, died on December 14, 1900.[10] Fuller's son-in-law, Harry S. Black, inherited the company. Black reorganized the company with a stock capital of $20,000,000, which made it the largest construction company in the world.[11] The new company became known as the United States Realty and Construction Company, headed by Black, while Judge McConnell headed the Fuller Company, a wholly owned subsidiary that managed the construction end of the business. One of the projects described in the announcement of the new company was "a twenty-story office structure on the flatiron at Broadway and Twenty-third street." Originally called the Fuller Building, this landmark would become known as the Flatiron Building.

The move to New York did not help the McConnell's failing marriage. They divorced, and in 1902 Judge McConnell married Mayo Methot. Various sources have described her as a "domestic servant," a "French governess," and the former wife of actor Humphrey Bogart. She was actually the aunt of Bogart's first wife,[12] also named Mayo Methot, although *that* Mayo hadn't yet been born when *this* Mayo married Judge McConnell. It's also doubtful that she ever worked as a servant, since she was a trained actress who had studied under actor/manager Richard Mansfield. She was the daughter of Minnie Methot, an internationally successful singer in comic operas. Judge McConnell was fifty-three when they married, and Mayo was twenty-two.

That same year, Jim McConnell made headlines for the first, but certainly not the last, time in his life. Jim's mother and sister were spending the summer in Highland Park, near Chicago.[13] Jim, who was then fifteen, and a seventeen-year-old friend named George Garrett drove from New York to join them.[14] This was an amazing adventure in 1902. There were no major highways. If you wanted to travel from one city to another, you took a train. Country roads were primarily unnamed, unmarked, dirt trails that wandered from one town to the next. There were no road maps. A brand-new publication, *The Official Automobile Blue Book*, gave motorists turn-by-turn directions to go from one town to another. One of the few "long distance" routes covered by the 1901 edition gave instructions on driving from Albany to Buffalo. These instructions included the following:

> Turn left, cross canal, and turn right on the street south of the canal. Where street crosses canal, turn left after crossing and ride to East Palmyra; turn left and keep alongside of railroad about four miles, then turn left across railroad to Palmyra.[15]

The roads on this section of the trip were described as "fair to poor" gravel and sand. Unfortunately for Jim, the *Blue Book* covered only a few metropolitan areas in eastern states. None were farther west than Buffalo.[16] He and George had to rely on directions from strangers. They often found themselves mired up to the axles in mud, since it rained twenty-eight out of the thirty-three days they were on the road. On their best day, they made 100 miles in nine hours.

On the basis of family and newspaper photos, the car they drove was a curved-dash Oldsmobile Model R. Jim had gotten the car three months earlier, perhaps as a birthday present when he turned fifteen.[17] This was a classic "horseless carriage." Tall, skinny bicycle wheels, no windshield, and a tiller instead of a steering wheel. The engine was underneath the car, so there was no hood. Just a bench seat for the boys to sit on and a tarp covering luggage and spare parts behind them. They caused three "runaways" on the trip—horses that bolted at the sight of the car and ran off with their wagons. They paid the farmers who owned the horses for the inconvenience they caused.

Driving a car like this on a long-distance trip was not for the faint of heart, and the fact that they successfully completed the trip speaks volumes for their courage, endurance, and resourcefulness. Jim's car was reported to be the first lightweight automobile, and only the second automobile of any description, to make the 1,000-mile trip.[18] They left New York on June 28 and arrived in Chicago on July 30. Jim was able to make all the required repairs himself, except when they broke a drive sprocket near Kendallville, Indiana. Jim and George had to

Jim's car. *NASM*

spend a night in a hay loft that night, while waiting for help to arrive from Detroit. When they finally arrived in Chicago, they were the guests of honor at a meeting of the Chicago Automobile Club. The trip also gave evidence of Jim's growing independence. Judge McConnell thought the trip was foolhardy at best, and when they ran into serious problems, he wanted to send someone to pick them up and ship the car by train. Jim told reporters that this just made him more determined to get through.

Back in New York, the Fuller Company completed the Flatiron Building and proceeded with other construction projects on properties owned or acquired by the United States Realty and Construction Company. Then Judge McConnell's success with the company came to a scandalous end. The skyscrapers that Fuller was building made extensive use of steel, so they needed to maintain good relations with the steelworkers' union, Local 2 of the International Association of Bridge and Structural Ironworkers. Local 2 was headed by Sam Parks, who had worked as a foreman for the Fuller Company in Chicago. According to some sources, Sam Parks was still on the payroll of the Fuller Company.[19] In June 1902, Sam Parks was arrested for extortion.[20] A number of small contractors had gone to the district attorney, complaining that Parks had asked for $1,000 to prevent union troubles. If they didn't pay, the steelworkers went on strike and Parks would demand $2,000 to end the strike. At the trial, it came out that Judge McConnell frequently let Sam Parks use his office for negotiations with these contractors, and the Fuller Company had cashed an alleged extortion check for Parks.[21] The prosecuting attorney tried to show that the Fuller Company had brought Sam Parks to New York to foment strikes on competing contractors. The judge stopped that line of questioning, but the damage was done. The questions asked before the judge blocked the prosecutor created enough of a stir that Judge McConnell felt obligated to issue a statement saying there was no truth in those allegations.[22]

The trial and the publicity about the relationship between Sam Parks and Samuel McConnell did considerable damage to the reputations of Judge McConnell and the Fuller Company. In an otherwise routine newspaper article about a political rally, one of the attendees was listed as "Judge Samuel P. McConnell (without Sam Parks)."[23] When the trial finally ended, it took the jury only eleven minutes to find Sam Parks guilty.[24]

The scandal outraged the directors of the United States Realty and Construction Company, which included prominent men such as Cornelius Vanderbilt and Henry Morganthau. They formed a committee to institute reforms in the construction side of the business. President McConnell resigned.[25]

This was a difficult time for Jim. Within a three-year period, his family moved from the house where he grew up to New York, he was sent to a boarding school, his parents divorced, his father married a woman who was closer to his age than to his father's age, and his father was involved in a scandal that made the front page of major New York newspapers.

Things weren't easy for Judge McConnell either. He went from being the respected president of the largest construction company in New York to being fired as the result of a widely publicized scandal. Presumably he resumed his private legal practice, but being accused of hiring an extortionist couldn't have been good for business. One of his previous clients had been the Vanderbilt interests,[26] but since Cornelius Vanderbilt was one of the directors who forced Judge McConnell to resign, it is doubtful that relationship continued. The judge was fifty-three years old, he had a new wife who would soon give birth to the first of three children they would have together, and he was out of a job.

His immediate financial situation must not have been too bad, since Jim continued to attend the Morristown boarding school, and in 1906 he transferred to the Haverford School, near Philadelphia, Pennsylvania, again as a boarding student.[27] The following summer, he entered the University of Virginia. His first two years were devoted to general studies (English, French, history, etc.), and then, not surprisingly, he began studying law. He performed very well academically, and he was involved in an amazing number of clubs and fraternities. He was a member of the Beta Theta Pi fraternity, and a member of the Theta Nu Epsilon secret sophomore fraternity. He was a member of O.W.L, an honorary literary society, and T.I.L.K.A., a society focused on student leadership. He was an assistant cheerleader and a member of the German Club, and he worked on the school yearbook, *Corks and Curls*, becoming editor in chief for the 1910 edition. He was a member of a club for students from New York state, being elected "Lord High Executioner" his first year and "President" his second year. He helped found the Aero Club and served as its first president.[28] Jim was also a member of the philanthropic Seven Society, although in accordance with the rules of that society, his membership was announced only after his death.[29]

Jim McConnell at UVA. *World's Work*

Jim with bagpipes. *NASM*

Jim also became famous (or infamous) for teaching himself to play the bagpipes while at UVA. He bought a kilt and Scottish garb of the MacConnell clan and provided musical accompaniment for various functions. This meshed well with one of his other activities, being an active member of the Hot Foot Society. To call this a "social" organization would be an understatement. The avowed purpose of the organization was to stage open-air parties at which beer from a wooden keg was freely distributed to all who wished to join the festivities.[30] Perhaps as a result of the beer consumption, elaborate rituals and practical jokes often took place. Jim was elected "King of the Hot Foot Society" in 1910, a singular honor. Years later, a friend of Jim's reminisced about a time when he and Jim had gone from a "goating" of the Hot Foot Society to a downtown carnival. Jim, dressed in his kilt, played the bagpipes while his friend, dressed as a Turkish prince, danced wildly.[31]

Jim made many friends at UVA. He was obviously enjoying himself, and he was making good progress toward a law degree. One of his professors later noted that Jim displayed "a hatred of the humdrum, an abhorrence of the commonplace, a passion for the picturesque."[32] He stayed in touch with his mother, Sarah, spending at least one Christmas vacation at her winter home in Florida. Then, on April 25, 1910, Jim withdrew from the university before completing the spring term. He listed the reason for his withdrawal as "Father's wish."[33]

Some sources claim that Jim was expelled, or pressured into withdrawing, because he placed a bedpan over the head of a statue of Thomas Jefferson that was about to be unveiled. Some versions go so far as to claim that President Taft was to attend the unveiling. This is highly unlikely. Although the Hot Foot Society had a reputation for staging elaborate pranks and would be permanently banned from the university the year following Jim's withdrawal,[34] newspaper accounts show that the unveiling didn't occur until June 15, 1910, two months after Jim withdrew.[35] President Taft was not listed as an attendee, and no mention was made of a bedpan or any other prank.

So why did the judge want Jim to withdraw from UVA? There's no written record of why he asked Jim to leave, but one possibility is that he encountered a financial setback. Whatever he was doing after he resigned from the Fuller Company failed to make headlines. His name appears as an ex-judge and ex-president in a few stories about minor political events, but with no mention of current employment. He was still living in a grand style, since the 1910 US Census shows that he, his wife, five children, one friend, and five servants were living in Westchester, New York. (Jim was listed as one of the children, since New York would have been Jim's legal residence while he was attending UVA, but his older sister, Julia, had by that time married and left home.) A short announcement in a 1909 newspaper showed that Judge McConnell had bought Keg Mountain (now called Dickerson Mountain) and Keg Mountain Lake in Westchester County, New York, for $50,000 (roughly $1.74 million in 2024 dollars.) He then spent $60,000 ($2.1 million in 2024) to build a house on the 500 acres he owned adjacent to the mountain he just purchased.[36] There was no mention of how much he had paid for the 500 acres. If he borrowed money to buy the land, expecting a quick turnaround, he might have been in trouble. There was a sharp drop in housing prices in 1910. One of Judge McConnell's descendants said that after he died, his estate included fancy china and luxury items, but very little money.

Regardless of the reason for the judge's request, Jim withdrew from UVA and moved back to New York with his family, who soon moved to Carthage, North Carolina. The judge had accepted a new position, general manager of the Randolph and Cumberland Railroad. While this sounds like an impressive position, the railroad consisted of only 19 miles of track. This was soon increased to 23 miles, including 4 miles under construction to a new town of "McConnell*."[37]

Mayo McConnell was the railroad's secretary, and Jim served as the railroad's industrial agent.[38] The railroad dreamed of extending its line to Winston-Salem, a distance of roughly 100 miles. There it could connect to a railroad that ran to Southport, North Carolina, which was expected to become a major seaport.[39] The railroad spent several years promoting bond drives to make this connection, but they were never able to raise the money.

The result was that Jim was the industrial agent for a railroad that had very little business. He also became the secretary of Carthage's newly formed board of trade,[40] and he joined the local state militia as a second lieutenant.

---

* McConnell, North Carolina, is still shown on some state maps, but there is no sign of a town there.

He created a booklet for the board of trade, extolling the opportunities that Carthage offered to any entrepreneur who wished to start a business in that town. The booklet provided specifics on the climate, history, and resources of Carthage. The introduction showed Jim's flair for dramatic use of the English language, declaring, "On her Eden-like islands the palm, fig, and orange trees of the semi-tropics are mingled with the moss festooned oaks of those fairyland forests. . . . A commercial El Dorado of this magnificent domain, in which are represented the charms of all climes, the resources of every continent, and the harvests of the world."[41]

Jim also created a similar, but less flowery, booklet describing business opportunities in all the areas served by the Randolph and Cumberland Railroad.[42] Instead of focusing on how wonderful the climate was, this booklet described crops, timber, mineral deposits, and other resources available to developers. The booklet was obviously a source of frustration to Jim, since he wrote to a friend that the two big railroads that he was assured would pay handsomely for the booklet failed to follow through. "The result is that I am the author of about the best territory development pamphlet that has never been published."[43] He was hopeful that he could eventually get the railroads to pay, but he worried that if they didn't publicize the booklet and get it into the hands of potential entrepreneurs, it wouldn't do any good. He said he wasn't doing enough work for the railroad alone to sustain himself, but his work was doing some good for the family, and that's why he was still on the job.

Jim kept in touch with his UVA friends while he worked in Carthage. One of his friends, Lewis D. Crenshaw, was singled out in the 1911 school yearbook as being "foremost" in creating the literary portion of the yearbook. Jim was credited with "literary contributions." Since Jim hadn't attended UVA that year, he had obviously worked closely with Lewis. Another close friend was Charles Chouteau Johnson, from St. Louis, who graduated from UVA with a bachelor of law degree in 1913.[44] Nicknamed "Chute" by his friends, for a time he lived with Jim in North Carolina.[45] They moved to New York and tried to start an Army-Navy business, but it quickly failed due to lack of experience and capital.[46] Jim moved back to North Carolina. Jim and Chute would later fly together in the Lafayette Escadrille.

In August 1914, war broke out in Europe. The events that started this war are so complex they are still being debated today, but several events would have caught the attention of an American who was sympathetic to France. Germany declared war on France. The German army attacked Belgium, killed civilians, and devastated Belgian cities as it marched through Belgium to attack France. After desperate fighting, the German advance was stopped, leaving most of Belgium and a large section of France occupied by the Germans. The French, and a much-smaller British army, were struggling to defeat the German army and liberate the lost territory.

The initial battles of World War I did not involve the grim trench warfare we usually associate with that war. Initially it was a war of movement, with cavalry charges, bayonet attacks, and field artillery behind galloping horses rushing to catch up with a retreating enemy. It was not yet obvious to the combatants, let alone to an observer thousands of miles away, that machine guns and bolt-action rifles had made that form of warfare obsolete. People who had not experienced these battles still held a romantic illusion of warfare. It's easy to see how a young man who had been forced to drop out of college, had failed to earn a living in New York, and was struggling to get paid for a booklet describing local crops would be intrigued when he learned that an American group in Paris was looking for volunteer ambulance drivers.

One of Jim's friends in North Carolina was Frank Page. Frank was the son of Walter Hines Page, the US ambassador to Great Britain. Mr. Page was also the founder of the *World's Work* magazine, one of the most popular magazines of the day, and a cofounder of the Doubleday-Page publishing company. Both would soon become important to Jim. Mr. Page was a North Carolina native, and his son Frank was trying to develop railroads and highways in the sandhill region of North Carolina. This, of course, aligned perfectly with Jim's attempts to publicize his father's railroad. In January 1915, Frank was surprised when Jim told him he was leaving the US to drive an ambulance in France. Jim felt that the war was the greatest event in history, and he would be missing the opportunity of a lifetime if he did not see it. "These sand hills will be here forever," Jim said, "but the war won't, and so I'm going. And I'll be of some use, too, not just a sight-seer looking on. That wouldn't be fair."[47]

TWO

The American Ambulance Field Service

Sarah McConnell wasn't the only wealthy American to spend extended periods in France. Before the war, a number of notable American families such as the Vanderbilts, Morgans, Chapmans, et al. had business interests and homes in France. There were also a number of expatriate Americans in France, working for American companies, working as artists, or studying at French universities. In 1906, these Americans created L'hôpital Américain, the American Hospital in Paris.[1] When World War I broke out, the hospital immediately began treating wounded soldiers. Volunteers used cars and trucks to carry the wounded from train stations to the hospital. The number of wounded who needed care quickly overwhelmed the small American hospital, so they rented a new, much-larger building in Neuilly (a section of Paris) that became the American Ambulance* Hospital.[2] The fleet of vehicles that transported the wounded from the field to this hospital was called the "American Ambulance Field Service." Much later in the war, when volunteers began driving supply trucks as well as ambulances, this was shortened to "American Field Service," the name by which it is still known today.

A former director of the US Mint and an assistant professor of economics at Harvard named A. Piatt Andrew wrote to the American Ambulance Hospital in 1914 to volunteer his services. Since he was not a medical

* The term "ambulance" originally meant "moving hospital," typically a military field hospital in tents that moved with the army. In the US and England, the word soon came to mean the vehicle that transported the wounded to the hospital, but during World War I the French used the term "ambulance" to refer to a military hospital as well as to the vehicles.

professional, the only job they could offer was driving a vehicle to transport the wounded. He immediately accepted and arrived in Paris in late December. Having only limited driving experience, his test to obtain a French driving license was not auspicious. "After nearly hitting a trolley, a flock of sheep, and an assortment of pedestrians (his licensing officer used the word 'assassin' during the test drive), Andrew was grudgingly given his license."[3] The hospital quickly realized he was more talented as an administrator than as a driver, and they made him the inspector general of the American Ambulance Field Service. It proved to be a wise choice. He quickly organized the ambulance corps and developed an excellent working relationship with the French army.

French army officials tightly restricted civilian access to the front. They were particularly suspicious of allowing citizens of neutral nations into an area where they could see troop movements, the location of artillery batteries and supply dumps, and other details that would be of value to the enemy. If nonmilitary ambulance drivers were to be allowed, they would have to conform to French military restrictions, regulations, and discipline. But how could this be required of noncombatant American civilians?[4]

Andrew had to wrestle with this and many other problems while he negotiated with the army over where his ambulances could be used. Initially, passenger cars and trucks loaned or donated by individuals were used to transport the wounded, but it was obvious that a vehicle designed to carry stretchers would be needed. Tests were conducted with Fiat, Peugeot, and General Motors ambulances. Additionally, Mrs. Vanderbilt worked with the manager of the Ford Motor Company's French assembly plant to have ten Model T chassis outfitted with wood and canvas ambulance bodies by a local carriage builder. She donated these to the ambulance service. While the larger ambulances were impressive on wide city boulevards, tests on narrow unpaved roads in the French countryside showed the Model T was the clear winner. It could wind through traffic on narrow twisting roads better than the larger vehicles. It could climb steep hills and mountains where previously only mules and horse-drawn wagons could navigate. It could navigate flooded roads that would "drown" a lower vehicle, and if a road was blocked, it could go cross-country. Surprisingly, it was also more comfortable for the patients than the larger vehicles with stiffer springs. On top of everything else, it was light enough that three or four soldiers could pick it up and move it if it got stuck in a ditch or a shell hole.[5]

Andrew was still negotiating with French officials when Jim McConnell arrived in Paris. Jim had left New York in early February, with five other American Ambulance volunteers, on the French Line ship SS *Chicago*. On board he met Marcelle Guerin, a young French woman who was sailing back to France with her mother. Her father was a professor who had taught in American schools, and Marcelle spent several of her childhood years in Brooklyn. She graduated from high school in 1914 and was planning on attending college in the US when the war intervened. Her parents did not want to sit idle in a neutral country while France was being invaded. Her father immediately returned to France. Her mother began wrapping up their affairs in the US, closing their apartment and making arrangements to store or ship their household goods. Marcelle took a whirlwind training program in nursing at Mt. Sinai Hospital. After completing their tasks in the US, Marcelle and her mother also sailed to France on the SS *Chicago*. On board the ship, Walter Lovell, one of the ambulance volunteers, needed his final typhoid shot. When he learned that there was a young nurse on board, he asked her to give him the shot. She got to know the "boys," and they got together frequently. They helped her celebrate her birthday, and a photograph from a McConnell family album shows a "Red Cross Rehearsal" on board the ship. Marcelle is in her nurse's uniform, and the boys are gathered around her, wearing slings and bandages and showing signs of distress. Jim has the choicest spot, lying prostrate on the deck with his head cradled in Marcelle's lap.[6] It appears that Marcelle is about to give him a sip from someone's hip flask.

Jim wrote to his sister Julia while on board the *Chicago*,[7] and he wrote his mother soon afterward.[8] He told his sister that they stopped at St. Pierre Miquelon (a French archipelago south of Newfoundland) to take on 350

A "wounded" Jim being comforted by Marcelle on board the SS *Chicago*. *NASM*

conscripts. The captain of the boat that ferried them to the SS *Chicago* said he was sorry to see such a large portion of the youth of St. Pierre Miquelon go, but they wanted to fight. He thought it would be all right because it was *la dernière guerre* (the final war). Jim wrote his mother that when they entered the harbor at Le Havre on February 10, they saw a liner that had been sunk by a U-boat. Two others had met a similar fate.

The ambulance drivers hadn't gotten their cars yet, so there was no real work. Jim had, however, been invited to have dinner with Mlle. Guerin, "who is quite the important person in Paris and now is in the Red Cross service."

Jim spent a few days getting uniforms and typhoid shots and being assigned a car. He was soon pulling regular shifts of ambulance duty, picking up the wounded at the La Chapelle train station in Paris and transporting them to various local hospitals. He lived with thirty-five other ambulance drivers in a barnlike dormitory on the roof of the new American hospital in Neuilly. Marcelle was working at the same hospital, but his ambulance duties kept him from seeing her, so he wrote her a letter. "If it gives me a certain amount of happiness to talk to you on paper, you won't begrudge me the pleasure, will you?"[9] He also described a wounded officer who had hidden his pet Skye terrier under his coat. The dog was discovered when nurses handed out sandwiches, and the dog began crying because it didn't get one.

Jim told his sister he was very enthusiastic about his work. The American volunteers were often mistaken for British soldiers because their uniforms were similar. There was a theater near the dormitory where he could see movies for free. He could get tickets to the opera house for one-fourth the normal price, but even with that discount he couldn't afford to attend. He said that the French people were very nice and Paris was a beautiful city, "and as for the *demi mondes* [prostitutes] one has to fight 'em off with sticks"[10] (prostitution was legal in France during World War I).

Not all the volunteer drivers were assigned to hospitals in Paris. Some were sent to cities closer to the fighting, where despite the official French policy, local military officials sometimes asked them to evacuate the wounded from the military zone. Jim's friend "Chute" Johnson had volunteered as an ambulance driver, and he was working at one of these cities. In Jim's letter to his sister, he commented that "Kid Johnson got his Ambulance busted up with shrapnel. He lost his way and got on a road that was under fire."

Jim kept busy for the next six weeks carrying the wounded from the train station at La Chapelle to hospitals around the city. He wrote letters to friends and family, and he found time to do a bit of sightseeing and to go for walks with Marcelle. In late March he wrote his mother that there were thousands of wounded coming in, and he was being called to carry them day and night. He said that Chute Johnson was in Paris for a rest, and that although they used to allow ambulances near the front, they weren't doing that anymore. He also described a zeppelin raid on Paris:

> The night of the 21st we had a call from two Zeppelins. The first ever visible over any of the Allies' cities. We were awakened by a dull, heavy boom, and the rapid fire of artillery. Our dormitory windows were the best seats for the show in town. We looked out and saw great searchlight beams playing into the sky. There was another thudding boom, as a second bomb was dropped, and just then one of the searchlights caught the airship. We saw her far above us glowing a silver white against the dark sky. Suddenly great balls of fire began to hurtle up towards the Zeppelin. The battery at the Trocadéro [an area of Paris near the Eiffel Tower] had gone into action with fusee [incendiary] shells. They look exactly like a giant Roman candle going off. The airship began to climb to get out of range. We heard a whirring, tearing roar as an aeroplane passed by overhead and saw her light streak along the sky*. There was another in a few seconds. They were mounting to the attack. They were too late. The searchlight lost the Zeppelin. We were just crawling back to bed when we heard firing from another direction. The giant searchlight on Mont-Valérien [a fort in the western suburbs of Paris] was blazing up into the sky. Suddenly the huge trim shape of a second Zeppelin loomed up in the great beam of light. She was very near us. We could see her gondolas. Bright flashes began to burst near her. They were firing shrapnel from the fortifications. This ship began to climb too and was lost. It was very still and on a floor below I heard a wounded man call to his nurse who was looking out of a window, "Now that you're up will you get me a glass of milk?"[11]

While Jim was ferrying patients in Paris, he met a man who was destined to become a close friend. Paul Rockwell had traveled to France with his brother Kiffin and joined the Foreign Legion in August 1914. In December, Paul's collarbone was broken by a shell explosion, and it triggered an inflammation that gave him back problems that were so severe he was

---

* Night flying was in its infancy and very risky in 1915.

Jim with Paul Rockwell. Paul is wearing his Foreign Legion uniform and appears to still be suffering from back problems. *UVA*

eventually invalided out of the Legion. A *New York Sun* article[12] said they met as college students in 1908. Paul was attending Washington and Lee University at the time, and Jim was attending the University of Virginia. The two campuses were less than 100 miles apart, so it's possible they met during college, but Jim later told his mother that he hadn't known Paul in the States.[13] Whether or not they had met before, they became good friends in France. Paul served as the unofficial historian of the Lafayette Escadrille, so they would see a lot of each other during the coming years.

On March 29, A. Piatt Andrew got French authorities to approve a test program using American volunteer ambulance drivers to evacuate the wounded from first-aid stations near the front lines. He quickly put together a team of sixteen men with twelve cars and sent them to help French troops fighting in the Vosges Mountains. This test team was called "Section Z." They made an immediate and very favorable impression. The nimble Ford ambulances were able to navigate steep, snow-covered mountain roads that were impassable to larger French ambulances, and the enthusiasm and dedication of their drivers were equally impressive.[14]

While Section Z was impressing the French *poilus* (frontline troops; literally, "hairy ones") Andrew worked out an agreement with French authorities that placed the volunteer drivers under the same military regulations and discipline as French soldiers. They would be paid five cents per day, the same as French soldiers, and would be issued the same rations. One significant difference was that French soldiers enlisted for the duration of the war, while American ambulance drivers signed up for a six-month term, which they could extend in three-month increments.[15] The American volunteers paid for their own transportation, clothing, uniforms, and personal equipment. As one put it, "The Americans not only had to be willing to risk their lives, they also had to pay to do it."[16]

It didn't take long for these changes to affect Jim. Andrew probably began pre-positioning ambulance crews before the Vosges experiment had been officially approved, since Jim wrote a farewell note to Marcelle in early

April. He closed with the words "And tho I may be gone a long time you won't forget Hâvre, the walks in the Bois, and that you are everything to me over here—or elsewhere for that matter."[17] On April 8, he departed with a team of ambulances and drivers, headed for a destination "near Nancy."[18] They were to be "Section Y."

The ambulance that Jim was driving was a remarkable vehicle. Today all that most people know about the Model T Ford is that it was the first mass-produced automobile, and it came in any color you wanted, as long as it was black. The first statement is true. Ford perfected the assembly line for automobiles and produced Model Ts in previously unheard-of numbers. The second statement was true for most of the years the Model T was produced, but factory colors were available for the first and the last several years of Model T production. What is overlooked by these statements is that the Model T was incredibly robust and reliable for its price.

Ford wanted the Model T to be a car for "everyman," and at that time most people in the US lived in rural areas. Ford had grown up on a farm, and he knew what kind of a car farmers needed. It had to be low cost, but high quality. It would be driven on some of the worst unpaved roads imaginable and sometimes driven across fields where there were no roads. He kept the price low by keeping the car simple, not by using cheap materials. The simplicity also made it easy to repair. The high quality came from the materials he used and the design of the car. He worked with an Ohio company to develop a new vanadium steel alloy that had ten times the tensile strength of any other metal being produced in the US—including Carnegie's armor plating.[19]

Before the Model T came along, few people knew how to drive. Shifting gears was especially troublesome for new drivers, since nothing even remotely similar was needed to drive a horse and buggy. Why you even needed to shift gears was a mystery to people who grew up with horses. Ford designed the Model T to use an ingenious device called a planetary transmission. All the gears were already engaged, so there was no need to shift gears. The car's motion was controlled by friction bands, which stopped some of the gears from turning and allowed others to turn the rear wheels. American author and essayist E. B. White wrote a tribute to the Model T Ford in which he described the transmission as "half metaphysics, half sheer friction."[20] Fortunately, a Model T driver didn't need to understand the metaphysics of how the transmission worked any more than a modern driver needs to understand how an automatic transmission works. They just needed to know how to use it.

To start the car moving, you pushed the left pedal to the floor. White pointed out that this was "as natural as kicking an old door to make it budge."[21] Once the car was moving, you could take your foot off this pedal, and the car would shift into high gear. Push the pedal halfway down, and the car was in neutral. Pushing on the center pedal put the car in reverse, and the right pedal was the brake pedal. Since your feet were busy pushing these pedals, you controlled the car's speed with a hand throttle. A hand-brake lever put the car in neutral and activated conventional drum brakes on the rear wheels (virtually all cars built during that era had rear brakes only). While these controls sound strange by today's standards, people who had never before driven an automobile had no problem learning how to drive a Model T. Ford continued to use planetary transmissions until 1928, and he abandoned them then only because higher road speeds made it necessary to use more than two gears. Diehard Model T fans complained bitterly about having to learn how to shift gears. Not until the advent of automatic transmissions did gas-powered cars become as easy to drive as a Model T.

Like most cars of the period, the driver started a Model T with a hand crank. The right way to do this was to pull up on the crank, giving the engine a quick flip. The wrong way was to turn the crank round and round in a circle. If you cranked it the wrong way and it backfired, the crank could spin around and break your arm. Jim wrote in his diary that a fellow driver "broke his arm cranking his car this morning. He will be out of commission for three weeks, so the surgeon who set it informed him."[22]

Once the car started, the Model T had a tendency to creep forward if the driver forgot to set the hand brake or if the brake was worn out. Even though the car was in neutral, a little bit of "drag" from the transmission bands was enough to make the car creep. E. B. White compared this to a friendly horse nuzzling him at the curb, looking for an apple in his pocket.[23] Some ambulance drivers didn't remember it as fondly. One wrote, "My old bus has a horrid habit of running forward when I crank it. I think I have more dread of cranking my car than of a German '*obus*' [shell]."[24]

Henry Ford was adamantly opposed to war. He strongly believed in President Wilson's warnings not to show favoritism to either side. He allowed his French subsidiary to sell Model T rolling chassis—cars without bodies—to the ambulance service, but only at the full retail price. No discounts.[25] Later volunteer drivers wrote of helping to make the wooden ambulance bodies themselves,[26] but Jim makes no mention of that in his letters. Presumably his team received ambulances that were made by the carriage manufacturer in Paris who built the original ambulances for Mrs. Vanderbilt. The ambulances were designed to hold three stretchers in the back—one on each side supported on legs, and a third stretcher hanging from the center of the ambulance roof. If stretchers were not needed, four men could sit on benches in the rear of the ambulance. In either case, an additional three men could squeeze onto the seat beside the driver. The ambulance could therefore transport three stretcher cases and three sitting wounded, or seven sitting wounded. Sometimes as many as ten wounded were actually carried, with some men sitting on the fenders or standing on the running board.[27] The ambulances were painted a slate blue (described as "wartime gray" by some) with Geneva red crosses on the sides and roof. There was no windshield or doors to protect the driver from the weather, but a canvas roof could be pulled out to extend over his head. Wooden storage boxes were built into the ambulance to hold tools, spare parts, and other items needed by the driver.[28] The drivers were not medics, so medical supplies were not carried, but the drivers performed most maintenance and repair of their ambulances, so the tools were a necessity.

The tools were undoubtedly a novelty to some of the drivers. When A. Piatt Andrew first began recruiting ambulance drivers, he was not looking for mechanics, chauffeurs, blacksmiths, or other people who knew how to drive and repair automobiles. He was looking for men who would make a good impression on the French, who would help him sell the idea of allowing American volunteers into the war zone. His recruiter in the US visited eastern prep schools and colleges, looking for men "of good disposition possessed of self-control—in short, a gentleman."[29] Once they got to France, they learned to clean spark plugs, repair punctured tires, replace broken springs, change friction bands in the transmission, decarbonize heads, and do everything else their ambulances required. In the days before antifreeze, they also learned to drain the water out of their cars when parking them in cold weather, to prevent the water from freezing and destroying the engine. A side benefit was that they could use the hot water they drained to wash up or to make "radiator cocoa."[30]

Jim drove one of these vehicles in a convoy of Model T ambulances to the town of Vittel, France. This was the location "near Nancy." There, they waited while Section Z showed the French what they could do. As it turned out, they could do plenty. They carried hundreds of wounded soldiers safely, day and night, in all kinds of weather. Frontline dressing stations sometimes called for an "American Ambulance Boat," because the Model T's could make it through flooded roads that stopped all other traffic.[31] The steep mountain roads were tough on brakes and transmission bands, which were designed for the flat farming countryside where Henry Ford had grown up. Drivers learned that they could use the reverse pedal like a brake to slow the car on steep descents. They used low gear to climb hills, low gear or reverse to control their speed going downhill, and brakes to slow down for curves. With care, a set of transmission bands would last ten to fourteen

Jim McConnell in his ambulance, with three unidentified French soldiers. *NASM*

days in mountain driving.[32] While this was not nearly as long as they were designed to last, roads like these wore out clutches on conventional ambulances too. Changing a clutch was a major operation for a professional mechanic, since it involved removing the engine or the transmission. Changing transmission bands was no picnic, but it could be done by the driver, using only hand tools and a moderate amount of profanity. Drivers on mountain roads also earned a badge of honor—a hole worn through the sole of their left shoe caused by standing on the low-speed pedal for hours every day.[33]

Driving these primitive ambulances on mountain roads could be harrowing, especially at night and in snow. A driver named Luke Doyle described a trip that nearly ended in disaster:

> When I got to the top of the mountain and started down, the roads had been broken and beaten down by munition wagons and were like a sheet of ice. I started down without chains, and with all my brakes on the car began to slide slowly down the road. It slid toward the edge of the ravine and the two front wheels went over; it stopped, I got it back on the road, turned the radiator into the bank on the other side and tried tying rags on the rear wheels to keep the car from going down, when a big wagon with four horses came down the hill behind me. It was so slippery that the horses started to slide down on their haunches, and, with brakes on, the driver could not stop them. The horses came on faster and they slid into the rear of

> my car, pushed it along for about six feet, and then nothing could stop it. It started down the road. I yelled to the wounded, "*Vous, jetez vous!*" [You! Throw yourselves!]. They understood and piled out just in time. The car ran across the road and plunged down into the ravine. There was a lot of snow on the side of the ravine, and it had piled up so that it stopped the car part way down, and it was not injured very much. It took nine men and as many mules to pull it out.[34]

Doyle was fortunate that all his wounded that night were walking wounded who could jump out of the ambulance, or the results could have been tragic. Despite incidents like this, and because the drivers proved themselves willing to take such risks to bring wounded soldiers to medical facilities, French authorities went from being skeptical to wanting as many American ambulances at the front as they could get. On the nineteenth of April, Jim's team received orders to proceed to the front. Their destination was the town of Pont-à-Mousson.[35]

THREE

Pont-à-Mousson

Military histories focus on major battles—strategic engagements that affect the outcome of wars and change the course of human history. World War I had its share of major battles, but there were also hundreds of lesser engagements, important only to those who fought in them. Battles where soldiers on both sides fought desperately and heroically to capture or defend local objectives. A hill, a section of trench, or an observation post might change hands dozens of times in fighting that went on for days, consumed tens of thousands of artillery rounds and millions of bullets, and left thousands of soldiers dead or maimed for life. Some of these engagements went on for months, but they don't receive even a brief mention in history books because ultimately they made no difference to the outcome of the war. Only the men who fought in these battles remember the bravery and the sacrifices of the combatants. Such was the case with the fighting around Pont-à-Mousson.

The town of Pont-à-Mousson is about 170 miles east of Paris, on the Moselle River. As the word "Pont" in its name implies, there is a major bridge over the river in the town. During the initial German invasion in August 1914, German troops captured the town. French soldiers dynamited the bridge during their retreat. A few days later, after the German invasion was stopped by the Battle of the Marne, German troops retreated to the more easily defended high ground north and east of the town, and the French reoccupied Pont-à-Mousson. They repaired the section of the bridge they'd dynamited with a temporary wooden structure.

The city of Metz lies about 16 miles north-northeast of Pont-à-Mousson. Metz was a vital railway center for the German army, so the Germans were prepared to defend the hills north of Pont-à-Mousson at any cost.

The French fortress of Verdun is about 35 miles northwest of Pont-à-Mousson. Between the two, almost directly west of Pont-à-Mousson, is the town of Saint-Mihiel. The Germans captured this town in September 1914, and German control of the territory between Metz and Saint-Mihiel blocked most French road and rail traffic to Verdun. German control of this territory also partially encircled Verdun, allowing them to threaten the fortress from three sides. The French were determined to push the Germans out of Saint-Mihiel, open the roads to Verdun, and threaten the German rail center at Metz. The Germans had no intention of letting them do that.

The German-held territory between Metz and Saint-Mihiel formed a "salient" or peninsula into the French lines. The classic way to remove a salient is to attack it at its root, cutting it off and encircling the enemy troops inside the salient. The eastern root of the Saint-Mihiel salient was the Bois-le-Prêtre, or "Priest's Woods," just northwest of Pont-à-Mousson. The French launched an attack here in October 1914. This battle would rage for ten months and would periodically flare up afterward until the Americans finally captured Saint-Mihiel four years later.[1] The French lost over seven

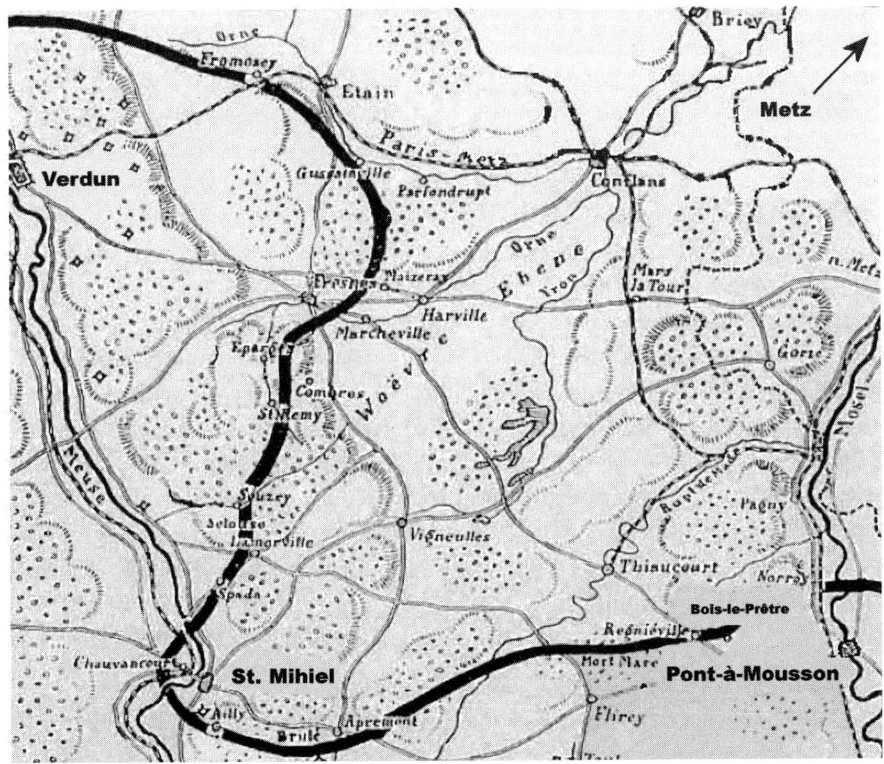

The St. Mihiel salient. *Public domain*

thousand men killed and twenty-two thousand wounded during the first ten months of intense fighting at Bois-le-Prêtre. German losses were almost identical.[2] That's why the French wanted an American ambulance team at Pont-à-Mousson.

An American engineer, Mr. A. R. Decker, managed an ironworks in Pont-à-Mousson before the war broke out. The rush of men called to arms at the beginning of the war shut down the factory, but Mr. Decker and a small group of caretakers stayed behind to keep watch. Extremely dedicated, Mr. Decker stayed put when the Germans marched into Pont-à-Mousson early in the war, and he was there when they marched out a few days later.[3] Decker also became a correspondent for the *Chicago Daily News*, so that newspaper kept close tabs on the fighting around Pont-à-Mousson. Decker published more than a hundred articles about the battle in 1915 alone. He described seemingly endless battles in the Bois-le-Prêtre and nearby sites. Artillery from both sides bombarded the trenches while soldiers fought with rifles, machine guns, bayonets, hand grenades, and clubs. Decker could see the explosions and occasionally distinguish individual soldiers from the windows of the house he was renting in Pont-à-Mousson. The town was, in fact, within rifle range of the trenches. German artillery often shelled the town. Sometimes they shelled the bridge, trying to disrupt French supply lines to the battlefield. Sometimes they shelled the ironworks. Sometimes they announced they were shelling in retaliation for the French shelling of towns that were now in German hands, and sometimes they fired shells seemingly at random, perhaps hoping to hit French soldiers who billeted in the town and frequented its cafés. Often they hit French civilians instead. There were a surprising number of civilians still in Pont-à-Mousson. About fourteen thousand people lived there before the war, but many people left as the shelling became more frequent. By September 1915, it was estimated that only about 1,500 civilians remained in the town.[4] Most of them worked in the cafés, bakeries, grocery stores, and other establishments that served the soldiers and the few remaining civilians. Many had sent their children off to live with relatives or with foster parents who cared for children from the war zone.[5]

A few highlights from Decker's articles give a feel for what the town was like before Jim arrived:

> **December 26, 1914**: The Germans conducted their largest bombardment of Pont-à-Mousson to date on Christmas Day. The bombardment was both cowardly and useless, since it was not directed at any military target.[6]

January 12, 1915: Citizens must restrict their movement to within ¼ mile of their home, which means they cannot tend their crops. Everyone must be off the streets and all cafés and such must close by 7:00 p.m. Soldiers are permitted in cafés only between 5:00 and 6:00 p.m. (very unpopular with soldiers who get twelve-hour passes to town that don't cover that hour). If a soldier gets drunk in a café, the café will be closed. Dogs found outside after 7:00 p.m. will be shot. Civilians are free to leave Pont-à-Mousson, but they cannot return, which prevents supply runs to nearby towns and cities. The cemetery is on one side of the river. When a civilian is killed on the other side, their family cannot cross the river to participate in the burial service.[7]

January 13: Fighting continues in the Bois-le-Prêtre. Decker watched shells explode in the same places where he saw shelling the previous August, showing that after five months of war, the position was back to where they started.[8]

January 20: Severe fighting continued as attacks and counterattacks captured and recaptured trenches. Decker could watch Germans bombard French positions from his third-floor window. Areas outside Pont-à-Mousson were also shelled as the Germans searched for French supply stockpiles.[9]

January 23: Pont-à-Mousson was shelled and an old people's home was destroyed, forcing the men and women to evacuate to Nancy. A German spy disguised as a French laborer was captured but escaped.[10]

January 27: A German airplane from Metz flew over Pont-à-Mousson and dropped a card that said the kaiser sent greetings to the residents on his birthday and would send some shells later on. When the first shells approached, a group of dogs immediately sought shelter. Local dog owners said they had noticed the same thing. Later another German plane passed over. Decker saw something glint as it dropped from the plane, and later learned a civilian had been killed by a steel arrow*, that transfixed him from head to foot.[11]

February 1: Things are amazingly quiet in Pont-à-Mousson. Most of the fighting in the Bois-le-Prêtre is being done underground, since soldiers on both sides dig mines under the other side's trenches.

---

* The steel arrows were called *fléchettes*. They were about the size of a pencil and were used by the Allies and the Germans before more-effective antipersonnel bombs were developed.

Decker notices there are few NCOs in the French units he sees, since they are specifically targeted by German snipers, and French officers seldom stay in the front lines.[12]

February 3: Pont-à-Mousson was struck by sporadic shellfire, close enough to Decker's house that he spent most of the day in his cellar. Later he learned that an eighteen-month-old baby boy was killed while sitting on his mother's lap. Others in the room were unhurt. He was the twenty-third civilian killed in Pont-à-Mousson.[13]

February 5: Decker realizes that he cannot overestimate the importance of aircraft in modern warfare. He saw at least fifteen French and German aircraft in the air today. German planes drop incendiary bombs on Pont-à-Mousson. The incendiary bombs look like an ordinary milk can: a handle at the top, and compartments filled with gasoline, kerosene, and phosphorus. An explosive charge is on the bottom, and it is about 2.5 feet long. Kids sell shell caps, fragments, etc. as souvenirs, but the price of arrows is dropping because the Germans have dropped so many of them. People are leaving the town as a result of the bombing.[14]

February 23: "Today the French take a trench and tomorrow the Germans retake it. No net advance is realized by either army. The principle [*sic*] result is to fill the hospitals and to keep busy the old man with the two wheeled cart who brings coffins for the dead."[15]

March 15: A chart comparing food prices in June 1914 to March 1915 shows that the price of most grocery items in Pont-à-Mousson has more than doubled. Some of that increase is due to the difficulty in transporting food to the city.[16]

March 16: The Germans planted five mines under French trenches and captured four lines of trenches after blowing the mines. French counterattacks took back most of the ground over the next two days. Stray bullets whizzed uncomfortably close to Decker as he watched the fighting from Pont-à-Mousson. All day long, a procession of ambulances brought the wounded back from the field.[17]

April 20: The warm spring weather has made the stench of decaying bodies in the battlefields around Pont-à-Mousson almost unbearable. Quicklime is being used to try to reduce the odor. Planned attacks are being delayed, but artillery duels continue.[18]

When Mr. Decker posted this last article, Jim and the rest of the ambulance drivers had been sitting in the town of Vittel France for eleven days. Vittel was about 50 miles south of Pont-à-Mousson. It was a classic case of "hurry up and wait." Presumably, the final arrangements to allow American volunteers into the war zone were taking longer than A. Piatt Andrew had anticipated. The name of Jim's team was changed from "Section Y" to "Section 2" of the American Ambulance Field Service. Ned Salisbury of Chicago was their leader. ("Section Z," which had been sent to the Vosges as a test, was renamed "Section 1.") Until they received their orders to proceed to Pont-à-Mousson, all Jim could do was wait, sip beer in a French café, and write to friends. On April 19, he wrote to Marcelle to describe how beautiful the countryside was, plead with her to write often, and say that they would drive to Pont-à-Mousson tomorrow.[19] The next day, he wrote to his sister to say that they would proceed to Pont-à-Mousson the following day. He also said that they were now under strict military rule and were eating military rations. He had listed his father as the person to contact if something should happen to him, but said if he was wounded, he wouldn't say anything about it but would go to the American Hospital to recover. "If I get potted [shot] and cash in I want no one to bother. I'll get them to plant me over here."[20] On the day after that, he wrote to Marcelle to tell her he was leaving that afternoon,[21] but later he wrote to Paul Rockwell to say that the trip had been postponed until the following day.[22] He also wrote to a friend from UVA, Lewis Crenshaw. He described his section as a handpicked squad with twelve ambulances. He was forbidden to disclose their destination (apparently a new restriction, since he'd disclosed it in several previous letters) but said it was "so near the damned Boche ["blockhead," French slang for a German soldier] that one is not allowed to smoke cigarettes at night for fear of drawing fire." He told Lewis that for all intents and purposes, he was part of the army now, and "subject to the shot-at-sunrise stuff." He also mentioned that he had made good friends with Paul Rockwell, who was engaged to marry "one of the richest and most prominent girls in France."[23] (She was Mademoiselle Marie Francoise Jeanne Leygues; Paul met her shortly after he was wounded. Her mother had hastily converted their chateau into a hospital, Paul was sent to that hospital, and Jeanne was working there as a nurse. Her father, Monsieur Georges Leygues, was an influential politician who after the war would become the prime minister of France.)

Finally, on April 22, the Americans were allowed to proceed to Pont-à-Mousson. Jim wrote to Marcelle and described it as a "delightful town" that was shelled regularly. The stores were open even though most had holes in them. They were located about 0.8 mile from the trenches. They heard cannon fire regularly, but almost nobody paid any attention. When a shot was fired at the town, they heard the sound of tearing parchment as it approached, followed by a tremendous crash. On their way to town, they had to drive through one stretch of road that was shelled regularly. One ambulance would dash through that stretch of road while the others waited.

When the dust cleared, the next ambulance would make the dash. He'd already made one trip to pick up the wounded, which took him to within 200 yards of the trenches.[24]

While he was obviously excited to finally get to their forward location and start picking up the wounded, he was deeply affected by a tragedy that happened the day they arrived. A German shell had killed two children who were playing in the street. This happened only 400 yards from where the ambulance crew was stationed. Jim told Marcelle that he walked by the location the next day and could hear the "breast deep sobs of the mother crying over the poor little mangled bodies of her only children."

Jim also said he met an American engineer in the town who dressed like he'd just stepped off Broadway. He was wearing an American fedora, tan shoes, an English raincoat, and trousers that were perfectly pressed and turned up. This was A. R. Decker, who wrote about the arrival of the Americans:

> Pont-à-Mousson has been successfully invaded by Americans. Twelve small automobiles equipped as ambulances with twenty or more American drivers and conductors have captured the town. It is true that, at first, the population was confused by the khaki uniforms and thought German prisoners were being conveyed to hospitals. But after being taken variously for German, English, and Russian, the American organization is now known and is being applauded.
>
> The little ambulances, I am told, are slightly disappointing at first to the French, who expect always something big and magnificent from America. But when they see the practical ambulances in action the French authorities are quickly converted to the serviceable automobile, which can go anywhere quickly and can transport comfortably the sick or injured. There are three stretchers which can be quickly removed so as to carry patients sitting up. The low body is evenly balanced upon an easy set of springs and hung upon the short chassis.
>
> The American volunteers are well quartered in the mess of the subofficers of the Chasseurs [light infantry or cavalry] who were located at Pont-à-Mousson at the commencement of the war. The mess hall had not been disturbed since the hasty departure of the Germans in September 1914. In the dining room the French cleaners found the remains of an untouched meal, left by the fleeing Teutons in their hurried retreat from Pont-à-Mousson. Only the rats had tasted the repast.[25]

Jim in his American ambulance uniform. *NASM*

The ambulance team was headquartered in a former French army barracks, which, as Decker pointed out, had been used by the Germans during their brief occupation of the town. Jim discovered that the building had running water and originally had gas and electricity as well, but those had been put out of service by shellfire. The telephone lines were frequently cut by shellfire as well, but since those were vital to the operation of the ambulance work, they were quickly repaired.[26] They initially shared this ambulance station with a team of French ambulance drivers, but after a few weeks it was obvious the Americans had the situation well in hand, and the French ambulance team was reassigned.[27]

Originally the Americans were billeted in the village of Dieulouard, about 5 miles south of Pont-à-Mousson, and spent only their duty shifts in the station, but most soon found places to stay within Pont-à-Mousson. Jim said the shelling in Dieulouard was at least as bad, if not worse, than the shelling in Pont-à-Mousson anyway.[28]

Jim wrote to his sister a few days after they arrived, and described the station as being "practically in Bois-le-Prêtre where the worst fighting in the St. Mihiel salient takes place." They were close enough to the front lines that the Germans could pot (shoot) at them with rifles, and German artillery 10 kilometers (6.2 miles) away could land their shots within a 50-yard radius. Jim described a local call that displayed the bravery, or the naiveté, of the American drivers:

> The day before yesterday the Germans opened up at 5. I was talking over agriculture with a French officer. There was a sickening whistle as the shell hurtled towards us and then the detonation as she hit the railroad. After only ten shells had gone off a call came in for two ambulances. The French drivers wouldn't go out. The French officer I had been talking to vanished after the first shot. A fellow named Willis* and I volunteered. It was regular 10-20-30

* Harold Buckley Willis, of Boston, Massachusetts. The two men would later fly together in the Lafayette Escadrille.

> stuff [ten shots, a pause; ten more, a pause; and ten more]. The crowd watched us from the tower of an old castle here and the door crowding populace cried out "Du bon Chance" [Good luck] as we descended the hill. Willis was sent in one direction after two badly wounded and I was pointed out the house where my blesse [wounded] was just on the other side of the tracks. I got my car across the sidings but couldn't make the main line. I stopped in the center of the railroad. A shell sizzed through the air and plunked down back of me. I went into the house for the blesse! Another shell came then and the men around the poor *ouvrier* [worker], who was lying in blood on a mattress, huddled against the wall. An old civilian said he would show me the way around to the door. Another shell landed in front of my car but didn't go off. We ran down between the tracks to the station, turned, and followed back to the other side of the door where I got my man loaded in. The thing I failed to do was to puff a cigarette out on the tracks. It was quite exciting and I will admit to being nervous. We got congratulated on our way back and that night the French officers came in to pay their respects. The report to the higher authorities was very complimentary to our squad.[29]

The same day, Jim wrote to his father and said that they were better housed, better fed, and treated better than when they were in Paris. They ate army rations, which were excellent—vegetables, bread, steak, or some kind of meat (much better than Carthage meat) and wine or a most excellent beer, followed by jam and coffee.[30] (Not all the Americans were as pleased as Jim was with the rations. One ambulance driver who served later in the war described the French army bread as "remarkable stuff. It comes in freight cars from the interior and is usually two weeks old before we get it. It is often brittle, like a piece of wood, and is about as palatable as soft pine. However it is supposed to be nourishing."[31])

The director, A. Piatt Andrew, visited them shortly after they arrived in Pont-à-Mousson, and carried letters back to post in Paris, ensuring quicker delivery and effectively bypassing the military censors. Jim gave him a letter to mail to Paul Rockwell in which he said the French were planning a major attack on the Bois-le-Prêtre. He said he liked the assignment, but "I'm getting tired of all this damned military stuff, saluting about 16,000 times a day and answering fool questions for soused soldiers. About half the town remains pickled all the time and grabs one around the neck saying 'Come with me to le Bois-le-Prêtre and we'll kill the Boche.' I've been on my good conduct here, tho I indulge in the most excellent beer."[32] (Jim apparently had a problem with binge drinking and was to embarrass himself on at least one occasion later on.)

The major attack that Jim wrote about began on May 1. A. R. Decker reported that the French captured two trenches in the "Quarter in Reserve" portion of the Bois-le-Prêtre. Four hundred prisoners were taken, and just 100 yards from the smoke and thunder, an American ambulance could be seen hauling the wounded.[33] The following day, he reported that the Germans recaptured the trenches the same morning that the French had initially captured them, the French retook them in the afternoon, the Germans retook them that night, and the French again recaptured them the next morning. The number of prisoners taken was scaled back to 130, and the Americans had evacuated over 200 wounded.[34] On the day after that, Decker reported that the Germans had retaken one of the trenches, leaving the French with a small net gain. He wondered if it was worth the cost.[35]

Jim was right in the thick of it. He sent two letters to his sister Julia, asking her to forward the first letter to their mother and keep the second for herself. (In his letters to his mother, Jim typically avoided anything that might upset her, while he was more forthright with his sister.) His letter to his sister said there was a big fight in which the French advanced 200 yards, took four trenches, and captured 150 prisoners. A wounded German sergeant kept calling out, "*Nicht kaput!*" (Don't kill me!) Jim carried his first German prisoner in one of his ambulance runs, "but he croaked just after arriving in the hospital." The roar of artillery was so bad they could hardly sleep.

> The heavy artillery has a strange roar when it's fired. The shell sounds just like an express train, hurtling thru the sky, and then as the singing whirr of a slowing down electric fan when it's going to hit. It's hard to distinguish one shell from another when the whole works lets loose. It's just a constant boom, roar, bang and a few kitchen stoves thrown in for the *mitrailleuse* [machine guns]. We work in front of the artillery and back of the trenches so get the benefit of all the racket. Yesterday morning an *obus* [shell] hit fifty feet back of one of our cars but didn't touch. Last night a large shell burst so close to Davis's car that it tipped it over on two wheels and a great chunk of the shell (*eclat* we call it) cut the top front of his car off, missing his head by ten inches. We have had some pretty close but that's about as near as one can be without being crammed into a field overcoat.[36] [The overcoat would have served as a shroud for burial.]

In the middle of a bombardment, when there was so much noise it was impossible to tell if a shell was approaching, he saw an old woman calmly working in her garden.

Jim wrote a similar letter to his father, but the letter was written over two days because he was interrupted by calls to evacuate more wounded from the front. He said they were removing the wounded from three different field stations and would drive about 66 kilometers (40 miles) on each trip, carrying the wounded from the front lines to the nearest field hospital. There were many airplanes flying over the battle, both French and German, and shrapnel from the antiaircraft guns fell near them.[37]

Things had apparently calmed down enough by the third day that he was able to write a long letter to Paul Rockwell. His description of the battle, hauling the wounded, the near miss on the ambulance, etc. was similar to what he wrote to his family, but he added some new information. He was glad to hear that Paul was going to be *reformé* (medically discharged from the Foreign Legion) so he could get on with his life and his upcoming marriage. Soldiers told him that in some places the trenches were only 30 inches apart. The French put a sandbag in front of their trench, only to have it stolen by the Germans. The next time they put up a sandbag, they watched, and when they saw it move they swatted the German on the hand with a shovel. When the ambulance drivers evacuate the wounded during the daytime, they encounter beautiful spring countryside once they get out of the war zone. "The road runs at the side of the velvet green bottom lands and between rows of beautiful tall trees that are now covered with the delicate green of spring. The hillsides have that entrancing miniature gardenlike appearance that the patches of green grass, brown soil, and yellow mustard plants give . . . one has to leave Paris to realize fully the meaning of 'La Belle France.'"[38] Their cameras had been confiscated; otherwise he could have taken some wonderful pictures.

Jim was surprised and piqued that he hadn't had even a line from "the Guerin individual" [Marcelle]. He wasn't at a loss for companionship, though. "I have scared up a village belle who has promised me I may call on her at night and *cause avec elle sous le jardin* [chat with her under the garden]. I get about two nights off a week and have a way of sneaking into my billet after eight so here's where I improve my French. I suppose it will end in a dose, but trust not."

His pique with Marcelle ended two days later when he was overjoyed to find a letter from her waiting for him when he went back to his billet at Dieulouard. He wrote her that when he made night runs from Pont-à-Mousson to the first-aid stations to evacuate the wounded, they had to creep along with no lights, not even cigarettes, and give passwords to sentries. French batteries were located in "startling proximity" to the first-aid posts. The French batteries were shooting at German batteries, and they were close to the front lines, so the Germans wouldn't have time to react to the noise of the incoming shell. Jim evacuated a dying soldier to the hospital, only to have him ask to be taken to his home in a nearby village so he could die there. He was going to do that, but a doctor at the hospital said the soldier wouldn't survive the trip.[39]

In the same letter, he said the war was an everyday affair to the people of Pont-à-Mousson, and they had reconciled themselves to it. Shops were open and children still went to school despite occasional shelling. He felt that his squad was doing good work, and he was comfortable and happy, "tho being so far away from you and not having the pleasure of seeing and talking with you keeps me from being content."

A few days later he wrote a note to Paul Rockwell, saying, "The factories are running, the cafés are crowded, and right now, between the roar of heavy artillery, I can hear the high pitched drone of children's voices reciting the lesson for the day in the little school across the garden from us." Their team was performing so well that the French ambulance team they had been working with was going to be reassigned to a different sector, leaving the Americans to handle all evacuations from the Bois-le-Prêtre themselves. The Americans were going to move out of their billets in Dieulouard and station everyone at Pont-à-Mousson, not just the on-duty crew. (Jim didn't know it at the time, but A. Piatt Andrew was about to send additional men and ambulances to beef up their team.) He mentioned receiving a letter from Marcelle, and also one from "no less a cutie than our little friend Elizabeth Baldwin."[40] Jim would have reason to write much more about "Betty" later in the war. (Betty Baldwin was a 1914 graduate of Bryn Mawr. She was the daughter of Professor and Mrs. James Mark Baldwin, a pioneering psychologist, who was teaching in Paris.)

On May 7, the German U-boat U-20 torpedoed and sank the British passenger liner *Lusitania*. In total, 1,198 people drowned when this unarmed passenger liner sunk, including 128 American citizens. Many people expected the US to declare war in response to this sinking, but the US response was limited to official diplomatic protests. American volunteers serving in France were outraged. Jim wrote to a friend in the US: "We heard the other day about the *Lusitania*. It's quite terrible, but our old Mother Hubbards in the capitol won't do a damn thing. America is a huge joke over here."[41] The letter was given to a courier who mailed it outside the war zone, so Jim could express his uncensored feelings about the war. "It's a hopeless, heartless sort of war. Nowadays the fellow that gets the jump on the other has everything. You can push on in, dig your system of trenches and God Almighty can't budge you. In the last attack the French took three trenches and advanced 200 yards, and to do it took an odd number over 40,000 men. . . . The new class [newly recruited or drafted soldiers who had just reached the age where they were eligible to serve] came up here composed of enthusiastic young men who sang and kicked up a racket and promised all sorts of things. They had their chance. A few *mitrailleuses* [machine guns] went into action and now there 'aint no new class.' . . . A gang known as the 346th has come down from Mort Mare to put in their lick here. I had coffee with the outfit this morning. They think they have come to a better post, but next week I won't be able to have coffee with them." On a cheerier note, he said that a soldier assigned to their support had previously been a chef in Paris, so their food was excellent. They had running water, hot showers, and electric lights when the shells hadn't broken the wires. He said he was having a glorious experience, and his only complaint was that his shoes were wearing out (a common complaint among the Model T drivers).

Jim's elation at having electric lights proved to be short lived. A. R. Decker reported that a new French offensive captured four trenches along a 500-mile front, but a German counterattack that night recaptured the trenches plus some French trenches. The French suffered five hundred wounded and two hundred dead in that one action, and many of the fifty Germans they captured were wounded.[42] Fierce fighting continued for the next several days, with both sides trying to consolidate their positions. Huge quantities of ammunition were expended, and many soldiers were killed or wounded in fighting over a 50-foot stretch of trench.[43] Jim wrote to Paul Rockwell that "a lot of very severe fighting during the last few days has resulted in a great deal of work for us."[44] He was living full time now at the advanced post in Pont-à-Mousson, but German shelling destroyed the lines that supplied their power. It also destroyed the shop where he used to buy pastries. They were expecting six new ambulances and drivers, which was good, because one of their ambulances was so severely damaged by shellfire that it had to be sent back to Paris for repairs.[45]

In his next letter to Marcelle, he apologized for taking so long to respond, but he had been working day and night evacuating the wounded and didn't have a single minute to himself. The *caserine* (barracks) they operated out of also came under shellfire. Jim described how a shell exploded just on the other side of a wall as he was parking his ambulance after returning from a call. He made a "graceful, yet rapid entrance into the *caserine*" before the next shell landed. He and his buddies stood in the doorway and waved other drivers into the shelter as they returned from their calls. He described them as ducking and scurrying as if they were "heading for shelter during a heavy rainstorm." Before the recent surge in activity tied everyone up, one of their ambulances was used as a hearse for the funeral of a very young *sous-lieutenant* (second lieutenant). His soldiers decorated the ambulance with the beautiful wildflowers that are now in bloom. His family was allowed to come near the front to attend the funeral, including his father, who had lost a leg in the Franco-Prussian War of 1870.[46]

A letter to his mother was, understandably, much more upbeat. There was no mention of fighting near his post or of shellfire. He described how beautiful the countryside was. He also reassured her that he was smoking less and drinking nothing (not even beer or wine), and his health was fine. He said it was hard to tell when he would be able to return to the States, since they were now part of the French army and could be released only as a unit, not as individuals.[47] (Either Jim didn't know the arrangements that A. Piatt Andrew had worked out with the French, or he didn't want his mother to know that he'd be eligible to come home in August, when his six-month enlistment expired.)

In mid-May, the Germans began shelling Pont-à-Mousson with larger-caliber, 210 mm shells. These did much-greater damage, and cellars did not provide adequate protection from them. Residents began leaving in greater numbers, schools were closed, and children were playing in the streets. They were playing war and imitated the sounds of incoming shells quite accurately. Plans were being made to send them away to a school out of the war zone.[48] Three hundred refugees, mostly women and children, fled the town in a single night. A German family living in a house near Pont-à-Mousson left their house temporarily, possibly to go shopping, and when they returned, French troops had commandeered their house and surrounded it with barbed wire.[49]

One of the large 210 mm shells landed 10 feet from an ambulance driven by a man named Curtin*, but it failed to explode. Jim said that if it had gone off, "we would have peeled him off the wall and sent him home in an envelope." Because of the general exodus of civilians from Pont-à-Mousson, he was now sharing a suite of rooms in a building across from their operating post with the team chief, Ned Salisbury. There were beautiful gardens outside, and he wrote to Marcell to ask, "Can't you get assigned to our section as Red Cross nurse? I'll guarantee to get wounded and then you can wheel me around the gravel paths of the aforementioned garden."[50]

A French lieutenant took Jim on a visit to the front lines. Jim was dressed in a French uniform and crawled behind the lieutenant between the first and second lines of trenches to drag in some dead bodies. Jim didn't keep low enough until a sniper's bullet zinged by. Later he was sitting in a trench talking to the lieutenant when they heard the screech of incoming shells. The lieutenant dove to the ground, covering his head with his arms, and

* Enos W. Curtin of New York.

Jim did likewise. Jim said if he hadn't followed the lieutenant's lead, he would have gotten his. "A large, robust, and very speedy chunk sang over my dome by a two foot miss and sunk in the edge of an excavation."[51]

Jim had an even closer brush with death as the month of May came to a close. He was picking up the wounded at their most advanced field post. The post was next to a French artillery position, and the Germans began shelling that position. He told Marcelle that "the blooming things were zizz-zizz-zizz-ker-banging all over the place and one shell went through a tree ten feet off. The first thing I knew was that something poked me a jab in the pack over my kidneys and I staggered a bit from the shock. A lieutenant asked me if I was wounded and came over to me. It was a huge joke for I reached around and pulled out a bit of shrapnel casing that hadn't gone into me at all. It just went through my uniform and when it encountered my tough hide it couldn't go any further. All I received was a bloody bruise that's nearly well now. Another fellow was with me and his car was quite badly cut up by the same shell."[52] Jim treated this as an amusing incident in his letter to Marcelle, but he obviously was well aware that if it hadn't been for the pack over his kidneys, the shrapnel wouldn't have had any trouble penetrating his tough hide. Mr. Decker described this incident, but in his description, Jim was more concerned than he admitted to Marcelle. Mr. Decker wrote that "Mr. McConnell of the American ambulance core was badly shaken by a shrapnel shell, which burst into fragments nearby. One of the fragments passed through the steering post of a car, damaged a tire, and carried off the top of the ambulance, but the Americans continued transporting many injured to the temporary hospital." He went on to add that a bombardment of Pont-à-Mousson killed eight soldiers and thirteen civilians, and it wounded forty-eight people. "The American ambulances had the gruesome work of removing the dead bodies being in a frightful condition."[53]

FOUR

With the American Ambulance Service

The fighting at Bois-le-Prêtre raged on, and so did the bombardment of Pont-à-Mousson. The Germans began using a new weapon against French artillery positions—a 42-inch high-incendiary shell filled with benzene that flowed into the dugouts where the artillerymen sheltered.[1] The American ambulances were kept busy evacuating wounded soldiers and civilians. For days on end, Jim was too busy to write anything more than a postcard that said he was too busy to write.[2] Finally things slowed down enough that he could write to his sister:

> Our section has been mentioned in Joffre's order of the day*. It's one of the highest honors a man can get. . . . Bravery under fire was one of the recommendations. About half of the crowd are scared to death half the time tho for some reason I very unfortunately achieved a reputation of being one of the nerviest in the section. Possibly from my run to the railroad tracks where shells were coming down. Anyway I have that burden, and now, tho I feel cold inside when I hear a shell whistle towards me, I needs must act as if I didn't care a whoop and never change expression. . . . I can't very well refuse to saunter out on any old mission no matter how warm it may be.[3]

* General Joseph Joffre was the commander in chief of the French army.

He went on to describe the shrapnel that hit him in late May as "a joke . . . it couldn't traverse my tough hide. I picked it out of my pack and then like a fool lost it. I only got a bloody bruise." He criticized the weak US response to the *Lusitania* outrage, saying, "The American nation over here is a huge joke as regards its maintenance of rights; its upholding of ideals or any cooperation towards the betterment of civilization—save from a monetary standpoint." (Not all Americans carried a lasting outrage over the *Lusitania.* Less than a year after the sinking, a song titled "Down in the U-17" became popular enough to be recorded by Billy Murray, a popular recording star.[4] Subtitled "A Musical Torpedo," the song depicts German submariners singing, dancing, and having a jolly time under the sea when they weren't busy fighting.)

The intermittent bombardment of Pont-à-Mousson was still going on. "In our last bombardment 31 were killed and 50 wounded. I picked up some of the dead. Women are awful looking dead. Their hair gets all bloody and falls down. German shells have a faculty of killing only women and children for the most part." In closing, he mentioned that he was being given two days off to write a sketch about the work his section was doing. That sketch would help change the US attitude toward the war.

Jim and his fellow drivers used Model T ambulances for their runs to first-aid posts near the front lines and to carry the wounded from these posts to forward hospitals in Pont-a-Mousson and nearby towns. In addition to the Fords, they brought a large Hotchkiss ambulance when they came up from Paris. It was too large and heavy to negotiate the narrow roads to the first-aid posts, but they did use it on occasional runs to move patients from forward hospitals to permanent hospitals farther back, or to a train station out of shellfire range, where the wounded could be transported to hospitals throughout France. A. Piatt Andrew sent them a large Pierce Arrow truck in June to use for similar runs.[5] Jim used one of these larger ambulances to carry the wounded to Nancy. A French officer there took him on an hour's tour of the city before he had to head back. He wrote a long letter to Marcelle describing that trip—and more. He apologized that the letter was disjointed, since he wrote it a few paragraphs at a time in between getting calls to drive to first-aid posts and evacuate the wounded. Excerpts from that letter give a feel for the daily life of an ambulance driver at the front:

> I had a very good tour of the place [Nancy]. It was a glorious day and I enjoyed it all immensely. The Place d'Alliance [town square] is a perfect little gem. The gardens, where we sat down to have a

drink—I would have you know that for a month now I have touched but lemonade and other soft thirst killers—were beautiful. It was Sunday and everyone was out strolling around. True there was something strange about the scene; the noticeable absence of men from twenty to forty. . . . I took an artillery captain back with me and as it was his first time at our part of the front the details of approach to the line were called to my attention by his questions and comments. At five fifteen we left the beautiful city in the quiet of its Sunday rest and at six we were in front of artillery that was in action. After we had followed the road for a few kilometers the captain called attention to an observation balloon, sharply outlined against the deep blue sky. Then we went thru villages where great crowds of soldiers were gathered. As we passed others one could notice the difference in the appearance of the men. Those in the towns farther back were cleaner and looked fresh; as we went on one could notice the boots and coats still covered with the dirt of the trenches and then we arrived at a town where the fronts of some buildings were torn by *éclats* [shell fragments]. We rolled on and suddenly came to a stretch of road on which the Germans can look and frequently shell. The captain covered his gold *galons* [stripes; i.e., rank insignia] with a map he was looking at. We then entered a town where I began to meet friends. They greeted us and some wanted a ride. Then we came to our town [Pont-à-Mousson] and its wrecks of buildings. We turned out toward the trenches; past cantonments where great numbers of soldiers I knew were resting. They would wave, and in the most advanced one a man ran up, stopped me, and gave me a ring he'd been making for me out of a piece of shell. "Why you know everyone here don't you?" said the officer. We had been hearing distant firing but now it became clear and sharp and we looked for wires that having been cut by shells might be too low to pass under. Up we went. There were no soldiers to be seen now and ahead we heard heavy firing. We rounded a bend and came upon a battery firing across the road just in front of us. Of course we could go no farther and so our dapper little captain with the usual profuse thanks dismounted and disappeared in the woods behind to circle the artillery. I couldn't quite get it thru my head that only three quarters of an hour before we had slipped out of a peaceful city.

The letter continues from a hospital in Pont-à-Mousson near the *caserine* where Jim was stationed.

I had a man in my car just now that had come within the zone of effect of asphyxiating, or however you spell it, shell. [The Germans began using gas warfare in April 1915.] He suffered in his breathing and at this moment one of the doctors came up to ask me where he could get ahold of Salisbury. . . . The doctor had just sat down next to me when we heard the tearing roar of a great shell overhead. It hit a house a hundred yards from us with a deafening explosion. We bent down to avoid the *éclats*. I asked the doctor what message I could carry to Salisbury. Instead of replying he got up and said "Come in with me." We entered the long corridor. A few seconds afterwards, not more than three I estimate, I saw a small group of *brancardiers* [stretcher bearers] in the next entrance to the corridor from us, crouch swiftly down. They had heard the whistle. Immediately the air became crushing. I was bent over. There was an overpowering detonation and it became dark. Glass, wood and plaster pelted and fell on me. I remember wondering what was coming down next and then I heard terrible shrieks above the din of falling debris. I tried to look down the corridor through the dense smoke and saw a man waving his arms and yelling crazily totter towards me. He grabbed my shoulder and moaned. You have heard a child cry after some shock. It was like that but this was a man and it made it seem worse. The clouds of smoke and dust cleared and twenty yards from me I saw one of the *brancardiers* on the floor. A stream of red blood was feeling its way through the coating of dust on the floor. An *éclat* had passed thru his chest. He had been killed instantly. Others were wounded. I went out and saw the great hole where the *marmite* [shell] had struck twenty five yards from where I was standing. . . . If it had been ten feet nearer it would have hit the corridor wall and bagged the whole bunch of us. I heard another coming and fell flat on my face. . . . The men began hurrying towards the cave [basement]. . . . First I went back to get this letter that I had placed on a chair in the corridor when I entered and found it all covered with glass and stones and plaster. I've cleaned it up as well as I can. The rough edges come from cramming it in my pocket. I'm sorry. Shells began coming at regular intervals. When it was time to go back to the *caserine* I waited until a shell went off and then made a dash for it. Got to the main street and was tangled up in broken telephone lines. I got them off and hit it up across the Place [town square]. Two of our fellows who were looking out from a sand bag shelter there said I just got away in time to miss two [two shells]. . . . There were a great many killed and several wounded. 60 casualties in all.

> We evacuated all the hospitals in Pont-à-Mousson last night and it was eleven before we finished . . . we could see part of the town burning from the bombardment and shrapnel bursting over to keep people from putting it out. . . . I'm going up there [to a frontline first-aid post] in an hour for an attack is in progress, and the wounded will be coming in from the trenches then. Shells are singing overhead and explosions are shaking my room but that doesn't bother us for it's only our artillery shooting and the Germans shooting back at the batteries. It's a fearful din tho.[6]

A few days later, Jim wrote to Paul Rockwell and said that all the hospitals in Pont-à-Mousson had been closed because of the bombardments. They now had to evacuate wounded from the front lines to Dieulouard, about 5 miles farther. The extra distance was a problem at night because they had to creep along a road that was jammed with caissons and supply trains, and they couldn't use lights. He described the shell that nearly killed him in the hospital, and said that near miss was what caused the French to abandon the largest hospital in Pont-à-Mousson. The explosion was caused by a 210 mm (8.25 inch) shell that landed in the courtyard just short of the wall Jim was standing behind; "Otherwise I wouldn't be here." His description of the blast was similar to what he wrote Marcelle, describing the concussion wave that caused him to double over as "suddenly the air turned into a crushing solid that took my breath away." He also said that the man who grabbed him, screaming like a child, hadn't been hit by anything. "It was the unnerving effect those big shells have."[7]

In mid-June, Jim wrote to Marcelle that they had been joined by a "British driver named Bushwell."[8] This was actually Leslie Buswell, a British citizen who would later write a book called *Ambulance No. 10: Personal Letters from the Front.* His impressions of the ambulance team at Pont-à-Mousson provide additional insight into the life of Jim and the other ambulance drivers. Buswell was billeted in a French house near the *caserine* that served as their headquarters and mess, and as he walked to breakfast the next morning, he could see the German trenches in the distance. It struck him that "a first-class rifle shot could pick one off."[9] After breakfast, a fellow driver offered to take him up to the lines in an ambulance and show him where they worked. "No one can realize the excellence of the Ford for this purpose until he has seen what they can do." Some of Buswell's additional observations:

> Every other night we have to sleep in barracks to be on duty any moment, and so we sleep on straw and don't undress. Every fourth night we are on duty all night and go to X___ [a first-aid post near

the trenches] and stay there in the car taking wounded to the first, second, and third base hospitals.[10]

In several places here the trenches are only fifteen or twenty metres apart and the French and Germans are on quite good terms. They exchange tobacco for wine and paper for cigarettes and then return and shoot at each other quite merrily. About Christmas or February, I am told, by soldiers who were then here, they used to walk into each other's trenches and exchange stories, etc., but now they have become *méchant* [nasty].[11]

The governor of Pont-à-Mousson was indignant when he learned the American volunteers were being paid a sous per day, same as an ordinary poilu. He thought they should earn at least as much as a sub-lieutenant.[12]

I took three wounded to the hospital this morning from X___ after they had only been in the trenches twenty minutes, having come straight from the Home Base. They talked so hopelessly about their chance of life. An old chap asked me yesterday if I would like a German rifle. "Well, rather," said I. He promised he would bring it to me at seven o'clock, unless an *obus* [shell] hit him. He did not come, poor fellow, but perhaps he forgot his promise. I hope so.[13]

It was a sad trip for me—a boy about nineteen had been hit in the chest and half his side had gone, "*tres pressê*" [hurry up!] they told me, and as we lifted him into the car, by a little brick house which was a mass of shell holes, he raised his sad, tired eyes to mine and tried a brave smile. I went down the hill as carefully as I could and very slowly, but when I arrived at the hospital I found I had been driving a hearse and not an ambulance.[14]

The French were very pleased with the work being done by the section at Pont-à-Mousson, and they expanded their territory to include the towns of Limey, Flirey, and Fey eu Haye—roughly a third of the way to St. Mihiel. Each driver spent one day out of every ten in Diulouard, using one of the large ambulances to carry wounded from the hospitals to a hospital train.[15]

A. R. Decker, the American engineer in Pont-à-Mousson, also noticed how pleased the French were with the American ambulance drivers. He wrote a very complimentary piece for publication in American newspapers:

The presence of the American ambulance section in Pont-à-Mousson has an important influence upon the morale of the French troops. This factor is not to be disdained, for in a long, grueling campaign

> the morale is everything. The concrete expression of America's sympathy for France's sacrifice is to no small extent buoying up the French hopes. . . . The ambulance section has been cited for the order of the day and decorated with the war cross. . . . The section at Pont-à-Mousson comprises twenty men, with seventeen Ford cars, a Hotchkiss, a Peugeot and a magnificent Pierce-Arrow. . . . These young Americans daily run risks more serious than the soldiers, who are somewhat sheltered by the trenches and dugouts. An ambulance running along a shell swept road is without any protection whatever. One car had the steering post pierced by a shell fragment and a spare tire torn off the top. . . . In one day McConnell escaped three times. He was hit by shrapnel, covered with debris by a "kettle," and deluged by a projectile that fell in the river. . . . The American ambulances are extremely popular with the French. During the early days of the "American invasion," when French and American cars divided the work, the French injured would dispute for places in the American cars. At the field hospitals a wounded soldier refused to accept a place in a French ambulance and insisted upon waiting for a ride down with "*une voiture Américaine*" [an American car]. Hardly a day passes without a soldier or an officer stopping me with the following conversation: "You are an American, aren't you?" "Yes," I reply. "Well, I just want to let you know that we appreciate the fine, noble work that your ambulance corps is doing. They are brave young men, seriously doing their work. I must say that our injured receive better care with them than with our own ambulance men."[16]

Decker also wrote that roughly 250 people a day were fleeing Pont-à-Mousson because of the shelling. Prices had doubled and in some cases tripled since the start of the war. Both sides used airplanes to direct their artillery, and battles between airplanes were becoming common as each side tried to keep the other side from carrying out their missions. "William Thaw, the American aviator, also flies in this vicinity. He has earned the nickname 'that mad American' because he flies at only 4,000 feet altitude above the German guns."[17] Within a year, Jim would be flying alongside "that mad American."

Jim wrote to Paul Rockwell in late June with questions about how Paul sold articles to newspapers and magazines. He said there had not been much fighting lately, and some days they handled only fifty wounded. They would get a rush of wounded when the *crapouillot* (literally a "little toad"—a French nickname for a trench mortar) were active, and then things would

Jim with one of the large ambulances, probably the "magnificent" Pierce-Arrow. *NASM*

slow down. One night they had a rush caused by a short but intense bombardment by 210 mm shells. There were many head wounds. One died in Jim's ambulance before he could get him to a hospital, and out of eleven operations at the forward treatment post, ten died. When they didn't have a rush of the wounded, though, Jim had time to write. He had just finished a seven-thousand-word article about their section for the ambulance authorities, and he thought he might be able to earn a little extra money by writing for publication. "I might not be able to send in anything worthwhile, but there's no use in not trying." He had approached Arthur Page, the editor of *World's Work* magazine and the brother of Jim's friend Frank Page, but Arthur told him it was hard to sell articles about what was happening, since people had grown bored with that. They wanted to know what was going to happen.[18]

American readers may have grown bored reading about what was happening, but that didn't stop it from happening. An American ambulance driver in Mourmelon le Grand, about 75 miles from Pont-à-Mousson, described the effects of artillery bombardments on that town:

> There is no form of devastation on earth that can compare to a town deliberately and completely wrecked by continuous artillery fire. On one side of the street the houses were blown into shapeless masses; the stone was not only scattered, but often crumbled into dust; the iron was tortured into fantastic shapes; the woodwork was ashes; on the opposite side were wrecks of houses with one wall or one triangular corner standing others had holes blown through them big enough for a two-horse team to drive in, yet still upright; here and there a single house had escaped destruction, but served only to emphasize the devastation around it; the roof of the church is gone, one half of the nave and entire transept is crushed in, and the tower is tottering; it was as if the huge hand of some demon from the clouds had lifted the entire village to unthinkable heights and in wanton rage dashed it back to earth.[19]

That Sunday, the *New York Sun* carried a half-page spread, with photographs, extolling the work done by the American ambulance drivers. A. Piatt Andrew described the work being done by all three sections, with special praise for the run that Jim McConnell and Harold Willis made to pick up wounded civilians during a bombardment of Pont-à-Mousson. He said their section carried 1,650 wounded the previous week, and at least 1,000 wounded per week since they arrived at the front.[20]

Another ambulance section based farther back picked up the work that Section 2 had been doing, taking the wounded from Diulouard to hospital trains, so Jim's section was able to use all their ambulances evacuating the wounded from the fighting around Pont-à-Mousson.[21]

Paul Rockwell's brother Kiffin, who was still in the Foreign Legion, had been seriously wounded during a bayonet attack in early May. Jim wrote to Paul to say he was glad to hear that Kiffin was recovering, but worried because that meant he would soon be sent back to the front. He also worried about Paul being sent back. "God knows he's [Kiffin's] done ten times his share and then some and I should think they would insist on his going in some branch that didn't have the odds stacked against one. . . . I hope they pronounce you a hopeless *réformé* so you can't go out and risk your old neck again. I'd hate like hell to see you go. You may not know it but I haven't a friend in the world I like better than you and am damn glad to have you say you find me a good pal."[22] A few days later, he wrote Paul to say that his article about the work Section 2 was doing had made a hit with their headquarters, and he might land a published article out of it:

> Hope so, anyway for finally, after writing me a number of letters telling me to return to America, my family has informed me that they will discontinue sending me even the small sums that I used to receive with much glee from time to time. Fortunately, the amounts were small so I shall not miss them so much.[23]

This would not be the last time his family expressed their displeasure at his voluntarily risking his neck for the French. With no extra money coming in from his family, Jim would have to get by on the five cents per day he earned as an ambulance driver.

Jim also told Paul Rockwell that the Americans were planning a big party for the Fourth of July. They had lots of food and booze, and a piano, and had set up a boxing ring in their *caserine* for a match between a Frenchman and one of the Americans. They were counting on the Germans to provide fireworks. "I'll drink to your health tomorrow. Then back on the wagon." On a serious note, he said the Germans sent fifty-three shells into the little cluster of houses where some of the forward first-aid stations were located. One was a station where Americans stayed when they pulled night duty, but none of the Americans were injured. Two of his friends among the French officers were killed. There was a terrific bombardment of the trenches going on, with fifteen thousand shells hitting the French trenches in twenty-four hours.[24]

Leslie Buswell also described the heavy fighting that was going on:

> For some days most of the French batteries had been leaving here for up north where a large army is concentrating, and the Germans (who know everything) attacked us at the most unfortunate moment—and by so doing won back in that short attack much of the land they had lost since December, the winning of which has caused France the loss of over forty thousand men! . . . We worked late and I got to bed at three-thirty, having carried some fifty wounded a distance of about ten kilometers—ten trips—two hundred kilometers [125 miles]! In all we carried away over three hundred and fifty crippled wrecks who three hours before were the pride of their nation and families! . . . I had a German *couché* [wounded] given me and I probed out the fact that there were some six or eight French waiting to be taken. "Oh, but he is seriously wounded—take him first!" . . . I shall always remember that in France the German went before the less wounded Frenchman![25]

The fighting went on for several days. The soldiers were tired. The ambulance drivers were tired. The doctors, nurses, and stretcher bearers at the forward hospitals were tired. Jim came back from night duty at the first-aid post to find a letter from Marcelle waiting for him. He wrote back before sleeping, and the strain of the nonstop work showed. He described returning from a run to a hospital, trying to fall asleep on a stretcher, and hearing the phone ring as another call came in:

> "*Monsieur Américain, un blessé urgent á C____.*" You get up and go out to the car and whirr up a long hill to a place in the woods. The poor, hard worked men at the *poste de secours* [first-aid post] are waiting. In the light of the illuminating rockets you see a much bandaged figure on a stretcher and between the reports of artillery you get instructions to go carefully but swiftly. That's hard, that two kilometers down into the town and you figure on every little bump or hole. Sometimes there's a new shell hole and you hit it. The poor fellow shrieks and you would give anything to have avoided the bump. We get so that we know the easiest way to take all the turns and what sides of the road are smoothest, but every second is a strain as we nurse the car down to the ambulance where the man will be operated on and evacuated the next morning. The cobblestone streets are the hardest proposition and then comes the hospital. You stop and go to the back of the car. The wounded man is groaning softly. You hurry into the bureau to wake up the attendant. "*Un couché gravement blesse*" [a seriously injured stretcher case]. The man slowly gets up mumbling about the toughness of the war and slowly ambles back into the building. Minutes pass. You go out to the car and try and explain the delay to the wounded man. One *brancardier* [stretcher bearer] comes out. When will the other come, you wonder. He's careless about that and wants to know if there are many more wounded. Finally you lose all patience. I know I do and think of the other *brancardier* still sleeping. Finally he comes out. The man is taken into the operating room and examined in a superficial way. They wake up a surgeon. He takes his time and after a short look turns away saying it's no use trying to operate and goes back to bed. The man is carried to a side of the room and the *brancardiers* go out. Oh, that hurts so after you have tried so hard to get the poor fellow down as easily as possible and hoped you could save his life. To have that indifference shown is very aggravating. You go up again after using up all your matches trying to pick out a *brancard* [stretcher] that

> isn't too bloody or broken and find a load waiting. Three *couches* [stretcher cases] and two *assis* [sitting wounded]. Down the hill you go again and then there's the same fight to wake up the hospital. (I am taking parts from last nights' work for it's fresh in my memory and typical of other nights.) I took the two *assis* in with me while I went to rout out the *brandardiers*. In the corner of the room the poor fellow I had brought before was making hideous noises. He seemed pitiful dying there all alone, and when I lit a match the two *assis* looked at him in a shocked sort of way. I went out to my *couches*. There was a long delay getting the men out. One was a trepan case [skull wound] and I said I'd take him down eight kilometers where a young doctor in a second evacuation hospital would take care of him all right. "Oh, we do all that here" said a *brancardier* and disappeared with the jolting stretcher. They didn't return for a long time. The remaining man and I passed the time cussing the gang out. "Here we go and get all shot to pieces and then they treat us like *cochon* [pigs]," he said. When the *brancardiers* came out he handed them a bit of his mind. "Remember you're not the only one," they said, and that got me furious. "You g---- d---- bunch of *embusqués* [literally, "ambushers," often used in World War I to mean slackers]. You sit around here all day and raise h---- when a wounded man is the cause of some work, just as if you blamed him for it. I hope to heavens you all get sent up and get a taste of it yourself." I said all that in English, but from the tone and the word *embusqués* they got my meaning perfectly and for the rest of the night things went better.[26]

Jim wrote to Paul Rockwell the same day, saying he hadn't slept for a couple of days and would be on call again that night. Calls came in throughout their Fourth of July celebration, so drivers were coming and going throughout the festivities. "The wounds are frightful these days and a good many die before we get them to the surgeons. The only consolation lies in the fact that the Boches are getting it just as badly. The damn swine are using gas and as an extra barbarism they throw petrol jets [flame throwers] on the choking soldiers."[27]

Jim also wrote to his mother that day. He was probably running on adrenaline at that point, unable to sleep because of the stress and feeling that he had to answer the letters that had piled up while he was working. He spared her the gruesome details of his work but vented his frustration on President Wilson's lack of action:

> I haven't had any sleep in the last 36 hours, but I don't mind the work for there's a great deal of satisfaction in helping the French to evacuate their wounded as quickly as possible, outside of the pleasure one derives from feeling that it all helps to beat the rotten Germans. . . . I don't see where Wilson has any diplomacy. It's Mexico all over again. He dictates what he's going to do. Everyone says "Hurrah, we're back of you." And then the outfit he calls to task does the very thing he has complained about and he proceeds to dictate again. Why, America is a huge joke. I will always be ashamed of my country for not having helped France and what she stands for in this war. Thank God I can help some and I'd do more if you would let me. I'd like to go to the trenches and take a chance on killing some Boches myself. The world would be hideous if Germany won this war and America is going to get a large share of the benefit of France's victory just by selfishly staying out of the war while this land pours out her life's blood.[28]

Jim told both Paul and his mother that the famous African lion hunter R. J. Cunningham had joined their unit. Cunningham became famous when he served as Teddy Roosevelt's guide on his 1909 African big-game hunt. Cunningham was British, so the section now had at least two Englishmen and a Hollander in their unit, in addition to the French support staff.[29]

The following week, Jim wrote to Paul to say that the Germans' July 4 attack captured several French 75s [field artillery] and one thousand French prisoners and took back all the ground the French had taken since January. He tried to see this in a positive light. "This small attack business means nothing but part of a process: the wearing down and killing of Germans. The big events will have to wait until next spring when Russia is supplied and has her new armies ready and England can lend a hand. The Russian retreats now are all in our favor. The Germans are being worn down. I wouldn't be surprised to see them meet with a disaster similar to that experienced by Napoleon this winter."[30] He also said that the piece he wrote about their ambulance work was very well received by the leaders of the ambulance service, and they were sending it to the US to try to get it published in *Scribner's* or *Metropolitan*.

Jim wrote to Marcelle a few days later and expressed similar optimism about the coming year. He thought the British attack at Gallipoli would open the Dardanelles by Christmas, so that the Allies could help train and supply the Russian troops (however, the Gallipoli campaign turned out to be a disaster). "Germany can be crushed into a heap from which she can never straighten out. We French will be the ones that will administer the final touch, as is fitting and proper, for France from the first to the last has fought the whole war." (Note that Jim now considers himself "French.") He then quoted a French trench mortar gunner, who told him,

> I tell you, you would laugh to see it. I shoot my *torpille* [torpedo]. She goes turning slowly over and over through the air and then drops right in the trench. Oh you see 'em go up. Legs and arms and heads. Rifles, helmets, and sacks. All go up at once. Once I saw a whole Boche go up. Perfectly good Boche. Only one leg missing. He went up. Way up thirty meters.[31]

Not everyone was as callous as that French gunner. Buswell wrote, "It is no good trying to make you understand what horror really is—you must see a bit of it as we see it here to be able to semi-realize what that place, the Bois-le-Prêtre, is like. It was known by the Germans when held by them as '*Hexenkessel*' (witches' cauldron) and as '*Witwenwald*' (widows' wood)."[32]

Jim's letters weren't only about the war, and they certainly weren't all as macabre as his description of the trench mortar. The French army tried to give its soldiers leave periodically, and since the American ambulance drivers were subject to military rules, that applied to them as well. Jim's section chief, Ned Salisbury, was granted an eight-day leave, which he was spending in Paris. Jim wrote to Marcelle and described Ned as "an awfully fine chap" who had stumbled onto a "most wonderful *affaire d'amour*" [affair of the heart]. He told her that Paul Rockwell "thinks you're a peach. Can't say as I dispute his taste." He signed the letter "affectionately" and then added a PS to ask if that bothered her.[33]

In several of Jim's letters to Paul Rockwell, Jim asked if Paul had set a date for his upcoming wedding. He wanted as much advance notice as possible so he could request leave for those dates. (There would be many delays before the wedding finally took place, but when it did occur, Jim served as Paul's best man.) In one of these letters, he described bombardments in a matter-of-fact manner, almost as if he were describing the weather:

> Our chief Ned Salisbury is in Paris for eight days at present. Queer, it had been quiet for almost eight days before he left. An hour after we commenced to get it. Today it started in again and stopped a few minutes ago. Up around the trenches all is fairly quiet save for the occasional shots and in the lines *crapouillot* and grenades.[34]

A few days later the town suffered a bombardment that Jim couldn't dismiss as though it were bad weather. They had a "normal" bombardment shortly after lunch, and when it died down, Jim began writing his sister. He was concerned because his mother had found out where he was stationed, and he was afraid she would worry too much. Everyone was excited about the new leave policy. Jim had spent the previous night on duty at an advance first-aid post, and "the place buzzed with conjectures as to how home would look." Jim thought he might get his leave in September.[35] His letter was interrupted by a new bombardment, and he didn't get a chance to finish it until two days later, when he described what had happened. Buswell described the bombardment in his book also.[36] The following narrative combines details from both sources.

Around 9:00 p.m., a woman began screaming, "*C'est les Américans*" [It's the Americans]. They rushed to the *caserine* and found most of the section in the cellar, but a French mechanic and the French orderly who took care of them were missing. The mechanic, a man named Gustrai, came staggering into the *caserine*. A shell fragment had gone through his cheek and cut off part of his tongue. His left arm was lacerated by shell fragments. They found the orderly, a well-liked man named Mignot, lying dead outside. Next to him lay a mother and her daughter, clasped in each other's arms, both killed by the same explosion. Jim had walked past that spot just minutes earlier. Jim rushed the mechanic and a civilian who had been injured by the shellfire to a hospital in a nearby town. They amputated the mechanic's arm in an attempt to save his life, but he died later.

When Jim got back to Pont-à-Mousson, he found it was badly shot up. Their *caserine* had been hit in two places. Nine of the drivers had been having a party in a house near the *caserine* before the bombardment started. The first shell hit in front of the house and blew them all to the floor. They ran into the basement just in time, since the next shell came into the room they had just left, and demolished it. The hats and coats they had left behind were in shreds. When the shelling near their house eased, they went out to look for the dead and wounded, then headed for the basement of the *caserine* when the shells came closer. When the bombardment stopped, they discovered that a shell had gone into the basement of the house they had been in, destroying it. They couldn't account for one of the drivers, so they began digging through the rubble. He showed up a little later, wondering what they were looking for.

The French lieutenant who was in charge of the section while Salisbury was on leave announced they would evacuate to Dieulouard the next day. Jim, Buswell, and many of the other drivers were furious. Pulling back to Dieulouard would delay their response when men in the front lines were badly wounded, especially at night, when they couldn't use lights. They would have to drive at a crawl from Dieulouard to Pont-à-Mousson and then begin crawling toward the front lines. Jim predicted they would have more smashups with trucks, wagons, and troops that also used the crowded road to Dieulouard.[37]

When Salisbury returned from leave, he agreed with the drivers that it was impractical to operate from Dieulouard. Instead, he found a mansion in Pont-à-Mousson that hadn't been shelled, and moved their operations there. It was actually closer to the front lines than the caserine, which made their runs to pick up the wounded a little shorter. It had been owned by a German before the war, which they assumed was why it hadn't been shelled. Jim was assigned a bedroom with a canopy bed and its own bathroom. A couple of the drivers were returning to the US, and they received new drivers to replace them. One of them was Waldo Pierce, whom Jim described as "the nut that started for Europe with John Reed* on a cattle ship and, not liking the cattle ship, jumped overboard when outside of Boston Light and broke a swimming record."[38]

July passed into August and the fighting continued. Military history accounts of the Bois-le-Prêtre say that the French stopped trying to capture the woods in August, but that wasn't obvious to the ambulance drivers. Both sides continued to pound the frontline trenches, both sides bombarded towns and cities on the other side of the lines, and both sides launched local attacks to capture enemy trenches. Jim mentioned a failed German night attack that resulted in the ambulance drivers having to evacuate "only" ninety wounded men. He described the front lines in a letter to his mother:

> The Bois-le-Prêtre has seen the most hideous form of fighting in the war. It's unbelievable the life that is led there. Men crouch in little caves that have been left, for hardly any trenches remain. Great shells, that whip the ground around them into a sea of moving earth, rain down almost continually. It seems impossible that men could stand it. They are blown to pieces rather than wounded. They gaze out over a wilderness of black, shattered tree stumps and putrid bodies they dare not reach to bury. They throw grenades and iron cased explosives across at the trenches so near to them. The rifle is hardly ever used save to carry a bayonet in a charge.[39]

---

* Waldo Pierce later became a famous American painter and was a good friend of Ernest Hemingway. John Reed would go to Russia during the revolution and write *Ten Days That Shook the World*. Years later, he was the subject of the movie *Reds*.

In describing what a difference the American ambulances had made, Buswell mentions the staggering number of the wounded that Section 2 routinely transported:

> I must tell you what happened to the wounded before our little cars came here—we carried over eighteen hundred last week and more than seventy-five hundred during July. . . . Here in former days they were re-dressed, and if there were room, stayed in the little shelter, or if not, they had to lie outside till a horse-wagon came to fetch them. Sometimes they would have to wait many hours before their turn came, and even the most urgent cases would not get away and arrive at the hospital for a long time. Hundreds of soldiers died thus. Now, with our little cars, an urgent case is at the hospital ready for operation in twenty minutes at the most, and generally about ten to fifteen—no matter what time of the day or night.[40]

He also described the hazards and rewards of driving an ambulance at Pont-à-Mousson:

> About ten o'clock I had a call to go to Auberge St. Pierre for two seriously wounded, and when I arrived there, the *médecin* chef told me that if I got them to the hospital quickly, they would have a chance of living. So "No. 10" tooted off down the hill—at what the plain warrior would term—"a hell of a pace." As I entered Montauville I saw no one about, but as I passed a *poste de secour* [first-aid post] a doctor rushed out and told me to take two more if I had room. . . . I noticed ahead of me three large motor-trucks and the thought struck me: "What if those are hit and contain ammunition." I was ten yards away when—bang!—I was half blown out of my seat—a shell had landed on the motor truck. Hardly believing I was not hit, I increased my pace and emerged from the smoke and blackness, doing at a good clip, safe and sound, but shaken.[41]
>
> A shell had landed near a kitchen, killing several and seriously wounding one soldier. He had a hole as big as your fist right through his back. "There is a chance if you can get him to the operating-room quickly," I was told. It was eighteen kilometres [11 miles] to the best surgeon; so off dear old "No. 10" and I started on our rush for life . . . through village after village, without moving the throttle, we sped on and on. Bump, bump, bump, what did it matter if I had to shake him about a little, he was unconscious, and every second

> counted . . . I drew up at the tent. In a second two *brancardiers* had the car unloaded—the surgeon in white was washing his hands—and thirty minutes from the time my charge was given into my care, he was lying on the operating-table. "He may live," said the surgeon. That was my reward! That is why I am happy.[42]

The shelling of Pont-à-Mousson continued. A. R. Decker continued to write newspaper articles about the results. Many described tragedy, but there were some miraculous escapes. A shell exploded underneath a bed where a man was sleeping. The man was thrown against the ceiling but escaped with a few minor bruises. Decker invited one of the ambulance drivers to have dinner with him, when a shell exploded outside Decker's house. The driver was sent flying across the table, accompanied by a lamp and the dishes, but was unhurt.[43]

Jim was, of course, right in the middle of the evacuations and the bombardments. He was nearly killed when a 4-pound shell fragment just missed the window he was looking through.[44] He wrote very little about his work during this period, though, possibly because it was no different than the work he had been doing since the section arrived in Pont-à-Mousson in April. Instead, he wrote about things that were new, even if they were trivial. He found a canister of excellent pipe tobacco that was left behind by a German. The American aviator Bill Thaw landed at a nearby airfield to avoid a storm (Paul Rockwell had served with Thaw in the Foreign Legion, so this was of interest to him). Paul's brother Kiffin requested a transfer from the Foreign Legion to Aviation. Jim wrote Marcelle, "I should think he'd be glad of the change, but for one thing work in Aviation is awfully monotonous after the novelty wears off." He was looking forward to taking leave in Paris, which was tentatively scheduled to begin on September 15. He wasn't certain if Paul Rockwell would be in Paris that week, however, and Marcelle had just moved into a new job at the hospital and wasn't certain she could get time off during his visit. Jim told her he was "counting the days" until he could see her again. He had mentioned Betty Baldwin in some of his letters to her, and apparently she asked him about Betty and some of the other women he had mentioned. Jim replied, "Good heavens Mlle. Guérin, don't worry about whether I'm going to see any girls while I'm in Paris. You mention Mlle. du Bouchet* and Mary Lines, for it's only you I want to be with."[45]

---

* Hélène du Bouchet was the daughter of an American surgeon, Dr. August du Bouchet. Dr. du Bouchet worked in Paris during the war, presumably at the American Hospital.

Jim also wrote to his sister shortly before he took leave. In the first part of the letter, he complained about America's lack of support for France, and in particular about "Grandma's" weak response to the Arabic incident. (Presumably "Grandma" was President Wilson. The SS *Arabic* was a British passenger liner that was sunk by a German U-boat. The *Arabic* was following a zigzag course, and the U-boat commander said he thought the liner was turning to ram him.) Jim's letter then turned to personal feelings, something unusual in his letters to his sister. "I've never felt as close to you until I got away over here. Some day when we all get rich, I will take you over for a sightseeing tour of this sector. Educate your children by a first-hand view of the war. I'm afraid you'll ruin Mitchell, tho, if you send him to Groton. That's the finest factory for self-satisfied snobs I've ever met."[46]

On September 14, 1915, the divisional chief surgeon presented Section 2 with a unit award of the Croix de Guerre (Cross of War). He also presented their section chief, Edward Salisbury, with an individual award of the same medal.[47] The next day, Jim left for an eight-day leave in Paris. That was the same day *The Outlook* magazine published his article "With the American Ambulance Service."

FIVE

Changing Gears

The Outlook was the third-most-popular news magazine in the US when they published Jim's article. In the days before radio, television, or the internet, people got their news from newspapers and magazines. Newspapers were read locally but magazines were read nationally, and news magazines therefore carried a lot of weight. Jim's article, with his name as the author, was featured prominently on the magazine cover.

The article carried additional weight because the introduction was by former president Teddy Roosevelt. Roosevelt disagreed with President Wilson on many issues—not surprising, since Roosevelt had formed the "Bull Moose" Party to run against Wilson in 1912—and he strongly disagreed with Wilson's neutrality policy. Discerning readers may have detected that sentiment in his introduction to Jim's article:

> The United States has played a most ignoble part for the last thirteen months. Our Government has declined to keep its plighted faith, has declined to take action for justice and right, as it was pledged to take action under the Hague Conventions*. . . . It has treated empty rhetoric and adroit phrase-making as a substitute for deeds. In spite of our solemn covenant to see that the neutrality of unoffending nations like Belgium was not violated; our solemn covenant to see that undefended towns were not bombarded . . .

* The Hague Conventions were international "rules of war." They were later replaced by the Geneva Conventions.

> our solemn covenant to see that inhuman and cruel methods of warfare—such as the use of poisonous gas—were not used, we have in a spirit of cold, selfish, and timid disregard of our obligations for others, refused even to protest against such wrong-doing. . . . What is even more serious we have wholly failed to act effectively when our own men, women, and children were murdered on the high seas by the order of the German Government. . . . But there have been a few individuals who, acting as individuals or in organizations, have to a limited extent by their private efforts made partially good our Governmental shortcomings.[1]

Mr. Roosevelt praised Jim and all the other ambulance drivers and said that every young man just leaving college should assist those who were "battling for the right on behalf of Belgium," or else prepare himself to help his own country if the US entered the war. (It is doubtful that Mr. Roosevelt realized Jim was the son of the lawyer who he had previously claimed had hands "dyed in blood" for helping secure pardons for the Haymarket Square conspirators.)

Like most of Jim's writing during the war, the article was written in an informal, present tense that drew the reader in and made them feel as though they were experiencing it themselves. Jim included small details of everyday life as well as the harrowing details of evacuating the wounded under fire. He opened with a calm, everyday scene:

> A small field ambulance with a large red cross on each of its gray canvas sides slips quickly down the curving cobblestone street of a quaint old French frontier town and turns onto the road leading to the *postes de secours* (dressing stations) behind the trenches, which are about two kilometers distant. The driver is uniformed in khaki and is in striking contrast to the hundreds of blue-gray clad soldiers loitering on the streets. A group of little children cry out "*Américain.*" And, with beaming smiles they execute a rigid though not a very correct salute as the car goes by. A soldier yells "Good morning, sir!" another "Hello Charley!" and waves his hand, while others not gifted with such an extensive command of English content themselves with "*Bonjour!*" and "*Camarade!*" The little car spins on past companies of tired, dusty soldiers returning from the trenches, and toots to one side the fresher looking sections that are going up for their turn.[2]

As the article continues, he describes the realities of war:

The mention of shell fire to one who has never experienced it brings to mind, in a vague sort of way, an association with danger, but that is all. To us who have seen its effects—the hideously mangled killed and wounded, the agonized expressions and streams of fast-flowing blood, the crumbling of solid houses into clouds of smoke and dust; to us who hear the terrible tearing, snarling, deep roar of great shells as they hurtle down the air-lanes towards us to detonate with a murderous, ear-splitting crash, flinging their jagged *éclats* for a half-mile in all directions, and sometimes killing French comrades near us; to us who live and work within shell range, not knowing when we too may be annihilated or maimed for life, it seems a very real and terrible menace, and for that reason to be banished from our thoughts.[3]

A kilometer up the climbing, winding road is a lone *poste de secours* in the woods just off the highway. The approach and the place itself are often shelled. There have been times when the drivers were under a seriously heavy fire on night duty; times when trees have been shattered and fallen across the road and huge craters made in the soft earth of the adjacent fields. A kilometer beyond is still another point of call, and from there one can look directly into one of the most fought-over sections of ground in the long line from the sea to Belfort. It is a bit of land that before the war was covered with a magnificent forest. Now it is a wilderness whose desolation is beyond description. It is a section of murdered nature. The black, shattered things sticking up out of a sea of mounds were at one time great trees. There are no branches on the split trunks now. No green can be seen anywhere. Where the trenches ran there are but series of indentations, jumbles of splintered trench timbers, broken guns, rusty fragments of shells, strips of uniforms and caps, shoes with a putrid, maggot-eaten mass inside. It does not seem possible that life could ever have been there. It looks as if it had always been dead. What testimony to human habitation remains is but mute and buried wreckage.[4]

A car with three stretcher-cases in the back, a slightly wounded soldier sitting on the seat next to the driver, and a load of knapsacks piled between the hood and the fenders, starts down from the *poste de secours*, spins on through a village full of resting troops, and turns on to the highway leading to the evacuation hospitals at the town eight kilometers below. At first the holes in the walls and houses along the way, and the craters in the fields where the *marmites* [shells] had struck, made one continually conscious of the possibility of a shell. Now one does not think about it, save to note the new holes, observe that older ones have been cemented up, and to hope that an *éclat* won't hit you at those exceedingly rare times when a shell burst ahead or behind.[5]

The work at night is quite eerie, and on moonless nights quite difficult. No lights are allowed, and the inky black way ahead seems packed with a discordant jumble of sounds as the never-ending artillery and *ravitaillement* [resupply] trains rattle along. One creeps past convoy after convoy, past sentinels who cry, "*Halte là!*" and then whisper an apologetic "*Passez*" when they make out the ambulance; and it is only in the dazzling light of the illuminating rockets that shoot into the air and sink slowly over the trenches that one can see to proceed with any speed.[6]

Early one morning there was an urgent call for a single wounded. The man's comrades gathered around the little car to bid their friend good-bye. He was terribly wounded and going fast. "See," said one of them to the man on the stretcher, "you are going in an American car. You will have a good trip, old fellow, and get well soon. Good-bye and good luck!" They forced a certain cheerfulness, but their voices were low and dry, for they saw death creeping into the face of their comrade. The driver took his seat and was starting when he was asked to wait. "Something for him," they said. When the car arrived at the hospital, the man was dead. He was cold and must have died at the start of the trip. The driver regretted the delay in leaving. Why had they asked him to wait? Then he saw that the ambulance was covered with sprigs of lilac and little yellow field flowers. The men knew the car would serve as a hearse.[7]

Well, there may be more interesting things in the future to write of the Americans serving at the front, and, again, their work may become dull. But it makes no difference to the Section. The men will do what is asked and gladly, for there is no work more worth while than helping in some way, no matter what, this noblest of all causes. One does not look for thanks—there is a reward enough in the satisfaction the work gives; but the French do not let it stop at that. The men from the trenches are surprised that we have voluntarily undertaken such a hazardous occupation, and express their appreciation and gratitude with almost embarrassing frequency. "You render a great service," say the officers, and those of highest rank call to render thanks in the name of France. It is good to feel

> that one's endeavors are appreciated, and encouraging to hear the words of praise; but when, at the end of an evacuation, one draws a stretcher from the car, and the poor wounded man lying upon it, who has never allowed a groan to escape during a ride that must have been painful, with an effort holds out his hand, grasps yours, and, forcing a smile, murmurs, "*Merci*"—that is what urges you to hurry back for other wounded, to be glad that there is a risk to one's self in helping them, and to feel grateful that you have the opportunity to serve the brave French people in their sublime struggle.[8]

The article was effectively illustrated with sketches by M. Bils, an artist assigned to record the war by the French General Staff.

Jim was on leave in Paris when his article was published. He was staying with Paul Rockwell, in a large suite of rooms that Paul shared with Mrs. Alice Weeks. Mrs. Weeks was one of the unsung heroes of the war. The wife of a Harvard professor, she and her son Kenneth had spent considerable time in France before the war. Kenneth was living in France, studying architecture and writing books, when the war began. He immediately enlisted in the Foreign Legion, serving for a while in the same unit as Kiffin Rockwell. When he wrote his mother that he expected to soon be given a week's leave, she left her home in Boston, sailed to France, and rented an apartment in Paris so she could see him when his leave was granted. She soon discovered that there were many Americans in the Foreign Legion who had no place to stay when they were given leave or, like Paul Rockwell, were recovering from wounds. She moved into a bigger apartment so she would have room for them. When she learned that there were others in the Legion who had no "home" in France—Russians, Italians, French, and Belgians whose homes were behind the German lines, and soldiers from French and British colonies around the world, she opened her home to them as well. They called her Maman Légionnaire, "mother" to the Legionnaires.

Sadly, her son Kenneth was killed before he was able to take leave, so she never saw him at her apartment. There were so many other Legionnaires who needed her help that she stayed in Paris to continue supporting the troops. She got involved with many charities in wartime France, and she made influential friends in the government whom she could talk to about soldiers' needs. When the US finally entered the war in 1917, she helped form organizations to give American soldiers the support they needed overseas. After the war, a grateful French nation made her a Chevalier de la Légion d'honneur (Knight of the Legion of Honor). Jim McConnell was just one of many hundreds of soldiers who found a little taste of home in Mrs. Weeks's apartment.[9]

Mrs. Alice Weeks. *North Carolina State Archives*

We have no surviving letters that Jim wrote during his leave in Paris, but that's not surprising. Men who escaped the war zone to spend a few days in Paris seldom used any of their precious leave hours to write. In Jim's case, he was staying with Paul Rockwell and visiting Marcelle Guerin every day, and since they were his two primary correspondents, he had no need to write. When he returned to Pont-à-Mousson, the workload was overwhelming, but he made time to write to Marcelle, thanking her for having spent so much time with him during his leave:

> I dare not count all the times I was at your apartment for fear of feeling ashamed of myself. I feel as if I had about lived there. It was all so delightful, and every thing we did I enjoyed so thoroughly. And then there was Versailles. It is hard to speak of that. It was a dream day—an exquisite harmony that your presence made me feel. There is no day in my life that can compare with that one. I'm back again at the old duty and now I do not know when I shall see you again. It depends a great deal of course on how my plans work out and what comes of my application. In a way I'd be an awful lemon to go back on Salisbury and the section but if in the future there's not much work here I will be of more use somewhere else.[10]

The last part of Jim's note refers to two changes to Jim's status. One, he had "re-enlisted" in the ambulance corps. His original six-month commitment would have expired about the time he went on leave, so he apparently signed up for an additional three months. Two, he had volunteered to become a pilot.

Jim later explained his reason for this as "All along I had the conviction that the United States ought to aid in the struggle against Germany. With that conviction, it was plainly up to me to do more than drive an ambulance. The more I saw the splendour of the fight the French were fighting, the more I felt like an *embusqué*—what the British called a 'shirker.' So I made up my mind to go into aviation."[11] His choice of Aviation over other branches of the French army was not surprising. He had driven a very primitive car from New York to Chicago and he later formed an Aero Club at UVA, so he was definitely interested in adventure and technology. Aviation was the newest, most high-tech, and seemingly most glamorous form of warfare imaginable, despite Jim's comment that it would get "monotonous" after a while. Aircraft from both sides flew over Pont-à-Mousson regularly, and Jim's reporter friend A. R. Decker had written about how aviation was essential to modern warfare. (His opinion about airplanes didn't appear to be changed by the fact that an incendiary bomb dropped from one started a fire in his house.[12]) At that time, there was still some semblance of chivalry among airmen. After one of the bombing raids on Pont-à-Mousson, a resident found a weighted note attached to a long streamer in their yard. The note provided information about the crews of two French aircraft that had recently been forced down behind German lines.[13]

Jim's friends undoubtedly influenced his decision as well. Paul Rockwell's brother Kiffin was just beginning his pilot's training and was writing enthusiastic letters to Paul when Jim took his leave in Paris. Jim's friend from UVA, "Chute" Johnson, enlisted in aviation in early September, shortly before Jim took leave in Paris. Jim had written to Paul about the exploits of an American pilot named Bill Thaw, and it's possible that Bill had approached him about becoming a pilot. Bill was trying to form an American *Escadrille* (flying squadron) within French aviation. Kiffin Rockwell's decision to become a pilot was influenced by Bill.

Bill Thaw was not the only person trying to form an American squadron. Another prewar American pilot, Norman Prince, had a similar vision. He came to Paris in January 1915, the same month Jim arrived, and tried for a while to sell his idea to the French authorities. Not having much luck lobbying as a civilian, he enlisted as a pilot and, like Bill Thaw, began trying to build an American squadron from inside the military.

Aviation was probably a "hot topic" of conversation among Jim's fellow ambulance drivers as well. Several of the drivers from Section 2 followed Jim into aviation, including Walter Lovell, Harold Willis, and Kenneth Marr. All these men would eventually serve in the American Escadrille, which Bill Thaw and Norman Prince dreamed of. Initially, the French were not particularly enthusiastic about the idea. They had plenty of French soldiers volunteering for aviation, and while they were willing to accept requests from Americans, they processed these requests through the regular channels and paid only lip service to the idea of an American Escadrille. Later, when it became apparent that a squadron of American volunteer pilots could help sway American public opinion, they would enthusiastically support the idea. In the meantime, Jim remained in the ambulance service while his request wound its way through bureaucratic channels.

While he waited, Jim had more than enough to keep him busy at Pont-à-Mousson. A. R. Decker wrote that war was becoming "commonplace" to the civilians. They sheltered in their cellars during bombardments and resumed work in their gardens afterward. A trumpeter warned of night air attacks, but that usually resulted in people going outside to look for the planes.[14] Buswell wrote that the section was being divided in two so they could cover an additional sector, but "Mac and I remain in Pont-à-Mousson."[15] This left them short staffed at a time when they were expecting a major attack in the St. Mihiel salient. "72 hrs of preparation," Jim wrote to Paul. "Some racket. Big show to come off in Bois de Mort Mare [Deadwood Pond] and near Flirey. We do work in that area, too."[16] The result was, as he wrote to Marcelle, that the remaining ambulance drivers were always on duty and were sleeping on the floor of the headquarters. "The days of splendid suites are over."[17]

Jim hadn't heard anything about his application to transfer to Aviation, but he wasn't in a hurry to leave the ambulance section anyway. The father of Ned Salisbury, their section leader, had suffered a stroke. Ned had to return to the US on emergency medical leave, and he asked Jim and Walter

---

* The French introduced steel helmets in late 1915, and the Germans and British soon followed suit. Until helmets were issued, soldiers in combat wore cloth or leather hats.

Jim strikes a heroic pose in his steel "fireman's helmet." *NMUSAF*

Lovell to take charge of the section while he was gone. Jim and the other drivers were issued metal *casques* (helmets)*. Jim said he "looks like a fireman" when he wore the helmet.

One significant event occurred during this period that Jim *didn't* mention in his letters. On October 5, 1915, he was awarded the Croix de Guerre (Cross of War) with star. The Croix de Guerre was created in 1915 to recognize individuals and units who distinguish themselves by acts of heroism involving combat with enemy forces. The star indicated that the action was significant enough to be mentioned in official military dispatches. The citation for Jim's award called him "a committed driver from the start, animated by an excellent spirit, has always shown courage and boldness worthy of the highest praise."[18]

On October 11, Jim wrote to Paul with three pieces of news regarding aviation. First, his application to enter Aviation had been accepted, provided he passed the medical examination. He told the French that he felt obligated to stay in his current assignment until Salisbury returned from the US, then he would go to Paris and enlist. Technically, he would be enlisting in the French Foreign Legion. US laws at the time stipulated that any American who took an oath of allegiance to a foreign state would forfeit their US citizenship. The Foreign Legion, however, did not require an oath of allegiance to France. It required only a promise to serve faithfully and go wherever the government ordered. Virtually all the Americans who voluntarily flew with the French did so by joining the Legion and then being detailed to aviation.

His second piece of aviation news was that the section had just received a new ambulance driver. "There is a good chap here named Haviland. . . . He came over to join the Canadian Artillery but couldn't get in without lying so he's out here. I've sent for blanks for him and if it goes through he will go into Aviation corps too." The "good chap" was Willis Haviland, who would, indeed, fly with Jim in the Lafayette Escadrille. The ambulance corps was proving to be a rich source of new pilots.

The third piece of news might understandably have dampened Jim's enthusiasm for flying a bit. He watched a French plane shoot down a German plane, and learned what happened to the aircrew.

> Haviland and I were on duty together at the *postes de secours*. A boche machine had crossed the lines and was flying somewhat to the rear of us. The enemy fliers had been bothering us all day. Our anti-aircraft batteries began firing at the enemy plane. The bursts of shrapnel were so thick that they merged into a long cloud bank.

> Suddenly a fast French plane shot out of the clouds and swinging alongside tho somewhat under the Boche, fired with a *mitrailleuse* [machine gun]. The enemy plane gave a sudden forward lurch, turned nose down and fell. A blue stream of smoke followed in its wake. It fell like a huge wounded bird, turning as it went, the sun glittering on its shiny surface as it tumbled like the white belly of a fish which shines when upward. It was a jolting, dead drop. Down it came, the soldiers on the ground yelling in delight. The machine crashed into the forest and I said to Haviland "Well there are two more good Boches." The French machine came swooping down in a giant circle. The crowd yelled its lungs out as an ovation. George Roeder* had been walking in the woods and the plane fell about four hundred yards from him. The wreck, he told me, was terrible. Nothing but splinters and torn cloth. The pilot had been cut in two. His legs had been thrown beyond the wreck. His face was flattened to about four inches and his liver was stuck on the motor in front. He had been killed by the machine gun but imagine the feelings of the observer who lived during that fall. His hands were clenched as if he had died in agony. Both were captains. . . . Well, maybe I'll take a header like that someday.[19]

A. R. Decker also witnessed this air battle and said that the Germans were flying an Albatros and that the French airplane was a "new model biplane**" that was much faster than the German plane, faster than any plane he had ever seen before. The machine gun fired through the propeller, which was protected by steel wedges.*** The victorious French pilot modestly accepted an ovation when he visited the crash site but was upset by the tragic fate of the German aircrew.[21]

The next day, Jim wrote his mother to thank her for the nice things she said about his article. He told her, "Some parts weren't bad, but others I didn't like. I had to write it off and on and as a result it has jerks in it." He also let her know that her last two letters had been opened and read by French censors. He told her about sleeping on the floor of the headquarters

---

* Jim misspelled the name as "Roder" in his letters. The correct spelling is used in this book.

** The plane was later identified as a Nieuport, an earlier model of the type Jim would later fly. The pilot was identified as Jean Doubrice, who was later killed in combat.[20]

*** The Germans had synchronized machine guns, which fired only when the propeller was not in the way. Steel wedges on the propeller to deflect the bullets were a crude and dangerous expedient used by some French pilots until the Allies developed their own synchronization mechanism.

but said it was actually better than sleeping in his sumptuous suite because they kept a fire going in the headquarters now that cold weather was setting in. He cut the letter short because he had to make an ambulance run.[22]

The ambulance work was slowing down as both sides prepared to spend another winter in the trenches, but there was still fighting going on. Jim wrote Marcelle that "a Hollander named Schroder* nearly got it yesterday. A shell hit so close it slewed his car around but neither he nor his wounded man were hit. We've got a special run of luck someplace." He closed the letter by asking her if she had "a little picture of yourself I might have" and jotted "see you in about 5 weeks now" in the margin. He was obviously expecting Salisbury to return soon, after which he would go to Paris and transfer to Aviation.[23]

A few days later, he wrote to a friend named Frank Tupper and explained why he wanted to become a pilot:

> I am at times ashamed of myself for doing this work when the fellows in trenches are running so much more of a risk and leading such a tough life, and as I feel just as strongly about the war as they do and believe it such a vital issue I am convinced that the decent thing for me to do is to mix up as a fighter and not remain in this soft position as a neutral. Then too, the crowd here is getting to be more and more a la sight-seeing in their viewpoint, and the new ones also are the typical flag-waving-superior-to-anyone-else-in-the-world type of Americans, and the insincerity of the average one gives me a desire to do something to clear myself of blame. Some of the new ones seem to delight in the fact that America is cleaning up a lot of money out of this slaughter; that for the gain alone they think America ought to stay out of the war, no matter at what cost to her honor.[24]

His letter to Frank had some lighter notes too. He told Frank he had just returned from an eight-day leave in Paris, his first vacation in six months, and said, "A French young lady guided me around Versailles, leading me by a gentle pressure on the hand from statue to statue, and so the place seemed perfectly wonderful."

Jim began to get serious about preparing for flight training and asked Paul to check with Kiffin to see what clothes he should buy before going to flight school. For example, he had heard that pilots needed a leather coat. Were those issued to pilots, or did he need to buy his own?[25] A few days later, he wrote Paul to describe negotiations and frustrations he was having

---

*Jim misspelled the name as "Shroder" in his letters. The correct spelling is used in this book.

trying to sell various articles to newspaper correspondents and editors. He also added a worried comment: "Never a word from little old bright eyes since I left Paris a month ago."[26]

Jim apparently received a letter from Paul later that day, since he immediately wrote to "bright eyes" herself:

> I have just received a letter from Paul in which he writes as follows, after mentioning you: "She looks like the shadow of death; seems on the verge of a breakdown. She has worked too hard." My dear little girl is it true that you're feeling so badly? You see, you've overdone it. You're too loyal and self-sacrificing and you've hurt yourself. It's all wrong to try and keep up, when it's a strain to do so, on your own account and for the sake of the wounded who need your care. If you break down what then? It may take you months to recover and all that time will be wasted. If you took things easier you could go right on. Isn't that so? I'm terribly distressed to hear you aren't your usual vigorous self. If you feel well enough and have the time won't you please write me and let me know how you are?[27]

Jim went on to say that he'd heard from "Chute" Johnson, who was at Pau, a flight-training school in southern France near the border with Spain. Johnson was discouraged because there were 250 men ahead of him, and he was afraid it would be months before he could even begin his training. Jim had a friend who was working to get Jim assigned to a training base at Avord, in central France, where he hoped the wait would be shorter. On a different topic, Jim said he got to visit the front lines, where he crawled in a tunnel that went under the Boches. (Both sides tunneled under the enemy's trenches to plant mines, which they detonated immediately before an attack.) A sniper took a crack at him as they were going through a shallow *boyau* (communication trench leading to the front line), but missed.

Jim's frustrations with editors continued. He appeared to be suffering from the eternal curse of writers—you submit a piece and never hear back. At least one of the editors was in Paris, and Jim told Paul that he was looking forward to meeting the editor in person. "Well, I'm learning now and am not afraid to meet our little friends. Every time they come across I can go 'em one better. I get my training from yelling at convoy drivers. Oh a choice lot of Billingsgate* that will simply floor them as soon as they open their mouths." Jim also asked Paul to do whatever he could to get Jim sent to Avord instead of Pau.[28]

---

* Cursing. From the Billingsgate fish market in London, renowned for its foul language.

Marcelle's reply to Jim's note has not survived, but it convinced Jim that Paul was right. She was working herself too hard. She may also have told him it was none of his business, since in his next note he admitted it was foolish of him to try to give her advice. "It's just your kind that's making for Frenchwomen the most glorious reputation in the world and we mustn't have you be done up by the strain." He also told her that his friends at Pau were telling him the outlook was hopeless. There were still 250 students ahead of them, and they were afraid it would take eight months before they finished their training.[29]

The next day, Jim received a letter from Paul that cheered him up considerably. Paul was feeling better, Paul's fiancée was returning to Paris, Kiffin earned his brevet (military pilot's license) and was spending a few days' leave in Paris, and Marcelle was looking better. Jim thanked Paul for the fact that he and Kiffin were trying to get Jim sent to Avord instead of Pau. He also commented on the weather, which was definitely becoming winter-like:

> The nights are cold—so cold you get numb. The trenches are pretty good now. Log matting floors raised for drainage in all *boyaux* and trenches up to 1st line and the *abris* [dugouts] are so deep and spacious that one is protected, warm and dry. Much better than last year. . . . Afraid I won't have any chance up at 148^{Bis} [Marcelle's address] after Kiffin appears in his flossy get-up before the button loving young lady. [Kiffin had a new uniform, with wings.]

Jim was also happy that Betty Baldwin would soon be returning to France after a short trip to America, and that UVA beat Yale 10–0 in a good, straight game of football.[30]

As October passed into November, the winter weather significantly reduced military activity around Pont-à-Mousson. A. R. Decker commented that the falling leaves made it possible to see the trenches from his house. No-man's-land was about 700 yards wide at the base of the ridge, 25 yards at the top. It did not appear to him that the lines had changed appreciably since September 1914. Artillery duels were still going on, and he speculated that metals could be profitably mined from the battlefield after the war.[31]

Mrs. Weeks had invited Jim to stay at her apartment when he came to Paris, and he replied that he hoped to be there around the first of December. He also said the atrocious weather was making it exceedingly difficult to evacuate the wounded:

> You never saw such a climate as this in your life. Starting at five, a heavy mist comes up which lasts until noon the next day. The only way you can tell there is something on the road besides yourself, is when you hit it, which damages the cars. We had one smashup last night and another car hit a man and knocked him ten feet, curling him around a tree, but did not kill him.[32]

They were still making ambulance runs in weather like that because even when no attacks were underway, men were killed and wounded every day from shellfire, snipers, and trench mortars. In the inhuman terminology of the war, this was sometimes referred to as "daily wastage."[33] The weather made ambulance runs harrowing, but the absence of major attacks made them infrequent. In a letter to Paul, Jim made a statement that has probably been made by soldiers at least as far back as Caesar's legions: "Being bored is 99% of war, isn't it?"[34]

Jim's family had still not accepted the fact that he was fully committed to supporting the French cause for as long as the war lasted. The husband of his older sister, Julia, Mitchell Follansbee, was a successful attorney in Chicago. He offered Jim a job. Jim described the situation in a letter to Paul:

> In dutch with the family for good now. Brother-in-law offered me a job that would pay $5,000 a year* if I made good. I turned it down. To avoid argument I informed my older sister, wife of said brother-in-law, that I was in French army and so it would do them no good to write.[35]

Technically, Jim was not in the French army yet, but as an ambulance driver in the war zone he was subject to French army regulations and was not free to come and go at will. It's not clear that he told them his "enlistment" would expire in December, but that would be rendered moot by the fact that he was planning to enlist in the French Foreign Legion (another detail he may not have told his family about). That enlistment *would* be for the duration of the war. He did, however, tell his family that after December 1, they should write to him in care of Paul Rockwell.

In the same letter to Paul, Jim said the ambulance section was planning a big Thanksgiving dinner. "I'm off the wagon that day and so if you hear any large rumbles from S.P. 84 [the postal zone he was in] don't think we're commencing a new battle."

---

*$5,000 a year was a handsome salary in 1915, the equivalent of $157,000 a year in 2024 dollars.

Jim told Marcelle about the breach with his family, but he described the issues to her in words that were surprisingly harsher than he used when describing it to Paul:

> For one thing they won't stand for my attitude towards the States, and for another because I won't go home and help out during the hard times prevailing. The last attempt to get me back consisted in an offer from my brother-in-law of a job that would pay me five thousand a year if I made good. I turned it down and told them to accept things as they were or to stop writing. I know I'm wrong, and mean, and a slob, and everything else, but I happen to be constituted that way and I [might] just as well be frank about it.[36]

Jim gave no indication of what the "hard times prevailing" at home were. Overall, the US economy was going strong, helped in part by the sale of war materials to the Allied powers, but the Randolph & Cumberland Railroad had failed in its attempt to extend its rail lines to Winston-Salem. His father's business might not have been doing well.

Jim and the rest of Section 2 got an unexpected honor on November 14. Jim described it in a letter to Paul:

> We got a phone message Sunday to go to the Mayor's and meet a high official. Five of us who were around the bureau went over. A number of big limousines were drawn up in the Place [town square]. One bore the flag of the President of the Republic. We were to meet Poincaré. We lined up inside the sand bag barricaded arcade. The President and his entourage passed. He stopped in front of us and said a few hasty complimentary words. Then he shook hands with each of us, saluted, and passed on. We strolled to the end of the arcade to watch the President and party go down a side street. A sentry there engaged us in conversation.
>
> "Did he shake hands with you?" he asked, addressing himself to Pottle*.
>
> "Sure did" says Pottle.
>
> "Hell, he isn't a bit proud is he?" was the comforting comment of the man on post.[37]

---

* Emory Pottle of Lago di Como, Italy, was a volunteer ambulance driver with Section 2.

Jim said he sent a description of the meeting to Paul Scott Mowrer, a correspondent for the *Chicago Daily News*. Mowrer's piece about it appeared the following Wednesday.[38] No reason was given for the visit of President Poincaré, but Jim's article in *The Outlook* magazine had caught the attention of other officials who then visited the section, so it's possible it was a factor in the president's visit.

As the end of November drew near, Jim began to make preparations for his departure. George Roeder had to take an ambulance to Paris for extensive repairs, and Jim was going to give him a "bag of junk" for Paul Rockwell to hold for him.[39] Jim also "got awfully reckless*" and bought a Kodak camera for 100 francs so he could take pictures of the place before he left. Jim expected Salisbury to return to the unit in a few days, and Jim was waiting to tell him about his departure before he announced it to the other drivers. Jim promised to drink to Paul's good health "to the point of exhaustion" at their Thanksgiving dinner.[40]

When Salisbury returned, his family matters were still in "a hell of a mess," according to Jim. "The only reason he's back is that he promised us he'd return." Roeder suggested that Jim wait until after the Thanksgiving blowout to tell Salisbury he was leaving, and Jim readily agreed. Jim wrote this to Paul the day before Thanksgiving, adding that he had "a really chic present for Bright Eyes," who was laid up from overwork.[41]

After the Thanksgiving celebration, Jim told Ned Salisbury that he wanted to transfer to aviation. Ned understood and supported him. Now Jim was just waiting for orders, which he expected in five or six days. Roeder was finally ready to leave for Paris, and Jim added three rolls of film to the "bag of junk" he'd given him earlier to take to Paul. Jim was going to take a short trip to the airfield at Toul to ask the pilots for advice on flight training. He thanked Paul for working to see that Jim went to the training school at Avord instead of the one at Pau and commented that it was "cold as a nun's navel" in Pont-à-Mousson.[42] The following day, he sent a postcard saying, "Please call off Avord Negotiations until I get to Paris. Have just received a long line of dope from Pau that leads me to think I'd better go there unless the dope's wrong. Will figure it out when in town."[43]

Now that Jim had "officially" announced he was leaving the ambulance service, he wrote a letter to A. Piatt Andrew to explain his decision:

---

* The "reckless" comment may have been because soldiers were forbidden to have cameras in the war zone, although many ignored that restriction. Jim was able to mention the camera in his letter because the "Hollander" Schroder carried it to Paris and bypassed the censor. Schroder had two brothers in the Foreign Legion. One of them had been killed in recent action, and the other had been badly wounded, so he was going to Paris on emergency leave.

> I've been thinking the matter over for a long time. I feel as strongly about the war as the French themselves. I believe it to be a war of freedom and civilization against despotic dictation and hideous ideals, and having this attitude I want to give up my capacity as a neutral—as a member of the Red Cross—and go into the fighting end. I told Ned about my leaving the day before yesterday. I regret exceedingly going out from the service, and leaving you, Ned, and one or two others in the A.A. that I like immensely. I trust, however, that I shall have the pleasure of seeing you from time to time and that my leaving this work will not result in any interruption in all the friendships I've made while with the A.A.[44]

Jim sent a brief note to Paul telling him he expected orders to leave on December 4 or 5.[45] The orders arrived, and his service with the American Ambulance corps came to an end.

SIX

Learning to Fly

"Norfolk-Southern has bought the Neidé Ry* and I arrived 5 hours & 20 minutes late." With that cryptic statement, Jim told Paul Rockwell he had arrived at Pau, France, ready to begin his flight training.[1] He also said that while sleeping on the train, he had put his foot in an officer's face, and the locals thought he was Belgian because they didn't recognize his khaki Ambulance Corps uniform.

All in all, Jim was happy to be at Pau. The students slept on boards in a barracks, but they had mattresses, sheets, and blankets, so he was comfortable. He was less enthusiastic about the fact that "they wake you up here with a fool bugle and then at sunset you have to stand around and salute the flag—all that sort of bunk like a prep school."[2] Jim hoped to begin his flight training in a few days. He said he didn't stand out as an American, since there were students from several countries, including a Filipino who bunked across from him, and several other Americans. His old friend "Chute" Johnson had just breveted (earned his military pilots license) and left that day for leave in Paris. Chute had been plagued with bad luck during his training and had crashed several planes, including one where his flying glove got caught in the throttle and he couldn't advance the throttle to rise or pull it back to land.[3] An American named Clyde Balsley also earned his brevet that day, and Americans Dudley Hill, Laurence Rumsey, and Paul Pavelka were working toward their brevet at Pau. All these men would later fly with Jim in the Lafayette Escadrille.

---

* Presumably the "Neidé Ry" was the railroad that brought him there. As a former employee of the Randolph & Cumberland Railroad, Jim would have had contempt for the Norfolk-Southern Railroad, or any other competitor in North Carolina.

Jim wrote to Mrs. Weeks to let her know he had arrived safely and to thank her for her hospitality when he was on leave in Paris. "They asked me if I wanted to be buried à la Catholic or Protestant," he told her. "I told them whichever gave the best send-off."[4] Jim's humor notwithstanding, flight training in wartime France did involve a significant risk. Clyde Balsley described three fatalities in two days,[5] and Kiffin Rockwell witnessed three deaths in one morning, two of which were men trapped in the wreckage who burned to death in front of students.[6]

One fatality that Jim may not have been aware of occurred while he was on leave in Paris. The first American ambulance driver was killed in action. Richard Nelville Hall, a driver with Section 1 in the Vosges Mountains, was called to evacuate wounded just before midnight on Christmas Eve. At roughly 2:00 a.m. on Christmas Day, 1915, his ambulance was hit by a shell, and Hall was killed.[7] Flying was more dangerous that driving an ambulance, but neither was a "safe" way to serve France.

The flight-training course that Jim hoped to begin in a few days was considerably different than flight training today. The French did have dual-control aircraft in which an instructor could teach a student to fly, comparable to today's flight training, but the dual-control trainers were large, heavy, and cumbersome compared to the small fighter aircraft, *avions de chasse* as the French called them, which were beginning to prove themselves at the front. There was a concern that students who learned on the heavier trainers would have trouble adapting to lightweight fighters, so the dual-control trainers were primarily used to train pilots who were expected to fly bombers and observation planes. Students who were expected to fly fighters learned to fly on small, lightweight, single-seat trainers. They received classroom instruction (in French) on *how* to fly, but they learned flying skills by doing. Their first flight was also their first solo. *Sometimes* they were given a joyride in a two-seat plane first, but it was strictly a joyride. They never touched the controls.

A Bleriot "Penguin." *Nordhoff and Hall:* The Lafayette Flying Corps

This training was not as suicidal as it might sound. Students were not simply turned loose in a fully functional airplane. They began their instruction in an airplane that was nicknamed a "Penguin" because it couldn't fly. It had a three-cylinder engine, a small propeller, and "clipped" wings that were too short to lift the plane off the ground. This plane was capable only of taxiing, and a student's first assignment was to taxi a Penguin in a straight line. This was harder than it sounds. Most World War I fighters were "tail draggers," with two wheels up front and a tail skid at the rear. On the ground, the plane sat at an angle, with the pilot looking up over the horizon. His view of anything directly in front of the plane was blocked by the fuselage, the engine, and, on most airplanes, the wings as well. The tail skid acted as a brake, and the wheels were not steerable, so to taxi the pilot had to speed up the engine and get the plane to move fast enough so the tail lifted off the ground. Then he could use the rudder to steer.

Speeding up the engine was an art in itself, since the Penguin, in common with all French fighters of the time, used a rotary engine. Rotary engines have the cylinders arranged in a circle around the crankshaft, like a conventional radial engine, but with a significant difference. Radial engines are like conventional car engines in that the cylinders stand still and the crankshaft turns. The propeller is fastened to the rotating crankshaft. With a rotary engine, the crankshaft stands still and the cylinders rotate around the crankshaft. The propeller is bolted to the cylinders. This type of engine was used in many early aircraft because it was lightweight and compact, and the spinning cylinders kept the engine cool. One of the disadvantages of rotary engines was that they were very difficult to control, and the pilot needed to adjust the fuel-air mixture as well as the throttle as he changed speeds or altitude. Another disadvantage was that the spinning cylinders acted as a giant gyroscope, twisting the plane in unexpected ways if the plane suddenly changed direction or if the engine suddenly speeded up or slowed down. With a novice at the controls of a Penguin, it was liable to do all of the above. The goal of Penguin training was for the student to start at one edge of a field, accelerate to 20 or 30 mph, and taxi in a straight line to the other end of the field. There, either the pilot or someone waiting for his turn in a Penguin would turn the plane around so the student could taxi straight back to his starting point. Ted Parsons, a Lafayette Escadrille pilot who began his training a few months after Jim, described a typical Penguin session:

> Start two at opposite ends of the field with practically the entire width of the field between them, and somehow they'd run together in a horrible collision in the center of the field. That is, it always sounded horrible, but usually repairs could be effected by the

> phlegmatic, betel-chewing Annamite [Vietnamese] mechanics within a very few minutes. Then there was the bugbear of ground loops*, or *chevaux de bois* (wooden horses on the merry-go-round) as the French so aptly named them. Once the Penguins started to turn in a ground loop, nothing could stop them except coming to a full stop with completely retarded motor. They'd whirl round and round like a dog chasing his tail. Then the red-faced, cursing neophyte would have to climb out, point his nose in the way he wanted to go and start all over again.[8]

Once the student mastered the art of taxiing in a straight line, he was given a plane with slightly longer wings. It couldn't sustain flight, but it could lift off the ground, rise to an altitude of 6 or 7 feet, and then descend. Students would cross a field in short hops to get a feel for takeoffs and landings. Parsons described the landings as such: "The sound was the general effect of an earthquake in a hardware store, but the miracle was that the ship seemed to suffer no particular ill-effects."[9] After a few days of mastering these hops, they were assigned to a plane that could climb to 30 or 40 feet. They flew this plane on a 1 km field so they had enough room to take off, climb, descend, and land without turning. Their next plane would climb to 250 feet. They flew this plane on a 3 km field so they could still take off, climb, and land in a straight line. Only after they mastered this were they allowed to try turning while in the air.[10]

Despite all of Jim's worries about the backlog at Pau and his attempts to get assigned to Avord, he was able to begin his training three days after arriving. He wrote Marcelle that he was very fortunate to have arrived when he did, since there were only seven students waiting to begin training ahead of him. Forty-five potential students arrived shortly after Jim did. The fact that he arrived on New Year's Day instead of extending his leave to include the holiday probably gave him a head start. Jim had already started training when he wrote to Marcelle, and he had already smashed his first Penguin. The training was keeping him very busy, and he had time to write only because it was Sunday:

> The chief trouble with this place is the fact that one never has any time to one's self. Today is *quartier libre* [free time] and so I have some time to write. Other days one hasn't even the opportunity to shave. That's really the truth. Even now the room is filled with

* In a ground loop the plane essentially spun around in circles on the landing gear, like a spinning top.

> a lot of young fools throwing bread at one another and it's so cold the pen moves with difficulty. As luck would have it I caught a cold and so appreciate your beautiful handkerchiefs more than ever. . . . Marcelle I don't know how to thank you for the pleasure you gave me while I was in Paris. I've never been happier and had it not been for the unfortunate incident it would have been perfect. Please do forget it . . . I've made friends and get along very well. It's about as good a place to learn French as a jail in Ohio. Everyone speaks English.[11]

Jim gave no hint as to what the "unfortunate incident" was. On the basis of later unfortunate incidents, he may have had too much to drink.

Jim dashed off a quick note to Paul and gave him an update on a few of the American students.[12] Jim was still taxiing Penguins, Pavelka had graduated to short hops, Hill was sent to train on Caudrons (big bombing aircraft), and Rumsey crashed again but was unhurt. (Rumsey, who had crashed several times already, got lost on a cross-country flight. He crossed the Pyrenees into neutral Spain, realized his mistake, and turned back to France and barely made it across the border before running out of fuel.[13]) Jim hoped that Paul could come to Pau for a visit, explaining they had every other Sunday off as *quartier libre*. A few days later, he sent a note to Marcelle, saying he hoped to finish Penguins within a week, if the weather cooperated.[14] "I am going to try my best to be breveted as soon as possible, for after that I will have six days permission [leave] and it will be possible to see you again—and read Spoon River* and just be near you and happy." He also sent a short note to Mrs. Weeks to let her know that everything was going well, adding, "We eat in a madhouse where one has to fight for a knife and fork."[15]

Jim finished his Penguin training sooner than he expected, since two days later he wrote Paul that he had graduated to "lignes droits" (straight lines) training to do hops.[16] He was concerned because Chute Johnson and Clyde Balsley had completed their training and been breveted on Bleriots, which were small, single-seat scout airplanes. Normally, pilots who were breveted on Bleriots were sent to a fighter school, but Johnson and Balsley had been sent to a Voisin school. Voisins were two-seat observation/bomber airplanes. "Hell, if they put them on the Voisin one might just as well take a Caudron—be perfectly safe and get breveted twice as quickly" (The dual-control Caudron training option had students fly with an instructor and bypassed the Penguin short-hops/long-hops training program).

---

* *Spoon River Anthology*, a book of poems written by Edgar Lee Masters, was published in 1915.

Jim in a Bleriot trainer; capable of short flights. *NASM*

The potential consequences of military training were being driven home by the fact that the school had asked Jim to make out a will. Jim told them to send his things to Paul. He asked Paul to forward his books, photos, souvenirs, etc. to his older sister, Julia. Paul should use whatever money Jim had to pay expenses and send the rest to his sister, unless it was only a little, in which case Paul should throw a party. "Give my clothes to the poor and tell Bright Eyes* I croaked muttering her name. Tell Betty the same thing."

Jim found little time to write over the next few weeks, but on January 24, he wrote Paul that he had recently learned the terrible news about Mrs. Weeks's son Kenneth. Mrs. Weeks had not received any letters from Kenneth since mid-June. There had been delays in mail from the Foreign Legion in the past, but week after week passed with no news. His unit had been involved in a major attack and had suffered many casualties, but none of the survivors knew what had happened to Kenneth. There were rumors that some Legionnaires had been taken prisoner and were being held in Belgium, where they were not allowed to write home. In late July, Mrs. Weeks received official notification from the French government that her son was "missing." They could tell her nothing more. She asked the US embassy for help, but in accordance with President Wilson's strict neutrality policy, they replied, "This agency knows nothing about those Americans who have volunteered in the Foreign Legion . . . and makes it a point to know nothing about them."[17] Finally, on January 2, 1916, the day after Jim arrived at Pau, Mrs. Weeks received official notification that her son Kenneth had fallen on the Field of Honor on June 17, 1915.[18]

* "Bright Eyes" was Jim's nickname for Marcelle. Presumably Betty was Betty Baldwin.

Jim wrote to Marcelle to say that for the first time, he spent his *quartier libre* in the town of Pau with a crowd from the airfield. They had a party then, but nobody felt like partying today. There were seven wrecks that day, one of which burned, and Jim thought that two of the student pilots had been killed:

> I saw one man on the piste [course] next to me waver and fall. There was a sickening, grinding crash and the machine turned over. I thought him killed. The men ran to him and pulled him out. He was stretched on the ground. Just then my monitor [instructor] signaled me to go ahead. I kissed myself good bye and started. *Mirable dictu* [Amazingly] I finished the day well and was passed to another division. I have now passed all the group I found myself with save one officer who is very good, and with fair weather and good luck I should have my brevet in sixteen days. I agree with you that one should not go too fast and I'm going to slow up until I get the *atterrissage* [landing] better. Sometimes I come down like a ton of bricks. One machine burnt up today. Gasoline tank exploded and a column of flame shot up. Discouraging sight.[19]

Three days later, Jim wrote to Paul and began with a rather puzzling observation. "Glad Bright-Eyes has struck off on another tack. She's fooling with fire, tho, when she tackles the Thaw*. *Tant Mieux* [So much the better]."[20] Marcelle knew Bill Thaw's sister, Mrs. Laurence Slade, and it's quite possible that she met Bill at the Slades' house in Paris. Perhaps she told Paul she was impressed by him? In any event, Jim either didn't care or was acting as if he didn't care.

The rest of the letter focused on aviation. Jim and Paul Pavelka expected to be breveted within the next two weeks, and Jim was still worried about the fact that Johnson and Balsley had been sent to a Voisin squadron. Jim wanted to know if any of Paul's growing list of influential friends could make certain that Jim and Pavelka could be sent to a Nieuport school. The Nieuport was the newest, fastest, and most effective fighter in the French

---

* Bill Thaw was one of the Americans already flying with the French who was trying to form an American squadron. He learned to fly in the US before the war, served as an infantryman in the French Foreign Legion, transferred to aviation, flew over several sectors with French squadrons, and would soon become the senior American officer in the Lafayette Escadrille. Ted Parsons wrote of him, "No matter where we were sent, Bill had generally been in that sector before. He always knew a houseful of more or less alluring young wenches in the next village or an attractive widow who owned a chateau with a grand wine cellar."

air service, and, like student pilots today, in 1915 every student pilot wanted to be assigned to a fighter squadron. "Unless I can get in a pull I'll be sent to a Voisin or some damned rotten thing," Jim worried. He closed by saying he needed to get to bed because "I have to file out again at six and my eyes need a good long rest. Was up an hour and a half with no wind shield or glasses and the orbs burn."

Jim's next letter to Marcelle didn't mention "tackling the Thaw." Instead, he wrote that he was making good progress in his flight training. He had finished all the stunts required for a civilian flying license and was about to tackle the harder military tasks. He expected to begin his cross-country flights in about a week, if his luck and the weather held out. He hadn't yet reached the point where flying came naturally, though, since the slightest distraction caused his airplane to wander:

> What I'm trying to figure out is how anyone shoots out of an aero. To run it is hard enough. Heavens if I try to move a hand to pull down my casque [helmet] or something the blooming thing begins to plop and dip and heave and run away.[21]

The stunts and tasks required to earn a military brevet varied over time, but when Jim was learning to fly, they typically included climbing to 6,500 feet or higher and staying at that altitude for an hour, making a triangular cross-country flight and landing at two different airfields about 50 miles apart, shutting off the engine at an altitude of 1,600 feet and gliding to a "dead-stick*" landing, and flying to another airfield at least 100 miles away.[22] More-advanced maneuvers such as loops, spins, and how to "shoot out of an aero" were taught in advanced training once a student had been assigned to a particular aircraft.

Jim wrote to Paul Rockwell on February 2 to say that he would begin his cross-country flights the next day. He hoped to complete his license requirements in two days, unless they insisted he have at least twenty-five hours of flight time before they breveted him. So far he had spent only twelve and a half hours in the air.[23] As it turned out, he got a few extra hours of flying time, because his attempt to complete his license in two days didn't go as planned. He found himself stranded at Mont-de-Marsan, a town about 40 miles north of Pau. He described his situation to Paul:

---

* A landing with the engine off, so the "stick" (propeller) is not turning.

> Here we are and as it's raining I figure I'll be here some time yet. I tried to do all my brevet in one day. Made my first two voyages in morning and then started on my triangle. To make it I had to start at noon, when it was blowing to beat hell. I had a terrible time. A Caudron man had a bad time of it and so you can figure what I got in a 60 hp Bleriot. (No 80's free.) I was to go to Pontoux [a town about 45 miles northwest of Pau]—the Caudrons go to Mont-de-Marsan. Just before I started a fellow gave me a few rotten directions and told me to watch for the Adour [a small river that runs between Pau and both destinations]. Well I went over a bit of a brook after flying for an hour and a half, saw no towns, and kept going. Country began to look like North Carolina and I turned back. When I hit the brook again—it turned out to be the river Adour—I saw a large town. Decided to give it the once over, then lo and behold I saw a large race course with hangars, a fire burning and a large arrow indicating the wind. Down I swooped with joy. To make it worse a wire had broken and my motor wouldn't cut off*. At ten yards from the ground I had sense enough to shut my essence [gas] and stop her that way. Made a good landing and felt content. "Pontoux isn't hard to find," I called out to the officer that walked up. "Pontoux!" says he in a surprised voice, "this is Mont-de-Masan." I would have beat it but one of my cylinders was on the bum and I had to send for a new motor. Now it's raining and I can't make my trip in the 48 hours allowed. Must do it again. I'm 30 kilometers from where I should have landed. Will get it right next time. I didn't have anything on but my leathers and the officer has reported me. I should have had a uniform and kepi. I'll probably get four days prison when I return which will delay my permission [leave].[24]

Although stranded, Jim's time in Mont-de-Masan wasn't entirely wasted, since he discovered that the nephew of General Joffre, commander of the entire French army, was also "en panne" [broken down] there, and they dined together.[25]

Jim spent another day stranded in Mont-de-Masan before the weather cleared enough for him to complete his triangle flight and return to Pau. Apparently his instructors waived the forty-eight-hour time limit, since they

---

* Because it was difficult to throttle a rotary engine down to a low speed, pilots used a "kill switch" on the control stick to turn the ignition off and on to slow down while landing. This caused the distinctive "Brrrp . . . Brrrp" sound you sometimes hear in movies of World War I planes landing.

Jim at Pau in his flight leathers and crash helmet (*left*) and in his French army uniform and kepi (*right*). *NASM*

gave him credit for successfully completing that test. They also didn't make him spend any time in "prison" (a detention cell on the military base, used as punishment for minor offenses). He completed his two altitude flights and sent a "Breveted!" postcard to Paul.[26] He sent a similar postcard to Marcelle, adding that they "faked up" his flight hours to qualify him for his license.[27] Now he was off to Paris to celebrate having earned his wings.

Jim enjoyed his leave in Paris. Perhaps a little too much. After he returned to Pau, he wrote a letter to Paul that was filled with remorse:

> Well here I am nursing myself in a room by means of milk. I hope to reduce my vibrations to not over ten times normal by the morning. I am heartily ashamed of myself. I should have died when I was a little baby. I hope I didn't get on the nerves of you or Mrs. Weeks. It was great in Paris and I thank you so much for letting me visit you and for all you did for me. I shall write Mrs. Weeks in a couple of days.
>
> I don't really see how Marcelle can forgive me. That makes twice, you see, and she's probably lost hope. I'm sorry. The girl is very dear to me and I hate the idea of having humiliated her. . . . You might tell Marcelle I can frame up some sort of a pledge that will result in my being sober when I go to see her.

> Lord I feel rotten. I guess I'll go to bed and ask God and his son Jesus to let me cash in.[28]

Jim apparently didn't spend all his Paris time with Paul, Mrs. Weeks, or Marcelle, since he added a postscript (possibly on the following morning, since it's written with a darker ink) to say that he was sending Paul a letter to give to "Yvonne in the Kodak shop."

Jim's leave in Paris prompted Marcelle to write to Paul Rockwell, one of the few letters from her that has survived. After expressing concern over the fact that Paul was down with the grippe (flu), she wrote about how pathetic Jim's behavior was. Mrs. Slade, the sister of American aviator Bill Thaw, invited Jim to come to a party along with thirty-four other guests. "Jim was the only one who distinguished himself." She understood that he had been under a great nervous strain at Pau, but she didn't think that his time in Paris did much to steady his nerves. "You know what a curse drink is!"[29] She said that Jim had written to her since his leave, but that letter hasn't survived.

Jim also wrote to his sister shortly after returning from leave. He thanked her for sending him some <u>real</u> socks and said that he flew at 7,000 feet that day, and his feet weren't cold. (Staying warm was a major challenge for World War 1 pilots, flying in an open cockpit with no heat and 100+ mph winds. The cold was especially intense during the winter and at high altitudes.) Then Jim gave her the good news about his advanced training:

> Was breveted the 6th of February, a month and a day from time I started in training and all within 15 hours of flight. On account of my record, etc., I was assigned to the best machine, a Nieuport, and have been kept at the Nieuport School here. I will leave here after finishing on that and go to general reserve near Paris and then to front. My job will be dueling and maybe special missions. In the first I try to shoot down Boche machines with my mitrailleuse [machine gun] and the second I can't tell you about*. Then again I may go as guard on bombardments but won't have any bombs, which is disappointing as I certainly would like to smear up a bit of German landscape just to square things a little.

---

* Early in the war, pilots sometimes landed spies and saboteurs behind the German lines. An American pilot named James Bach crashed while trying to take off and return after landing a spy. He was captured and became the first American POW in World War I. Jim McConnell certainly would have been aware of James Bach's fate.

Jim also said that the "excellent authority" who told him he would be commissioned as a lieutenant after being breveted was "a bit off." He was promoted to corporal instead. That meant he didn't have any extra money to send to their mother, as he had hoped. He suggested that the work he was doing in France was their family's contribution to the Allies, so his sister should give whatever money she was going to give to the Red Cross to their mother instead. "Things are more squared up viewed in that light."[30]

As Jim began his Nieuport training, there was a major development in the ground war—a development that would soon affect him and many other American pilots. On February 21, the same day that Marcelle wrote to Paul about Jim having "distinguished" himself while on leave, the Germans launched a major attack at Verdun. This developed into one of the most terrible battles in the history of warfare, and it became the longest battle of the war. Hundreds of thousands of French and German troops were consumed by the battle, and it dominated French military planning and logistical support. This would create confusion and equipment shortages that frustrated Jim during his training, and as the battle raged on, it would suck Jim and other American pilots into its insatiable maw.

SEVEN

Advanced Training

"February 22, 1916. Washington's Birthday. He started a good nation and it went wrong. Just as girls do."[1] With that cheery observation, Jim began his correspondence from his advanced training. He was very happy to have been selected for Nieuport training, since that meant he would be flying a fast, maneuverable fighter instead of a slow, cumbersome, bombing or observation plane. He liked the school, but he hoped to complete his training quickly. His letter to Paul Rockwell also mentioned that "Skipper"* (Paul Pavelka), who started flight training shortly after Jim did, had gone missing on his final test before earning his brevet. Jim didn't sound particularly worried, since getting lost and landing at the wrong airfield was not unusual for student pilots.

> Skipper finished up everything save one altitude, and went up for it at 3:00 p.m. this afternoon. It is 8:15 p.m. now and no one knows where he is. He probably wandered off someplace and was forced to land. He should have come back to earth at 4:15 at the latest.

Paul did turn up safe and sound. An altitude test required a pilot to climb to a specified altitude, stay at that altitude for an hour, and land at the training field he'd left from. He carried a recording altimeter in his plane to prove he'd met this requirement. Somehow Pavelka wandered off course

* Paul Pavelka had a serious case of wanderlust and had held a variety of jobs around the world before the war. His most recent job before joining the Foreign Legion was as a commercial seaman, which led his Legion buddies to call him "Skipper."

and landed at an airfield near Tarbes, about 40 km from Pau. He must have spent the required time at the correct altitude in the process, since he passed that test and was given leave in Paris to celebrate his new wings. Jim gave him a roll of film to take to Paul Rockwell, along with a note that asked Paul to take the film to the Kodak shop to have it processed. He apologized for any inconvenience this might cause, but added it would give Paul a chance to "gaze upon the titian haired young lady [Yvonne, who worked at the Kodak shop]."[2]

Nieuport fighters were developed from prewar racing airplanes. The Nieuport factory produced a bewildering variety of models during the war, which looked very similar but had evolutionary improvements as the science of aviation advanced. Most were single-seat aircraft, although a few two-seat models were made. A distinguishing feature was that they were sesquiplanes, literally "one and a half-winged airplanes." They looked like a biplane from the front, but the bottom wing was significantly narrower than the top wing; hence the "half wing" designation. The narrow bottom wing reduced drag and gave the pilot better downward visibility while still providing the structural rigidity and some of the lift of a conventional biplane. Powered by a rotary engine, Nieuports were fast and very maneuverable, but also difficult to fly.

Because Nieuports were tricky to fly, Jim began his advanced training on older, slower planes. He told Paul, "I passed from the small powered to the higher powered Morane and may get the Nieuport in a few days." Jim did not specify which Morane he was flying, but it probably was a Morane-Saulnier Type L "Parasol" or similar (the Parasol designation came from the fact that the wing was over the pilot's head, like a parasol).

A Nieuport 11 in flight. The narrow bottom wing is clearly visible in this image. *Wikimedia Commons*

Morane-Saulnier Type L "Parasol." *Wikimedia Commons*

Jim wrote to his mother the same day to tell her he was back at Pau, where he would learn to fly the Nieuport, "the fastest and finest." He liked the fact that there was just a small group of pilots in the Nieuport school, and they had more privileges than the beginning students. The pay raise that went along with his promotion to corporal, as well as the additional money he was paid for flying, made things nicer too. Apparently his family had still not fully accepted his decision to join the military instead of returning to the US to accept the job his brother-in-law had offered him. "I do not regret for a second what I've done," he wrote. "In fact I've much more respect for myself now. . . . Don't think I can leave the Army and go into business until after the war. That is impossible. One is shot if one tries to leave." He closed the letter on a reassuring note. "I think it [the war] will end this summer. Don't worry about me. I've had a run of luck that will carry me through and when it's over we can get together and live happily ever afterwards."[3]

Several Americans had been trying to convince the French to form a squadron of American volunteer pilots since long before Jim started pilot training. Norman Prince and Bill Thaw were leading this effort. They received some verbal support from French authorities, but little actual progress. The French had no shortage of men who wanted to become pilots, as evidenced by the 250-student backlog that preceded Jim at Pau. The French already permitted Americans to join the French air service by way of the Foreign Legion and fly with French squadrons, as several Americans were already doing. The authorities did not see a need to group the American pilots into a single squadron. It might be a nice idea, but they were busy fighting a war for their nation's survival and didn't have time to pursue nice

Pittsburgh Press headline, December 27, 1915. *Author's photo*

ideas. All that changed over Christmas 1915. The same leave policy that allowed Jim to spend eight days in Paris in mid-September allowed three American pilots to take leave in the US over Christmas. Bill Thaw, Norman Prince, and Elliot Cowdin were stunned to find reporters waiting for them when their ship landed in New York. The presence of three American pilots who had flown combat missions over the trenches created headlines across the country.

The publicity given to the American aviators made the French authorities sit up and take notice. American newspapers had been covering the activities of individual Americans serving in the Foreign Legion, the ambulance service, and in various French flying squadrons since the war began, but they were generally small stories, printed on page 8, or page 11, or wherever the newspaper had space. The Christmas leave headlines opened their eyes to the publicity value of grouping American pilots into a single unit. Suddenly an American escadrille was more than just a nice idea. It was a way to sway American public opinion to the French cause. More materials, more loans, a tougher stand on German atrocities—who knew where it would lead? Establishing an American escadrille became a high priority.

Trying to rush any major project inevitably causes confusion, and the fact that the Battle of Verdun erupted while the French were trying to set up an American squadron added to the chaos. Jim wrote to Marcelle that

> there are so many orders coming through daily that I do not know where I shall end up. First off it was decreed that Americans should be *perfectioned* [final combat training] at Belleville [Le Plessis-Belleville, about 25 miles northeast of Paris], where Kiffin, Thaw, etc. are at

> present, and then that all should be *perfectioned* on Caudrons. Today it has been ordained that Americans should train as well as be *perfectioned* on Caudrons so as to supply the heavy machines needed for the American escadrille. So far I've dodged them and am going ahead on the Nieuport with which I am doing well.[4]

The orders to train Americans on heavy Caudron bombers may have stemmed from the fact that Bill Thaw, who gained headlines in America, flew Caudrons. Norman Prince and Elliot Cowdin flew Voisin bombers, which flew the same type of missions as Caudrons. The only problem with this plan was that Thaw, Prince, and Cowdin had just been assigned to train on Nieuports, since the French needed Nieuport pilots at Verdun. More confusion followed. Jim was told that he would not be sent to the General Reserve* at Belleville but would instead be sent to the General Reserve at Le Bourget, just outside Paris. Two days later, he was told that he would be sent to Belleville after all.[5] An American pilot (and former ambulance driver) named Laurence Rumsey who had been sent to the Voisin school at Avon was sent back to Pau to learn Caudrons instead. When he arrived, he was sentenced to eight days of jail time because he was missing part of his equipment. "Shoes or something,"[6] Jim wrote. Then he disappeared for a week. Jim hoped he hadn't deserted, since there were rumors that several Americans had deserted already, including two who supposedly had intentionally landed in Germany**.

Meanwhile, despite the push to train Americans on Caudrons, Nieuport students were being rushed through the school because they were needed at the front. Except to Jim's frustration, he wasn't doing much flying because of the weather. Snow, sleet, and slush were keeping him grounded. When he did fly, it was in a Morane, since he hadn't been able do enough flying in that plane to graduate to a Nieuport. When the weather was too bad to fly, the students honed their skills at the rifle range or drilled. Jim discovered that the way the French drilled was different from the way he'd learned in the North Carolina militia. "When they yelled 'Shoulder Arms' I did it the US way and crowned a fellow on the head."[7]

---

* Groupe des Division d' Entrainement, or GDE. A "pool" where pilots who had finished their formal training awaited orders to the front and polished their skills while waiting.

** An American bicycle racer named F. C. Hild reportedly deserted to the US from flight training during the opening months of the war, and William Frey was charged with desertion after he failed to return from leave in the US upon completion of flight training in November 1916. Neither is known to have gone to Germany.

When the weather improved a bit, Jim got to do some flying, but the long grounding due to bad weather showed:

> Nearly killed myself today. Missed the trees on rising from the ground by 50 centimeters [20 inches]. Caught hell and it will be a couple of days now before I pass to Nieuport.[8]

It wasn't just flying that was giving Jim problems. In the same letter, he said that his efforts to sell articles and photos to the newspapers weren't working out, and he suspected they were using materials he'd submitted without giving him credit or paying for them. And Yvonne, the "titian haired beauty" at the Kodak store, had written Jim to say he must never try to speak to her in or out of the store. "Maybe she has some fool notion about 'I'm not that sort of a girl' and wants us to understand it when we near the sacred precincts of her pulchritudenous [*sic*] person. *Je M'en Fou* [I don't care]." And, to add to his frustrations, aviation students were now forbidden to go into the town of Pau. A student was soused and kissing a girl in town when a general passed. The aviator didn't see him, didn't salute, so now the town was off-limits. Jim went there only twice a month (he had been "on the wagon" since his leave in Paris), but that was the only place they could buy things.[9]

Rumsey finally showed up. He was sentenced to fifteen days in infantry prison because he took a detour to Paris on his way to Avord (Paris is about 125 miles north of Avord, so it was a *long* detour). This was on top of the

Jim next to a training Nieuport. *NASM*

eight days in the local jail he was sentenced to for showing up without his snow boots. Nonetheless, the French authorities were considering assigning Rumsey to Nieuports instead of to Caudrons. Paul Pavelka, on the other hand, who showed up on time and never got into trouble, was being trained on Caudrons. And when American pilots Clyde Balsley and "Chute" Johnson, who were providing air defense for Paris, heard about the formation of an American squadron and asked to be trained on Nieuports, their commander blocked the request (he was later overruled).[10]

By mid-March, Jim had finally gotten to fly a Nieuport, and he liked it very much. He began on the 23-meter Nieuport and hoped to soon progress to the 18-meter*. The weather had improved, and they finally had enough airplanes at Pau so that he could fly at least three times a day.

Jim wasn't particularly excited about being part of an American squadron, especially not if it held him up or meant he'd have to fly Caudrons. Kiffin Rockwell was in a similar position. He had been trained on Nieuports, spent months at the General Reserve in Le Bourget before being sent to the general reserve at Belleville, and was still waiting for orders to a combat unit. Kiffin fumed at the delay. He wanted to go to the front and fight Germans, and he didn't care if he was assigned to a French or an American unit. Both he and Jim were being delayed by the confusion over forming the American squadron.

Jim realized that he wasn't proficient enough to go to the front yet, but he hoped to be ready soon. He had written to a captain at the airfield near Toul, which he visited while he was working in Pont-à-Mousson, asking to be stationed there. He thought that since he already knew the countryside and the front lines there, that would be a good place for him. He told Marcelle that if the Toul assignment didn't work out, he might volunteer to fly on the Russian front.[11] One of the reasons he suggested the Russian front was because his mother was "threatening" to come to France. Jim was afraid that if she did that, she'd make a big scene every time he left her to return to the front.

The weather continued to improve, and Jim put in long hours flying Nieuports. He usually got up at 5:00 a.m. and worked until dark.[12] He found time to write only when rain or other bad weather kept him from flying. Then he typically wrote letters to several different people on the same day. He filled Paul Rockwell in on the status of the American students

---

* Pilots often added to the confusion caused by the variety of similar-looking Nieuports by referring to their planes not by the Nieuport model number but by the number of square meters of wing surface. The 23-meter Nieuport was *probably* a Nieuport 80, a trainer version of the Nieuport 12 two-seater with an 80 hp engine. The 18-meter was *probably* a training version of the Nieuport 10 two-seater.

at Pau, adding personal details such as the fact that Dudley Hill was collecting money to buy "a swank uniform for Skipper [Paul Pavelka]."[13] There was no standard uniform for French aviators in World War I. Pilots typically wore the uniform of whatever branch of the service they'd been in before transferring to Aviation. Skipper's Foreign Legion uniform had seen hard use in the trenches, but he didn't have enough money to buy a new one, so his friends surprised him with one. (As a corporal, Skipper was earning the same pay as Jim: twenty-five cents per day plus an additional twenty cents in flight pay. Jim said that didn't quite cover his expenses for food and cigarettes.[14])

Jim also wrote about his progress in these letters. He felt that he was making good progress, but "the perfection of a '*Pilote de Chasse*' [fighter pilot] takes longer than any other. It will be several weeks before I get out. The men flying Voisins, Caudrons, and Farmans take but a short time but we take longer at the finishing school than it took us to get our brevet."[15] He was finding landings to be the most difficult part. They were not allowed to make a rolling landing but were instead expected to make the wheels and the tail skid touch down at the same moment and stop (often called a "three-point landing").[16]

The hazards of flying were very much in evidence. Jim told his sister that "a chap I liked best of any here" was sent to the front and, within a few weeks, was wounded in an aerial duel. He survived but had a leg amputated as a result. In one day at Pau, three Nieuports, a Morane, a Caudron, and two Bleriots were wrecked. One of the Bleriots fell from over 2,000 meters (6,500 feet) before landing on its back and sending the pilot to the hospital. Another pilot was sent to the hospital after crashing on a cross-country flight, and a Caudron pilot was killed when he crashed while trying to make a landing. And at the General Reserve at Le Bourget, where Clyde Balsley had finally gotten his application for a transfer to Nieuports approved, Balsley was horrified to watch his commander and good friend kill himself while trying to fly a Nieuport. "I would quit the aviation today if I could," Balsley wrote in his diary. "This is the tenth comrade I have had killed in accidents since I joined. And in a day or two I am to commence my training on the Nieuport. What chance will I have with only a few months training if he with 5 years could not control the machine?"[17]

Jim almost had a fatal accident himself when he was spiraling down for a landing and didn't pay enough attention to his angle of descent. Suddenly his plane flopped from the side into a vertical dive. He had been warned that if this happened, his controls would be reversed (i.e., the rudder would point him up or down and the elevator controlled right or left). He managed to work his way out of the dive, but observers on the ground told him they thought the fuselage would snap because he straightened out so quickly.[18]

On March 26, the *New York Sun* newspaper published an article about the Americans who were training at Pau.[19] The article quoted a student who "after months of work at the front with the American Ambulance" was learning to fly. This article may have been a confirmation of Jim's suspicion that the correspondents in Paris whom he was trying to sell articles to were using the information he submitted without paying for it. The unnamed student is quoted as saying that as soon as he arrived at the school, he was asked if he wanted to be buried as a Catholic or a Protestant. Details in the article indicate that the material was submitted shortly after Jim arrived at Pau, including the fact that "H. Hill" (actually Dudley Hill) was being discharged because of poor eyesight. Dudley was, in fact, blind in one eye, and the medical staff began processing his discharge when they discovered it. He managed to earn his brevet before they finished. School officials decided they couldn't discharge him as being "unfit for flying" when they'd just issued him a pilot's license, so they let him stay.

If Jim even knew about the *Sun* article, he wouldn't have given it much thought, since the following day he received news of a serious tragedy that affected him personally. On March 24 the British channel steamer *Sussex* left Newhaven, UK, headed for Dieppe, France. Passengers were just sitting down for lunch when a German torpedo struck, shearing off the bow and killing all the diners and stewards in the first-class saloon*. The ship began listing badly and was in imminent danger of sinking. The crew began evacuating passengers on lifeboats, but several were damaged and sank. Miraculously, the *Sussex* stayed afloat, but she drifted so far off course that she was not spotted until 11:00 that night. Newspapers had already reported that the ship had been sunk and that no passengers survived.[20] Professor Mark Baldwin was on board that ship, returning from giving a lecture at Oxford. With him were his wife, Helen, and his twenty-five-year-old daughter, Elizabeth "Betty" Baldwin.

Jim wrote to Paul, hoping that Paul could provide him with more details:

> I have just seen yesterday's *New York Herald*, and in it about the Sussex murder. Betty and her father and mother are supposed to be killed. I would appreciate it very much if you could let me know the truth

* The Germans had temporarily suspended their U-boat blockade of Britain after the *Lusitania* outrage but resumed the campaign in February 1916. Unarmed merchant ships were not supposed to be attacked without warning outside the "war zone" around England, and passenger ships were not to be attacked anywhere. The arming of merchant ships and the British use of "Q-Ships"—armed navy vessels disguised to look like unarmed merchant ships—meant that surfacing to warn the crew to abandon ship was suicidal. It was often difficult to identify ships through a periscope. The German *UB-29* mistook the *Sussex* for a minelayer.[21]

> of things. I can't believe somehow that the little girl I'd looked forward to seeing for so long is dead. She wrote me last saying the boat they were to sail on had been held, that it would leave in a few days.[22]

Marcelle Guerin read a newspaper article about the death of the Baldwins and sent a letter of sympathy to Jim. Then she learned that the Baldwins had <u>not</u> been killed, although Betty had been seriously injured, and she telegrammed the update to Jim. He received the telegram and replied to it before he received the letter.

> Your comforting wire has just been received. I cannot thank you too much for sending it. It was wonderfully thoughtful and very fine of you to think of my worry and send me the wire. Yesterday's papers held out no hope. . . . The *Herald* I saw today told of the recovery of Betty's body. I got ahold of a Bordeaux paper having later news. In it was a note from Prof. Baldwin to Mr. Harper saying that he and his wife had escaped unharmed but that Elizabeth was seriously wounded and they were watching over her in the hospital at Winereaux in Pas de Calais.
>
> What a terrible thing it was. I was quite unstrung after the news yesterday and it reflected in my flying. I tipped over on landing and damaged a Nieuport. First bad landing I've made or first thing I've broken.
>
> Thanks again, Marcelle, from the bottom of my heart.[23]

Jim received her sympathy letter the following day and wrote to thank her. He also provided some details on the Bleriot that had fallen from over 2,000 meters, landed on its back, and sent its pilot to the hospital on March 21. Marcelle had read about that accident in the papers and worried that the pilot might have been Jim. He reassured her that the pilot was a man named Le Compte who was taking his altitude test. He apparently fainted from the thin air and lost control of the airplane. It was a miracle that he wasn't killed, but he was definitely suffering from the effects of his crash. "His hair has turned gray. His eyes have a dull, senseless look, and he does not recollect much of his former life. He does not know who he is, and he stoops."[24]

Betty Baldwin was still unconscious, and her recovery would be slow. Jim would continue to worry about her in the weeks and months to come. In the meantime, efforts to form an American escadrille were heating up and were causing more confusion at the training schools. Jim vented his frustration to Paul:

> This damned Aviation bunch in Paris has goon wild. First they put Rumsey on Voisins, then send him back here to Caudrons and they put Skip there too. Then they move both to Morane to pass to Nieuport along with Hill. Then they order them all off. In three days Rumsey, who had done well on Morane, was sent to the G.R. [General Reserve] on Caudrons, Skip back to Morane, and Hill to Caudrons at this school. In addition they find out about me and sock me into A.E. [American Escadrille] I had it planned to go to Toul. I'm tired of trying to figure anything out.[25]

Jim had to make about twenty more flights in the 18-meter Nieuport before they sent him to join Thaw et al. at Belleville, although there were rumors that the Belleville pilots were going to be brought back to Pau to go through a yet-to-be-formed "battle school." Jim asked Paul to remind the correspondents in Paris that Jim had sent them several articles, and he'd like to be paid if they use them. "Am short and so the few francs due would help out." On a more positive note, "Skip is resplendent in his new dark blue uniform, corporal's stripes and [a chevron] on the arm for having been wounded."

On April 4, Jim received definite orders to proceed to the General Reserve at Plessis-Belleville. He wrote to Paul, Marcelle, and Mrs. Weeks to say that he hoped to be able to spend a day or two visiting with them in Paris en route. He told Paul he'd received a letter from Betty Baldwin's mother. "Her daughter is not conscious yet. Her right side is paralyzed and she is a mass of bruises. Specialists from England, however, tell her that Betty will eventually recover tho it will take a very long time."[26] His note to Marcelle said it felt strange to be nearly finished with his Nieuport training. He used to look up to the students in his position, but now that he's there, he doesn't feel as if he knows much about flying.[27]

Jim enjoyed a few days leave in Paris on his way to Plessis-Belleville, and, to everyone's relief, there were no more "unfortunate incidents." After he arrived at Belleville, he wrote Marcelle to say that it was delightful to see her again, and he thanked her for making him feel at ease, adding that he had been afraid to look her in the face again. He was very optimistic about his new assignment, saying that the camp was a delight after Pau. He was free to do as he pleased, and it pleased him to go ahead as fast as he could. He already had more hours flying Nieuports than most of the pilots there, so he hoped to be able to fly the "Baby"* right away. He expected to leave

---

* The Bébé or "Baby" Nieuport was the Nieuport 11. This was France's premier frontline fighter at the time. As the name implies, it was smaller than the less nimble training Nieuports that Jim flew at Pau.

Jim the fighter pilot. *NASM*

for the front with the other American pilots within the week. Almost as an afterthought, he added, "A chap burnt up in a machine here yesterday. His gasoline tank exploded and no one could get to him."[28]

Jim may have had more hours in Nieuports than the other pilots, but he still had not yet flown a combat aircraft. He had never fired a machine gun in the air, never engaged in mock dogfights, and never practiced formation flying or other combat tactics. This was not a deficiency on his part; those skills were not yet part of the training program for fighter pilots. The French would soon create advanced training programs to cover these topics, and his friend "Skipper" Pavelka, who was only a few weeks behind Jim, would benefit from some of these classes, but when Jim went through pilot training, the whole concept of a fighter pilot was so new that the classes had not yet been developed.

Jim's initial optimism about the training camp at Belleville was not necessarily shared by his fellow pilots. Kiffin Rockwell, who was there when Jim arrived, described it as "rather God-Forsaken country."[29] American pilots who passed through Belleville later in the war called the hotel where the pilots stayed "a rotten little hotel" and a "ramshackle place, with beds on three legs . . . broken-down chairs, walls covered with hideous paper, and dust and grime over everything."[30]

Jim's letter to Marcelle was written when he first arrived at Belleville and hadn't yet flown there. He was still "running from bureau to bureau" processing into his new assignment. The following day, he wrote to Paul to say that "after Pau with all their damn rules this is a paradise," but there were so many pilots and so few airplanes that it was difficult to fly. He hadn't been able to "butt in yet. That's what you have to do—fight for a ride."[31] The shortage of planes was not the fault of the organization at Belleville. The fighting at Verdun was creating such a demand for aircraft that even the first-line fighter squadrons couldn't get the Nieuports they needed. Kiffin Rockwell discovered this when he wrote to a friend of Norman Prince's named Saint-Sauveur, who commanded a fighter squadron at Verdun. Kiffin, Prince, and another American pilot named Victor Chapman were fed up with cooling their heels at Belleville waiting for the American Escadrille to be formed. They hoped that Saint-Sauveur could cut through the red tape and get them assigned to his squadron. His reply is illuminating:

> I should be very pleased to have in my escadrille for some time my personal friend Norman Prince, Chapman, and you, but I am afraid it is impossible to obtain. The situation is this: we are ten pilots having only eight airplanes. Every day we break one or two on the awful landing field of this country. The company Nieuport produce,

> they say, 3 airplanes a day. All the production is for the aviation around Verdun; they give me all the airplanes they can, and I never can have more than eight available. You will understand easily that under those conditions I am unable to ask what you wish.[32]

The lack of aircraft and waiting with nothing to do at Belleville didn't dampen Jim's ardor for France. He received a letter from an old friend in the US, Ward McLanahan, in which Ward expressed some pro-German sentiments. Jim wrote back and expressed his disagreement quite strongly. Jim was particularly disgusted with the lack of a strong US response to the German submarine warfare, not surprisingly, considering Betty Baldwin's experience. Jim described the US response to the U-boat issue as follows:

> There were but two alternatives—war or disgrace—and America chose the latter. . . . America may come into the war now but she can never regain the respect of the world. . . . I have become ashamed of my American birth and seriously contemplate becoming a Frenchman and remaining here after the war is over.[33]

Although progress toward creating an American escadrille seemed excruciatingly slow to the American pilots, there was progress. On March 14, while Jim was making his first flights in a Nieuport at Pau, the director of French military aeronautics formally announced plans to organize an Escadrille Américain. Two days later, he released a roster of pilots for this squadron: Bill Thaw, Norman Prince, Elliot Cowdin, Kiffin Rockwell, Clyde Balsley, Lawrence Rumsey, Charles "Chute" Johnson, Victor Chapman, and James McConnell.[34] The squadron would be commanded by a French officer with a French second-in-command, but these officers had not yet been selected. This announcement created the "madness" that Jim complained about while he was at Pau, as various officials in the chain of command for the training school tried to guess what type of aircraft this escadrille would fly. On April 9, Capt. Georges Thénault was selected to command this new squadron, with Lt. Alfred de Laage de Meux as the executive officer. Finally, on April 16, 1916, the Escadrille Américaine* was officially formed as N.124.[35]

---

* This would later be changed to Escadrille Lafayette, the name that became famous.

When the squadron was officially formed, there were a few changes to the roster. Balsley, Rumsey, and Johnson were changed to "replacement pilots," possibility because of the shortage of Nieuports or possibly because it was felt that there were too many pilots with no combat experience. They would join the squadron later. Bert Hall, a pilot with combat experience, was added to the roster in their place. A brief description of the "founding members" of the squadron follows:

Bill Thaw of Pittsburgh, Pennsylvania, was a student at Yale University in 1913 when he was bitten by the aviation bug. He dropped out of school and learned to fly at the Curtis School of Aviation. He engaged in stunt flying and air racing before the war and was in France preparing for an air race when the war started. He offered to fly his plane for the French, and when they turned down his offer, he donated his plane to them and joined the French Foreign Legion. He fought in the trenches until December 1914, when his request to transfer to aviation was approved. He flew Caudron bombers, earned a commission as a lieutenant, and briefly flew Nieuports at Verdun before joining N.124. As the only American commissioned officer in the unit, he exercised unofficial command under Capt. Thénault.

Norman Prince of Pride's Crossing, Massachusetts, earned a law degree from Harvard and was practicing law in Chicago when he became interested in aviation. He obtained his pilot's license in 1912, using an assumed name because his father considered flying to be frivolous. While growing up, he spent many months at his family's estate in Pau France, and he immediately sided with the French when the war broke out. He decided to volunteer his services to France and enrolled in a flying school in the US to improve his skills. While at the school, it occurred to him that a squadron of American pilots would encourage the US to support France. He sailed to France in January 1915 and tried to convince the French to form such a squadron. Discouraged by the lack of enthusiasm the French showed for his idea, he volunteered his own service and entered aviation through the Foreign Legion. He flew bombing and observation missions in a Voisin bomber and was selected for Nieuport training in February 1916.

Elliott Cowdin of Rockaway, Long Island, New York, earned a degree from Harvard in 1907. He joined the American Ambulance Service in November 1914 and drove an ambulance in the Belgian sector. In February 1915, he transferred to Aviation and learned to fly Voison bombers. He flew bombing and observation missions alongside Norman Prince, earning the Croix de Guerre for seriously damaging an enemy aircraft on June 26. Shortly after this event, he was trained to fly Nieuports and flew pursuit missions with several French squadrons. In February 1916, he was assigned to N.65, flying at Verdun alongside Bill Thaw. He was credited with shooting down a German LVG aircraft on April 4, probably the first confirmed victory by an American fighter pilot. He was awarded the Medaille Militaire for this victory, the first American to receive that medal, and he received a second palm on his Croix de Guerre.

Weston Birch "Bert" Hall of Higginsville, Missouri, was one of the more colorful, and controversial, members of the Lafayette Escadrille. The only founding member who did not attend college, Bert worked at a variety of occupations before the war, including farmhand, railroad worker, circus employee, and chauffeur. He was driving a taxi in France when the war broke out, and he didn't hesitate to join the Foreign Legion. He served in the trenches alongside Bill Thaw and Kiffin Rockwell. He volunteered for Aviation with Bill Thaw in December 1914, claiming he knew how to fly. Ironically, the French accepted his application before they accepted Bill's. They put him in an airplane and told him to show them what he could do. What he could do was zigzag across the airfield and run the plane into a hangar. When asked why he didn't tell them he couldn't fly, he replied that he thought he *might* be able to fly. They admired his guts for trying and sent him to flight training. After completing his training, he was sent to the front, flying observation missions in two-seat Morane-Saulnier "parasol" monoplanes. As the air war heated up, these planes were fitted with machine guns and given the additional mission of attacking German planes. Later they were equipped with two-seat Nieuport 10 aircraft, flying the same types of mission. In January 1916, Bert was assigned to the flight-training school at Avord as a Nieuport instructor (veteran combat pilots were often sent to training schools to give them a break from the stress of combat).

Kiffin Rockwell was born in Newport, Tennessee; spent his high school years in Asheville, North Carolina; and was living in Atlanta, Georgia, when he left for France, with the result that all three states claimed him as their own. The son of a Baptist minister who died when Kiffin was less than a year old, Kiffin was raised by a strong-willed, resourceful mother who put herself through medical school while raising three children. Idealistic and adventurous, he thrilled to stories of the Civil War told to him by his grandfather. He attended the Virginia Military Institute for half a year, briefly attended the Werntz Preparatory School in preparation for an appointment to the US Naval Academy, then transferred to Washington & Lee University. Still unable to decide what to do with his life, he dropped out of Washington & Lee, traveled across the US and Canada and worked various marketing jobs, and was living in Atlanta when the war clouds broke over Europe. He and his brother Paul left for France the week that war was declared, and joined the Foreign Legion. Paul was soon wounded and invalided out of the war, but Kiffin fought in the mud and horror of the trenches until he was shot through the leg during a bayonet attack in May 1915. He met Bill Thaw while convalescing in Paris and, finding that his leg wound made marching difficult, volunteered for aviation. He proved to be an excellent pilot and was trained to fly Nieuports after being breveted in October 1915. He was anxious to be sent to the front upon completing Nieuport training, but, as plans for an American squadron slowly evolved, he spent months waiting for orders at Le Bourget and Belleville. Kiffin was not good at waiting.

Victor Chapman of New York City was one of the few people on Earth who was more idealistic than Kiffin Rockwell. He had been extremely close to his mother, who, tragically, died when he was seven years old. Following her death, he became very protective of his younger brother Jay, but five years later, Jay fell into a river and drowned while Victor watched helplessly from the riverbank. After Jay's death, his father said that Victor constantly put himself in harm's way and felt truly alive only when faced with danger. Victor graduated from Harvard in 1913. He was visiting England with his father and stepmother when the war broke out, and, over his father's objections, Victor traveled to France and joined the Foreign Legion. He served as a machine gunner and, despite the daily threat of snipers and artillery, found life in the trenches to be boring. He never got to participate in any of the glorious attacks he dreamed of. In August 1915, he transferred to Aviation, serving as a Voisin gunner/bombardier with Norman Prince and Elliot Cowdin. He entered pilot training at Avord in September. There he met Kiffin Rockwell, and the two became close friends. He completed Nieuport training just in time to join the American Escadrille.

Captain George Thénault was chosen to lead the squadron. A career army officer, he learned to fly in 1913 and spent the early months of the war flying observation missions in a Caudron and dropping *flechettes* on enemy troops. He had the distinction of being perhaps the first pilot to be brought down by enemy fire, when his engine was disabled on August 7, 1914, while flying at an altitude of 3,600 feet. Fortunately, he was able to glide back to the French lines and report that planes were <u>not</u> invulnerable to rifle fire at that altitude, as had previously been believed.[36] Later, Bill Thaw flew Caudrons in Capt. Thénault's squadron, and Bill recommended him to lead the American Escadrille. Unknown to the Americans, the French Foreign Office gave Thénault written orders not to impose the strict standard of discipline that would be applied to a normal French Escadrille.[37] The French wanted favorable publicity from this new unit, not stories of pilots sent to jail for overstaying a three-day pass to Paris. The pilots remembered Capt. Thénault for his "tact and diplomacy" when dealing with them, although his patience must have been strained to the limit by this group of rowdy Americans. He found a way to retaliate, since the pilots also remembered him for his excruciating piano playing, which caused even his pet dog Fram to howl in protest.

As his second-in-command, Thénault chose French lieutenant Alfred de Laage de Meux. Lt. de Laage began the war as a cavalry officer and was seriously wounded when he was shot in the thigh during the first month of hostilities. Realizing that machine guns had ended the era of cavalry charges, he transferred to aviation after recovering from his wound. He served as an observer/gunner on Farmans and, with the help of squadron pilots, taught himself to fly while serving at the front. He earned his brevet without ever attending flight school. Known for his aggressive flying and absolute fearlessness, he had shot down one plane and had two of his own planes damaged beyond repair by enemy fire when Capt. Thénault chose him for the job. He proved to be an admirable choice. While Capt. Thénault had to remain somewhat aloof from his pilots, Lt. de Laage became well liked and greatly respected by the Americans he commanded.

Of the seven Americans assigned to Escadrille Américaine N.124, four—Thaw, Prince, Cowdin, and Chapman—were the sons of millionaires. McConnell and Rockwell were middle class, and Hall had a decidedly rough-and-tumble background. The stress of combat in the coming months would lead to some bickering on the ground, but in the air they fought as a team. The "N" in the unit designation "N.124" indicated they would be flying Nieuports*, specifically the single-seat Nieuport 11.

The Nieuport 11 was 19 feet long with a 24-foot wingspan. It was powered by an 80 hp LeRhone rotary engine, giving it a top speed of 97 mph and a ceiling of 15,000 feet. At this point in the air war, German planes had synchronized machine guns, meaning that the gun could be mounted immediately in front of the pilot and would fire only when the propeller was not in the way. The Allies had not yet developed an effective synchronization mechanism, so the Nieuport had a Lewis machine gun mounted on the top wing, where it fired over the propeller. This was a drum-fed machine gun, and each drum held forty-seven rounds of ammunition. The gun could empty this drum in less than six seconds, so the pilots carried extra drums of ammunition. Changing drums in flight was a challenge, since the pilot had to fly the plane with one hand while tipping the gun back and changing drums with the other in the 100+ mph wind blowing back from the propeller. Doing this in level flight was difficult, but doing it while maneuvering and

---

* Later in the war, the squadron was equipped with Spad aircraft, and the designation changed to "SPA.124."

trying to avoid enemy fire in a dogfight could be a nightmare. Fortunately, although the German planes were better armed, the superb handling of the Nieuport 11 evened the odds. Victor Chapman described flying a Nieuport 11 as follows:

> The Bébé is the smallest and latest model. . . . It is a most delightful machine and responds so quickly and precisely. . . . Monday I went out for the fifth time on it, and climbing to 1,000 meters [3,300 feet] I looped the loop a couple of times. . . . It is a beautifully balanced machine and it responds in a twinkling to the commands. Besides one has a great feeling of security and strength in its robust form and powerful motor. My! It is heavy for its size. To land well one must let it fall from about a yard and a half, taking care that the tail is well down at the time. . . . The first time I put my hand over for direction . . . it came over so fast that I wanted to climb on the upper side of the fuselage.[38]

Capt. Thénault gave a more practical assessment of the Nieuport 11. "They excited the jealousy of other pilots with slower and more bulky airplanes. They were mere lambs; we were wolves. In war it is better to be a wolf."[39]

The seven American pilots received their orders to report to the new squadron on April 16. The following night, Norman Prince gave a party in Paris to celebrate. Jim McConnell was able to attend the party, along with Bill Thaw, Kiffin Rockwell, and Victor Chapman. Kiffin's brother Paul also attended, along with the three "replacement pilots" who would join the squadron later. After the party, Jim, Norman, Kiffin, and Victor boarded a train that was to take them to their new assignment. It was the dawn of American combat aviation.

Kiffin Rockwell next to Elliot Cowdin's Nieuport 11. Three extra ammunition drums can be seen in a rack beside the cockpit. *W&L Archives*

EIGHT

Lounging at Luxeuil

After traveling all night on a supply train, Jim, Kiffin Rockwell, Norman Prince, and Victor Chapman arrived at their destination at Rosenay, in the Champagne hills overlooking Reims. They quickly discovered that no one knew why they were there. After some initial confusion, the authorities at Rosenay discovered that their orders were wrong, and they *should* have been sent to Luxeuil-les-Bains, about 150 miles southeast.[1] They loaded their gear into trucks and were given a ride to Epernay, from which they could take trains to Luxeuil. They spent the night in Epernay, and Jim sent a postcard to Paul Rockwell:

Villa Chatigny today. *Author's photo*

Jim McConnell (*left*) plays pool with Kiffin Rockwell (*right*) in Luxeuil. Victor Chapman talks to Madame Voge in the background. *VMI Archives*

> Dope was wrong and we find we are heading for original stomping ground, where we meet Thaw. Amusing trip so far. . . . Riding in tractors as if we were somebody but Prince has so much stuff we need a freight car. Will have another night's trip before settling down where we belong. Kiffin's happy.[2]

The next day they took a train to Lure, where Capt. Thénault met them with a squadron car and took them to the airfield outside Luxeuil-les-Bains. Jim said that the captain's "cheerful" greeting was "Sixty-two pilots were killed last month."[3] Jim enjoyed the ride to the airfield. "Lolling back against the soft leather cushions, I recalled how in my apprenticeship days at Pau I had to walk six miles for my laundry."[4]

Luxeuil-les-Bains is located near the Vosges Mountains, about 75 miles south of where Jim drove ambulances at Pont-à-Mousson and 35 miles northeast of the Swiss border. It was popular with tourists before the war, renowned for its mineral baths (les Bains means "the baths"). Jim observed that these were the same baths "where Caesar's cohorts were wont to besport themselves."[5] The pilots were quartered in an elegant chateau, Villa Chatigny, next to the baths. They ate at L'Hôtel Lion Vert* (the Green Lion Hotel),[6] a small family-run hotel that served excellent food. Jim described their accommodations in a letter to Marcelle:

---

* Capt. Thénault wrote that the pilots stayed and ate at the Hotel Pomme d'Or (Golden Apple), but Jim's letters plus the writings of other pilots make it clear that they didn't stay there until their second tour at Luxeuil.

> We have splendid quarters, eat with the Captain and Lieutenant at the best hotel and have an orderly to shine shoes, take care of rooms, and arrange for our baths which we take at the famous springs next door to us. *E'est dure cette sale guerre!* [It's hard, this dirty war!][7]

The French undoubtedly assigned the American Escadrille to a quiet sector to begin their combat operations, in part because they wanted positive news reports about the new squadron, but also because it made sense from a military standpoint. Any new unit needs time to sort itself out, time to learn to work together, and time for veterans to teach those without combat experience how to survive in a hostile environment. To some extent the luxury at Luxeuil was the "luck of the draw" for those assigned to that quiet sector. As the war progressed and the squadron was sent wherever air support was needed, the pilots would sleep in tents, unheated hangars, and slit trenches. Indeed, while Jim was telling his orderly to prepare his bath, Carol David Winslow, an American volunteer assigned to a French escadrille, was living in a tent and showering beneath a punctured gasoline tank while someone poured water into it.[8]

There was definitely a military need for the American Escadrille at Luxeuil. Shortly after the first four pilots arrived, Capt. Thénault introduced them to Captain Felix Happe, the commander of a bombing squadron operating out of the Luxeuil airfield. Renowned for his fearlessness and for his flaming-red beard, Capt. Happe was nicknamed "Le Corsaire Rouge" (the Red Pirate). Capt. Thénault described the Maurice Farman bomber that Happe flew as "prehistoric."[9] The variant that Happe insisted on using was powered by an 80 hp rotary engine and was slowed by so many bracing wires that it was nicknamed the "chicken coop*." With enlarged wings, larger fuel tanks, and a full bombload, the plane could barely make 50 mph. Happe removed the machine gun to save weight for bombs and armed his observer with a Winchester carbine. As a result, the plane was a sitting duck for enemy fighters and for German antiaircraft guns. Capt. Happe chose to fly this plane because it could carry a large bombload on a 300-mile round-trip mission. This meant it could reach several industrial complexes in southwestern Germany, including the zeppelin factory at Friedrichschafen. Miraculously, Capt. Happe survived many such missions unscathed, even though his plane was riddled by antiaircraft fire and German fighters. The crews who flew with him were not so lucky. They desperately needed fighter cover.

---

* Happe's squadron flew the Maurice Farman F.11 "Shorthorn" and the slightly improved F.40 variant.

When Capt. Thénault and the four American pilots entered Capt. Happe's office, he was writing names on eight small boxes. "These boxes contain the eight 'Croix de Guerre' I am sending to the families of the eight pilots who were brought down by the Germans the last time we bombed Habsheim Arsenal. . . . I know *escadrille de chasse* [fighter squadrons] do not like to accompany us, but it is my belief that they would find more game if they did. Now if you had been with us on my last trip, I should not have this sorry task. . . . Hurry up, and get ready as quick as you can, so that we may do some good work together."[10] Capt. Thénault thought this introduction made a deep impression on his pilots. It did, but the impression was not entirely favorable. Victor Chapman wrote, "I thought his eye glittered as he related the satisfaction of his last victim. I believe he prides himself on having lost as many *pilotes* as any other two Captains in France." Kiffin wrote that he was "a man absolutely without fear and at the same time a regular ogre for other people's lives."[11] Jim described Capt. Happe's speech as follows:

> After we had been introduced, he pointed to eight little boxes arranged on a table. "They contain Croix de Guerre for the families of the men I lost on my last trip" he explained, and he added: "It's a good thing you're here to go along with us for protection. There are lots of Boches in this sector." I thought of the luxury we were enjoying: our comfortable beds, baths, and motor cars, and then I recalled the ancient custom of giving a man selected for the sacrifice a royal time of it before the appointed day.[12]

In any event, it would be some time before the Americans could escort Capt. Happe's bombers. For one thing, Capt. Happe's second-in-command had convinced him that, in light of the casualties they suffered during day missions, they should try their hand at night bombing until they were issued better aircraft.[13] The American Escadrille's Nieuports were tricky enough to land in broad daylight. At that point in the war, none were equipped for night flying. The second reason the Americans could not escort Capt. Happe was that they did not actually have any airplanes. In *Flying for France*, Jim wrote that the "trim little Nieuports" were waiting for them when they arrived at Luxeuil, but he was exercising a bit of literary license to make the book flow better. The truth was that their planes had not yet arrived, and it would require many telegrams and phone calls from Capt. Thénault to secure aircraft for his pilots.

The French were going all out to support the American Escadrille. Jim said the squadron had "eleven new Fiat trucks, two staff cars, four trucks [probably larger tractor-trailer rigs], and all sorts of tents, etc. There are over 70 men in the escadrille." French authorities promised they would soon receive brand-new Nieuport 11 fighters, but given the fact that the Nieuport factory could barely keep up with the losses at Verdun, equipping a brand-new squadron at Luxeuil would take awhile. In the meantime, as Jim put it,

> In the Ambulance I was a driver and did repairs and ran around on orders. Here we have the driver come for us, an adjutant sees that our orderly does what we want, and for the first few days it's hard to get used to, especially after being a 2nd class soldier at Pau. The whole thing reminds me somewhat of the custom in ancient days of treating a man like a king before the sacrifice of his blood to the gods. But I don't care what the motive is so long as the treatment lasts. What I want is to get a chance at some Boches, and I'd trade in all the comfort for that.[14]

With no planes, the pilots had plenty of time to get acquainted with the airfield, the town, and the surrounding countryside. Capt. Thénault described the airfield as

> the fine aerodrome of Luxeuil, then the largest and most beautiful of the Army Zone. It was over two miles long, perfectly flat, and surrounded by a circuit of high hills, the last outposts of the Vosges Mountains. The French used one end of it; at the other were grouped British airmen of the Royal Navy, Canadians, Australians, and South Africans. I found quarters for my pilots in the little town of Luxeuil-les-Bains . . . where very few troops had ever been stationed.[15]

Because few troops had ever been quartered in Luxeuil, he added,

> Perhaps during the forced inactivity, there were some love adventures or sentimental affairs. They were young; soldier's life was not very safe. My men had a fair chance to die within the next few months. So being only human, they needed the comfort given by the love of a sweetheart.[16]

Jim expressed similar thoughts, although in a slightly less poetic form:

> Paul, this burg has Paris looking like a city designed after the heart of the late Anthony Comstock*. Why it's an effort to avoid being raped. I've obliged a couple but have settled down to occupy myself with a very interesting looking young lady of Italian birth. She is quite nice and not on the boards. Rosa is her name, and believe me Rosa is endowed with a beautiful form, graced with many charms and shows more animation than any I've seen in a long time. They're not used to soldiers here and so things flow our way.[17]

Captain Thénault borrowed an unarmed Nieuport 10 two-seater from another squadron so his pilots could maintain their flying skills. It was a great idea, but the day after he borrowed it, Norman Prince rammed the plane into a hangar. Not seeing any reason to hang around an airfield without any planes, he talked Capt. Thénault into giving him a twenty-four-hour pass to Paris. Jim wrote, "Prince can't stand the horrors of our warlike existence and is beating it back to Paris to stay until our machines arrive. Kiffin and I are disgusted."[18] He also described the wrecked Nieuport to Marcelle, adding, "If these old pilots are no better than he is we're going to have a rotten outfit."[19]

While waiting for the aircraft to arrive, Capt. Thénault used the squadron touring car to take his pilots, or at least those who had arrived so far, on tours through the mountains. They were going to be flying over this rugged terrain, and there were very few open areas where planes could land in an emergency. The few open areas and airfields that did exist were surrounded by trees, power lines, and other obstructions that made landings hazardous. They needed to see these potential landing sites for themselves. The captain was also concerned that their future area of operations was bounded on one side by the border with Switzerland, and the neutral Swiss did not take kindly to military aircraft violating their airspace. Knowing how easily novice pilots got lost, especially when the threat of encountering an enemy aircraft at any moment discouraged careful map reading, he used these tours to show the pilots landmarks and other ways to identify the Swiss border. The trips provided an excellent opportunity to combine business with pleasure, as they drove open cars through the mountains in the Alpine spring weather. The captain knew the location of several inns, which provided excellent lunches, Alsatian wines, and local *kirschwasser* (cherry brandy). Jim wrote to Marcelle that he had never had such a wonderful tour, with myriads of glittering cascades tumbling from the snow-capped peaks providing a ravishing sight.[20]

---

* A US postal inspector famous for promoting strict Victorian morality.

The first American Escadrille pilots at Luxeuil in front of an unarmed Nieuport 10. *Left to right*: Jim McConnell, Kiffin Rockwell, Capt. Thénault, Norman Prince, and Victor Chapman. *W&L Archives*

Bill Thaw, Elliot Cowdin, and Bert Hall finally broke free from their previous assignments and arrived on April 29.[21] This brought the American Escadrille up to full strength, counting Norman Prince, who had gone to Paris. Elliot was awarded the Medaille Militaire the following day for shooting down a German plane during his previous assignment with N.65 at Verdun. He was granted an eight-day leave, a common reward for shooting down an enemy plane, but before he left, the new pilots received a request from Captain Happe:

> The famous Capt A--- [Happe*] here called on us to volunteer to accompany him on his bombardments. The valiant American

* Jim had probably never seen the name spelled out and misinterpreted the French pronunciation as "App."

Touring in the Vosges Mountains. *Left to right*: Victor Chapman, Jim McConnell, Kiffin Rockwell, Lt. de Laage. Presumably the figure standing in the car is Capt. Thénault. *W&L Archives*

> Aviators couldn't see it at all, nor could Capitaine Thénault or Lieut. de Laage. As far as I can see there are only four of us who will make the ripple. Cowdin was awarded the Medaille Militaire. The day the news came was when the Capt. called for volunteers and so it was tough on Eliot C. Prince is 3 days late on the 24 hr. permission Thénault gave him. This seems more of a social than military outfit.[22]

Jim reiterated that point the following day in a letter to his college friend Lewis Crenshaw, saying, "The majority of the Americans couldn't see it and declined, leaving four of us to do the job. It's a damn shame to crawl after the way we've been treated."[23] Jim didn't specify which four pilots he thought would "make the ripple," but presumably he was thinking of himself, Kiffin Rockwell, Victor Chapman, and Bill Thaw. Jim may have met Bill Thaw prior to Thaw's arrival at Luxeuil, and not just because Jim "distinguished himself" at a party given by Bill's sister. Bill had been actively involved in forming the American Escadrille, and he was good friends with Paul and Kiffin Rockwell, having served with them in the Foreign Legion. Everyone who ever met Bill seemed to be impressed by his outstanding leadership. He was also the only commissioned officer among the Americans in the squadron, so Jim would have expected the best of him. Jim had already taken a dislike to Norman Prince and Eliot

Cowdin, and although he had not yet expressed any opinions on Bert Hall, it would soon become clear that he considered Bert a liar and a braggart, but a capable pilot.

Jim was not shy about expressing his views about his fellow pilots. In a postcard to Paul Rockwell, he included an ambiguous comment: "There is fearful class to our escadrille."[24] Months earlier, he had told his sister that Groton was "the finest factory for self-satisfied snobs I've ever met."[25] Norman Prince was a graduate of Groton and had a law degree from Harvard. Elliot Cowdin and Victor Chapman had degrees from Harvard as well. Bill Thaw had attended Yale. Prince, Chapman, and Thaw were the sons of millionaires. Kiffin Rockwell had attended Washington and Lee, but his background was middle class at best. Bert Hall ran away from home before finishing high school. He definitely did not come from a wealthy family.

The issues that caused division among the pilots were not limited to class and wealth. It takes time for any new military unit to bond into a team, and in the case of the American Escadrille, this bonding was slowed by the fact that they had no airplanes, and hence no immediate mission. Jim, Kiffin, and Victor were straight out of pilot training. This was all new to them, and they were eager to learn as much as they could about flying combat missions. They were also straight out of an environment with strict military discipline. Norman Prince, Elliot Cowdin, Bill Thaw, and Bert Hall had all spent the past year flying in combat. The rules were relaxed for veteran pilots, since they needed to "decompress" after each combat mission. If there were no planes to fly, why not decompress in Paris instead of twiddling their thumbs in some provincial town? Jim would provide additional opinions on his fellow pilots in the months to come.

Jim wrote to Marcelle to say that spring had arrived in all its beauty, but their planes had not. "They would have served so well this morning. A Boche flew over and let us have three bombs. Killed one of our drivers and wounded five others. We could have brought him down easily if any one of us had had his machine."[26] His lack of combat experience, or combat training for that matter, showed in the fact that he thought it would be "easy" to shoot down an enemy plane. In the same letter, he admitted that he had his first opportunity to fire a machine gun on the ground that morning, but he would not be able to shoot one from a plane until he actually got into a fight. When that opportunity did arrive, he would discover just how difficult it was to shoot down a plane that was maneuvering and shooting back.

The squadron's long-awaited airplanes began trickling in during the first week of May. They arrived by train, unarmed and unassembled, along with a few specialists from the Nieuport factory to help assemble the planes and adjust them as needed to suit each individual pilot. Three turned out to be the Nieuport 11 "Bébés" they had expected, with an 80 hp Le Rhone rotary engine. The other three were Nieuport 16s—essentially the same aircraft but with a larger 110 hp engine.[27] The Nieuport 16s were assigned to the officers, Thénault, de Laage, and Thaw, while the Nieuport 11s were assigned to McConnell, Rockwell, and Chapman. Cowdin was on leave in Paris, and when Prince finally returned from his leave, he was sent back to Paris to pick up a Nieuport 11 for himself.

Jim's plane was not one of the first to arrive, and he wrote to his mother to describe the life he was leading while waiting for an airplane:

> From Pau to here was like a change from jail to a palace. Our meals at the best hotel in town are really too good, for I am eating more than I should. We are at perfect liberty and due to the fact that we are still awaiting our machines my life so far has been the lazy existence of a summer resorter. I get up at 8:30, my orderly orders my bath, and I go to the Thermol for a dip in the warm waters that since the Romans' time have benefitted the pilgrims to Luxeuil. Then I motor down to the field to see what news there is of my aeroplane and to get the mail. Then back to our villa where I write until 12. Then I walk over to the hotel passing the Thermol en route where I drink some of the water. In the afternoon I walk or practice shooting with revolver and mitrailleuse [machine gun]. After supper we take our coffee and liquors in a café where the seven of us Americans gather. Of course, this lazy life will end as soon as the machines arrive and then too we may move from here, but until then I am enjoying the vacation about as much as anything in my life.[28]

He also said he had received a letter from Betty Baldwin's mother, who said that Betty had made remarkable improvement. She was still unconscious most of the time, but they were hoping for an eventual recovery.

A few days later, Jim was able to take his plane for a test flight. He described it as such: "It's pleasant to have one's own aeroplane and a crew to boss. I was worried for I'd never flown a Baby, but got away with it all right."[29] (Jim had flown Nieuports during his advanced training, but never a Nieuport 11 "Baby," the smallest and most agile model.)

Early aircraft did not come equipped with a neatly arranged instrument panel. The pilot sat in what amounted to an open tube, a tube already crisscrossed with braces, wires, and flight controls. A few critical instruments might be factory mounted, such as a fuel gauge on the side of a fuel tank, but for the most part, instruments were custom mounted to suit a pilot's preferences, and line of sight on the basis of his physique.

Regulating (adjusting) the machine gun was especially critical when the gun was mounted on the top wing. The pilot used a ring sight—concentric circles and crosshairs made of wire—near the nose of the plane to aim the gun. The gun itself was mounted about 3 feet above this sight, so if the gun was perfectly level, the bullets would go about 3 feet above whatever the pilot was aiming at. To correct this, the gun was usually tilted down a bit. The gun was "sighted in" for a specific distance, and at that distance the bullets would strike the target exactly on the aiming point. If the plane was closer to the target, the bullets would hit high, and if the plane was farther away, the bullets would hit low. The pilot had to judge the distance to the target and aim accordingly. Tracers, bullets with an incendiary filling that burned brightly enough to be seen in flight, were just coming into widespread use in early 1916, and these helped the pilot aim. But with only forty-seven rounds* in an ammunition drum, roughly a five-second burst, the pilot couldn't afford to waste shots spraying tracers like a garden hose to aim the gun.

The other key aspect to regulating the gun was to adjust the mounting so the gun would tip back to a position where the pilot could change ammunition drums once he had fired his forty-seven rounds. The pilot would pull a wire to release the gun, and the wind would swing it back, "cracking your skull if you raised your head a little too high."[30] If the pilot was still conscious, he would remove the empty drum, replace it with a full one, and push the gun back up to latch it in place. All this had to be done while the pilot was wearing heavy gloves and goggles, struggling against 100+ mph wind, and possibly maneuvering in a dogfight. It was important to adjust the positioning of the gun so it would be as easy as possible for the pilot to do this, and the best positioning would vary slightly on the basis of the physique and preference of the pilot.

Even when perfectly regulated, a machine gun mounted on top of a pole on the wing would vibrate significantly when fired. The result was that the bullets would spray in a wide pattern, rather than concentrating on the aiming point. This was one of the reasons that experienced pilots tried to get as close as possible to an enemy plane before opening fire.

In addition to adjusting the guns, instruments, shoulder harness, and other details to the pilots' physiques and preferences, each pilot painted a personal motif on the sides of his plane so they could be easily recognized

---

* Much later, a ninety-seven-round drum was developed.

Kiffin Rockwell regulating his gun (*left*) and a Lewis gun tipped down for reloading (*right*). Note that the mechanic on the far left is loading cartridges into a Lewis drum. *W&L Archives and public domain*

in a dogfight. Jim initially painted "MAC" on the sides of his plane, but sometime during the first few weeks of operations, he changed that to a white footprint, commemorating his reign as "King of the Hot Foot Society" at the University of Virginia.

On May 13, the squadron was ready for their first operational patrol. Capt. Thénault chose Kiffin Rockwell to lead the patrol in a V formation, with Chapman and McConnell flying behind him on either side. Capt. Thénault flew at the rear of one side of the V, while Thaw flew the rear position on the other side. The captain and Bill Thaw were the only two on this patrol with combat experience, and they flew at the back so they could keep an eye on the new pilots. The captain soon discovered just how inexperienced these pilots were, particularly in terms of formation flying. Jim described the flight from his perspective:

> Never having flown over this region before, I was afraid of losing myself. Therefore, as it is easier to keep other airplanes in sight when one is above them, I began climbing as rapidly as possible, meaning to trail along in the wake of my companions. Unless one has had practice in flying in formation, however, it is hard to keep in contact. The diminutive *avions de chasse* are the merest pinpoints against the great sweep of landscape below and the limitless heavens above. The air was misty and clouds were gathering. Ahead there seemed a barrier of them. Although as I looked down the ground showed plainly, in the distance everything was hazy. Forging up above the mist, at 7,000 feet, I lost the others altogether. Even when they are not closely joined, the clouds seen from immediately above, appear as a solid bank of white. The spaces between are indistinguishable. It is like being in an Arctic ice field. To the south

Jim with two unidentified mechanics and freshly painted "Hot Foot" motif. Note that the mechanic (*center*) is still holding the paint and paintbrush. *UVA photo*

> I made out the Alps. Their glittering peaks projected up through the white sea about me like majestic icebergs. Not a single plane was visible anywhere, and I was growing very uncertain about my position. My splendid isolation had become oppressive, when, one by one the others began bobbing up above the cloud level, and I had company again.[31]

Jim also wrote that he had never flown above 7,000 feet, so the 10,000-foot altitude of this patrol was a new experience. He had to take long, deep breaths in the rarified atmosphere, and even in his fur-lined flight suit he was shivering from the bitter cold.

Capt. Thénault's perspective of that flight differed slightly from Jim's:

> One pilot went alarmingly far from the rest of us; it was MacConnell [*sic*]. Dazzled by the sun, he no longer saw the other planes, and was making off dangerously toward Switzerland. Alas! Poor neutrality! Another diplomatic incident in perspective. I opened up my 110 hp and managed to overtake MacConnell and by making signs succeeded in bringing him back into line. He and I had lost sight of the others, but black shell-bursts northeast of us showed their course. We dived

> towards the black smoke blobs and soon after joined the patrol, circling round a little southwest of Mulhouse, just above the forest of Nonnenbruch, and the anti-aircraft battery hidden there.[32]

Jim's near violation of Swiss airspace was not the only surprise in store for Captain Thénault that day. Antiaircraft fire—machine guns at low altitudes and exploding artillery shells at higher altitudes—was not as accurate during World War I as it was during World War II, but it could still be deadly. Experienced pilots tried to avoid antiaircraft fire, and when they could not avoid it, they flew out of range as quickly as possible, changing directions and altitude frequently to throw off the gunner's aim. Rockwell and Chapman appeared to be enjoying the antiaircraft fire, deliberately flying through the puffs of black smoke that were left as each shell exploded, essentially taunting the furious gunners to fire more shells. Jim joined them in this game as soon as he and the captain returned. Thaw was circling above, keeping an eye on them and probably wondering what in the hell they were trying to prove. Ironically, his airplane was the only one that was damaged by the fire, and that damage was minor. (Pilots learned to avoid *all* known antiaircraft batteries because it was sometimes hard for the gunners to distinguish friend from foe. A French antiaircraft battery in Pont-à-Mousson celebrated their extraordinary achievement of shooting down three airplanes in one day. Their enthusiasm was only slightly dampened when they learned that only one of the three planes had been German.[33])

Once the patrol re-formed, Rockwell led them over the German airfield at Habsheim, dove to a lower altitude, and performed aerobatics over the airfield as a challenge to the German pilots. Capt. Thénault assumed the Germans must have been patrolling elsewhere, since they had never been reluctant to fight. Rockwell eventually gave up and led them back to Luxeuil, where they landed safely.

Although they had not needed to fire their guns, Capt. Thénault must have had them change drums during the patrol, and, in his words, "The try-outs had been rather unsatisfactory." Chances are, none of the new pilots had ever before tried to do this while flying. They were eager to go out on another patrol, but the captain insisted that they spend the afternoon flying around their own airfield, practicing changing drums. He said they "deemed themselves lucky when the wind did not carry the drum away before they had fixed it in place."[34]

Norman Prince and Elliot Cowdin returned from Paris that night, bringing a reporter and a motion picture film crew with them. The next day, the pilots were posed and filmed in a variety of situations. Jim wrote,

> Today the army moving picture outfit took pictures of us. We had a big show. Thirty bombardment planes went off like clock-work and we followed. We circled and swooped down by the camera. We were taken in groups, then individually, in flying togs, and God knows what-all. They will be shown in the States. If you happen to see them you will recognize my machine by the MAC, painted on the side.[35]

Each pilot was filmed individually standing in front of a Nieuport. Motion pictures were a relatively new invention, and the pilots had probably never been filmed before. They smiled nervously and tried holding their hands in different poses, obviously reacting to the directions of the cinematographer as well as the jeers of their fellow pilots.

One of the group photos showed the pilots clustered around Capt. Thénault for a "mission briefing." Capt. Thénault directed mechanics wheeling Nieuports out of a hangar, and the pilots gathered for another meeting in their flight suits. Capt. Happe's bombers were filmed as well, and the planes were filmed taking off for a mission, with the American pilots protecting the French bombers. The weather was bad that day, with a low cloud ceiling, so the pilots were nervous about maneuvering so close to the ground. Once the filming was complete, Cowdin and Prince went back to Paris with the reporter and film crew.

Victor Chapman wrote that both Kiffin Rockwell and Bert Hall were very upset by this, but for different reasons. Kiffin did not feel that the Americans should be given publicity until they'd done something to earn it. Bert was upset that they had to risk their necks so that someone else could make money.

Jim McConnell posing for the cinematographer. *UVA photo*

Captain Thénault "briefing" his pilots for the film crew. *Left to right*: Kiffin Rockwell, Capt. Thénault, Bill Thaw (*hidden behind the captain*), Norman Prince, Lt. de Laage, Elliot Cowdin, Bert Hall, Jim McConnell, and Victor Chapman. *W&L Archives*

"Think of the honor," Victor said.

"Oh no," Bert replied. "Give me the cash."[36]

With the first patrol and the film crew out of the way, the pilots got down to business. All the pilots flew patrols whenever they could, singly or in pairs, looking for German planes. The Vosges front was a quiet sector as far as flying was concerned, which meant that encounters with enemy aircraft were rare, and patrolling in large formations was not required.

Bill Thaw came close to scoring the squadron's first victory when he took off early on May 17 to intercept a bomber he heard over the airfield. He fired at it and saw it plunge straight down,[37] but ground observers reported that it recovered and landed under apparent control. This meant it was not credited as a victory*.

---

* The French would not credit a pilot with a victory unless the victory was confirmed by a ground observer or by a pilot not assigned to the same unit as the pilot claiming a victory. While frustrating to the pilots, especially when presumed victories occurred too far behind enemy lines to be seen by ground observers, the static trench lines in World War I meant that most dogfights occurred within view of ground observers. In the heat of combat, pilots seldom had time to watch a plane until it hit the ground, and it was fairly common for a pilot and his squadron mates to be "certain" that a plane was destroyed only to have ground observers watch it recover and fly back to its base.

The following morning, Kiffin Rockwell was flying a solitary patrol over the lines when he spotted a German LVG two-seater about 2,500 feet below him. Experienced pilots tried to "stalk" two-seaters, using cloud cover or the sun to hide their approach, or approaching from behind and below, where the observer's vision and field of fire were blocked by the fuselage and the tail of his own plane. Kiffin was not an experienced pilot. Like Jim, Kiffin had never been taught how to fight in the air, and he may have never fired a machine gun while flying. In the Foreign Legion, Kiffin had been taught how to attack with a bayonet. Charge the enemy, ignore enemy fire, and get close enough to jab him in the belly. That was the technique Kiffin used to attack the LVG. He dove straight at the enemy plane, ignored the bullets that were striking his plane, and waited to fire his gun until he was so close he had time to fire only four or five rounds before he had to jerk his plane to the right to avoid a collision. Those four or five shots were enough. The observer fell back against the pilot, the pilot slumped to one side, and the smoking plane dove toward the ground. A pillar of smoke rose up from where it came down. Ground observers watched the fight and accepted the smoke as proof that the plane had crashed*.

Jim McConnell sent a telegram to Paul Rockwell, saying, "Kiffin has brought down a Boche."[38] Paul was just starting to take a bath when it arrived, and the telegram excited him so much that he did a barefoot war dance around the room.[39] Jim McConnell wrote that all Luxeuil smiled upon Kiffin—particularly the girls.[40] The Escadrille Américaine had its first victory.

The same day that Kiffin scored his victory, the squadron got orders to move. They were being sent to the inferno of Verdun. They were still very much a "green" squadron, Kiffin's victory and the prior experience of some pilots notwithstanding, and they still had much to learn about combat tactics and operating as a unit, but the situation at Verdun was too pressing to spend any more time practicing at Luxeuil.

The Germans bombed the Luxeuil airfield on the night of May 19–20, killing five support troops and destroying three trucks, but the squadron was able to borrow trucks and depart on May 20. Most of the pilots flew to their new assignment. Norman Prince, finally returning from Paris with his new plane, ran out of fuel and crashed flying *to* Luxeuil, so he finished his journey

---

* German records do not show the loss of any airmen on May 18. It may be that the records were lost, or it may be that the pilot managed to recover control of the plane after it disappeared from the ground observer's sight, and that both the pilot and observer survived the forced landing and fire.

by rail. Elliot Cowdin was still in Paris, so he would pick up his plane and join them later. And Jim McConnell was left standing on the airfield at Luxeuil, watching the other pilots fly off. The pilots had been doing a lot of flying during their final days at Luxeuil, and Jim broke two longerons (wooden fuselage braces) when landing.[41] According to Kiffin, it was not Jim's fault. The plane had been poorly built, and the longerons broke when they shouldn't have, but that did not change the fact that Jim's plane wasn't flyable.[42] To add to Jim's frustration, the squadron had been equipped with spare longerons, but those had been destroyed by an earlier German bombing raid.[43] So Jim was stuck in Luxeuil. "God knows when I'm going to get away from here," he wrote Paul, "but I hope soon. I'm alone and it seems queer."[44]

NINE

Verdun

The city of Verdun is about 35 miles northwest of Pont-à-Mousson, on the other side of the German-held St. Mihiel salient. It had been a strategically important, heavily fortified city since the days of the Holy Roman Empire. In the late 1800s the French undertook a major construction program, surrounding the city with twenty-two massive, earth-sheltered concrete forts. It was considered impregnable.

Unbeknown to the Germans, by 1916 the French had stripped most of the troops and guns from the forts. In 1914, German 420 mm (16.5 inch) siege guns destroyed concrete forts at Liege, and the French worried that the forts at Verdun would prove equally vulnerable*. German offensives since 1914 had focused on the eastern front while they maintained a defensive posture in the west. The French believed that they could safely remove guns and troops from Verdun to use elsewhere. The Allies planned several major offensives for 1916, but they weren't expecting the Germans to attack. They certainly didn't expect an attack at Verdun.

Ironically, one of the reasons the Germans decided to attack Verdun was because the city was so heavily fortified, it had become a symbol of French strength. General Eric von Falkenhayn, chief of the German general staff, thought the French would throw everything they had into the defense of Verdun. The French had lost heavily in several disastrous attacks in 1915—the losses at Pont-à-Mousson had been trivial by comparison—and General Falkenhayn believed they were near the breaking point. He didn't have enough troops in the west to achieve a major breakthrough, but he

* As it turned out, the earth-sheltered forts at Verdun survived bombardment by the 420 mm guns.

thought if he applied enough pressure on a narrow front, the French would exhaust themselves trying to defend it. Essentially, he planned a war of attrition. He would mass the largest concentration of artillery the world had ever seen around Verdun, launch just enough of an attack to threaten the city, and use his artillery and machine guns to decimate the French troops who rushed to defend it. His goal was to bleed the French army white. If his attack succeeded in capturing the city, it would be a great moral victory, but even if the city eluded him, its defense would destroy the French army.

Falkenhayn realized that artillery was going to dominate this battle, and aerial observation was critical to the success of his artillery. Therefore, before the battle he transferred a hitherto unheard-of number of airplanes to Verdun in an attempt to sweep the skies of French aircraft and make certain only German eyes could direct artillery fire. He assigned 168 planes to the Verdun front. Only twenty-one of these were single-seat fighters,[1] primarily because the whole concept of a fighter airplane was new, and neither side had many of them. These fast, maneuverable, and well-armed aircraft were generally assigned piecemeal to squadrons that flew two-seat observation and bombing planes, to provide protection for those planes. To prevent the French from observing the artillery and troops massing for the attack, all German aircraft, including fighters, flew what were called "barrage patrols," maintaining an even spread of aircraft across the entire front. These patrols were flown from dawn to dusk to deny the airspace to French aircraft. At first the barrage patrols were successful, but the increased air activity and other intelligence sources made the French suspicious that the Germans were planning *something* at Verdun. They had no idea how big the planned attack was.

When the attack began, the German artillery pulverized the front lines. Heavy artillery and siege guns pounded the French lines and fortresses, while long-range artillery destroyed rail lines and other supply routes. The St. Mihiel salient already blocked many of the main roads to Verdun, and German artillery destroyed all but a single road leading to the city. This road became known as Voie Sacrée, the Sacred Way.

In keeping with Falkenhayn's plan, German troops didn't attack until they felt that the artillery had destroyed the opposition. Then the troops advanced cautiously, occupying the devastated landscape and stopping when they encountered resistance until their artillery destroyed it.

Initially, the attack was a success. The Germans made significant advances in the opening days of the battle, even capturing Fort Douaumont—the largest and strongest of the forts at Verdun. The French frantically rushed troops and artillery to Verdun along the Voie Sacrée. An unending stream of supply wagons, trucks, ambulances, and marching troops filled the road day and night. Repair crews worked around the clock to repair the road as fast as it was cratered by long-range German artillery that harassed traffic along the route. These reinforcements stemmed the tide of the limited German attack, and the French massed artillery on the hills on both sides of the battlefield. Verdun became a killing zone for the Germans as well as for the French.

The German public was thrilled when newspapers announced the early successes, and they expected their army to capture Verdun quickly. Falkenhayn had not told them this was to be a battle of attrition, not a battle to capture the city. Even his field commanders didn't know that. The pressure on Falkenhayn to capture Verdun overwhelmed him, and he began to rush more troops into the battle. It became like the fighting at Pont-à-Mousson, only on a much-larger scale. The battlefield was confined to a front 20 miles long and at most 4 miles deep. It covered an area smaller than Brooklyn, New York. It is estimated that sixty million shells were fired into that narrow strip, or fifteen shells for every square foot of churned-up earth.[2] "Officially" the battle lasted ten months, until December 1916, but fighting continued throughout 1917 and 1918. Total casualties for both sides in 1916 were estimated to be 420,000 dead and 800,000 wounded,[3] but there was so much confusion and so many men were missing in action that the numbers are incomplete. Men simply disappeared at Verdun, their bodies so pulverized and scattered by artillery that it was impossible to account for them.

The air war didn't go the way Falkenhayn had planned, either. The barrage patrols had been effective against the small number of planes the

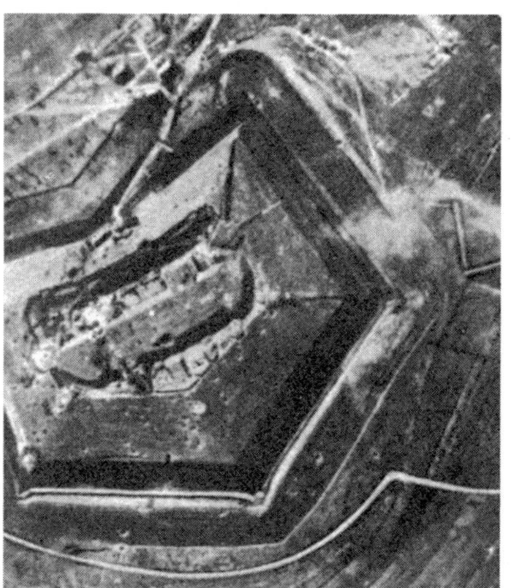

Fort Douaumont before the Battle of Verdun (*left*) and after bombardment (*right*), when Jim said it looked like "tracings of a finger in wet sand." *Wikimedia*

French initially had at Verdun, but the French quickly rushed an additional two hundred aircraft and aircrews to the battle. The German barrage patrols spread their planes thinly across the battlefield, and the French now had enough aircraft to overwhelm the barrage patrol at any given point*. The Germans in turn recognized that scattering their fighters throughout other aviation units was not effective. At the urging of their leading ace, Oswald Boelcke, the fighter planes were grouped together at forward airfields with telephone connections to German antiaircraft batteries. These batteries called the nearest fighter unit when French aircraft crossed the lines, so the German fighters could intercept them. Verdun became the first major air battle in history, and the first in which both sides fought for air superiority. Within a month, seventy French pilots were lost at Verdun.[4] General Philippe Pétain, commander of all French forces at Verdun, told his chief of air operations, Major Charles de Tricornot de Rose, "De Rose, I am blind; sweep the skies for me."[5] Major de Rose began organizing French fighter aircraft into offensive units, similar to what Boelcke was doing on the German side of the lines. Both sides recognized the need for more fighter planes.

* Today, *concentration of force* is recognized as one of the basic tenets of airpower, but air fighting was brand new in World War I, and the tenets were developed as a result of experiences like this.

Fort Douaumont as it appeared to the soldiers who fought there. *Wikimedia*

This was why Thaw, Prince, and Cowdin had been trained to fly Nieuports and sent to Verdun before the American Escadrille was formed. This was also why the escadrille had been suddenly ordered to leave Luxeuil while it was still learning the ropes.

While Jim waited impatiently for the parts he needed to repair his plane at Luxeuil, the rest of the pilots flew to an airfield near the tiny village of Behonne, northwest of the city of Bar-le-Duc. Capt. Thénault described the airfield as being "dreaded for its difficulties," being situated on the narrow summit of a hill, bordered on three sides by deep ravines, and frequently swept by strong crosswinds.[6] There were several other units stationed at Behonne, but Capt. Thénault called upon the billeting officer in town even before he reported to the commanding officer at the airfield. The billeting officer assigned the Americans to a villa that had been abandoned by its owner, who had fled to the South of France with his family. The villa was located right at the gates of Bar-le-Duc.[7] Bert Hall described it as

> about half way between our flying field and the town. It was situated up on a little hill, not very high. There was a winding stone stairway running up to the door with flower beds all around. It was really a lovely spot.[8]

The pilots appreciated the villa on days when the weather prevented them from flying, but when flying was possible, they did little except grab occasional meals and short snatches of sleep at the villa. The pace of operations was exhausting. After only two days of flying at Verdun, Kiffin Rockwell wrote, "This is a regular hell around here in the way of excitement and the world going crazy. Impossible to express with words one's impressions. I am badly played out for lack of sleep."[9] Pilots were generally assigned to one or two squadron patrols over the lines every day, and they were encouraged to fly as many voluntary patrols as possible. The Voie Sacrée wound its way through Bar-le-Duc, and the endless stream of men and materials going into the battle reminded them of why they were there. The much-smaller stream of exhausted survivors stumbling back from the battle, with ravaged uniforms and vacant stares, drove home the importance of their mission. The more freedom that German aviators had to direct artillery, the fewer French troops who would live to stagger home.

Capt. Thénault described how air operations were conducted. Patrols were flown at three different altitudes—a low patrol at 1,000 feet, a middle patrol at 6,000 feet, and a high patrol at 12,000 feet. A plane at a higher altitude had the advantage over a plane at a lower altitude, since altitude could be traded for speed. A plane at a higher altitude could dive on a lower plane, make a high-speed attack on the lower plane, and then use his superior speed to climb out of range and prepare to make another attack. This was especially true during World War I, when engines didn't produce enough power to let planes climb quickly. The patrol at 6,000 feet could provide protection for the low patrol, but planes from the low patrol could not climb quickly enough to help the patrol at 6,000 feet if that patrol was attacked. The patrol at 12,000 feet protected the patrol at 6,000 feet. Later in the war, as aircraft performance improved, planes flying at 12,000 feet were vulnerable to attacks from above, so the high patrol flew even higher. By the end of the war, they approached 20,000 feet.

A little-discussed but serious danger that Capt. Thénault also described was that of flying through an artillery barrage. Without radio communications, there was no way for pilots to know where the artillery was firing or for artillerymen to know if there were friendly planes in the vicinity. Pilots depended on the "big sky, little plane" principle for their protection. When flying over Verdun, where hundreds of thousands of shells could be fired in a single day, the sky didn't seem so big anymore. Capt. Thénault described the threat as follows:

> During our flight, we heard the roar of the nine-inch shells; sometimes we even saw them in the form of a passing flash. In aviation slang, we called them "*les gros rats noirs*"—the big black rats. The smaller ones were not seen but there was no little danger of being caught on the trajectory of any of them. Occasionally a plane would burst literally into fragments, which meant that a big shell had hit it in full flight. It is really surprising that accidents of this nature did not happen more often, especially in the case of low patrols, which were always in the zone where these trajectories were the thickest. On account of this ever present menace over one's head, it is easy to understand why the low patrol was not the most popular.[10]

Jim received sporadic updates from the pilots at Behonne while he cooled his heels at Luxeuil. Bert Hall shot down an Aviatik on May 22. Two days later, Bill Thaw shot down a Fokker during an early-morning voluntary patrol. "No credit to me," he said afterward. "It was plain murder. He never even saw me."[11] (Despite stories of chivalry in the air, successful pilots resorted to "plain murder" whenever they could. In war the objective was to shoot down the enemy's planes, not to vanquish an opponent in a fair fight.)

Later that same morning, Capt. Thénault led a squadron patrol over the lines. He knew that the German aviators at Verdun were experienced and skillful, and he wanted to give his pilots time to learn their trade before risking them in major dogfights. He gave them strict orders not to attack unless he "see-sawed" his airplane as a signal.[12] Nevertheless, when they spotted a group of German two-seaters, Victor Chapman broke formation and dove to attack. The other pilots followed, to protect Victor. It was an extremely risky move, since the Germans were well behind their own lines and so low that the Americans were exposed to ground fire as well as fire from the German planes. Fortunately, there were no German fighters providing top cover for the two-seaters, but the two-seaters showed they could hold their own against the Americans. Bill Thaw was hit in the left arm, just above the elbow. The bullet shattered the bone. Bleeding profusely and in great pain, Bill fought off unconsciousness as he struggled across the lines and landed in the first open area he saw. French soldiers dragged him out of the plane and carried him to a field-dressing station, where they managed to stop the bleeding. An American ambulance from Section 2, Jim McConnell's old section, took him from the dressing station to the nearest hospital.[13]

Kiffin Rockwell's windshield was shattered by a German bullet, and his face was peppered by fragments of the bullet and the windshield. Bleeding profusely, he thought his nose had been shot off (it wasn't). He disengaged from the dogfight and streaked for home, convinced he was the victim of an exploding bullet*, a projectile that was banned by the Hague Convention.

The other pilots disengaged and managed to return safely, but Bill would not be able to fly again for months. Capt. Thénault wanted to send Kiffin Rockwell to a hospital, but Kiffin wouldn't hear of it. He made a quick trip to Paris to reassure his brother Paul and Mrs. Weeks that he was OK and then returned to the squadron, only to learn that Capt. Thénault had given his plane to Norman Prince. Norman was a more experienced pilot than Kiffin, and Capt. Thénault probably thought that Kiffin needed time to recuperate, but Kiffin was incensed.

---

* The term "exploding bullets" was commonly used to refer to soft-nosed, hollow-point, or similar ammunition designed to fragment upon impact. Its use was banned by the 1909 Hague Convention, a precursor to the Geneva Convention, because it caused unnecessary suffering. Both sides accused the other side of using exploding bullets, although many historians are skeptical of these claims. The pioneering World War I aviation historian "Arch" Whitehouse, himself a World War I pilot, stated flatly that "there is no reliable record of explosive bullets in the air armament of the Germans during 1914–18."[14] At the time, however, the Lafayette pilots were thoroughly convinced the Germans were using explosive bullets.

The news of his friends' injuries must have been very frustrating to Jim, since he could do nothing to help. He was still stranded at Luxeuil, waiting for the fuselage brace he needed to repair his plane. He sent a postcard to Paul Rockwell, saying, "Have time, but nothing to write about, even for Mowrer."[15] (Paul Scott Mowrer was a newspaper correspondent for the *Chicago Daily News* who sometimes bought articles from Jim.) Jim kept up with the squadron news through letters and a visit by Lt. de Laage.[16]

With Bill Thaw in the hospital and Kiffin Rockwell temporarily out of action, Capt. Thénault requested replacement pilots from the reserve. The first to arrive was a man who was destined to become a legend—Raoul Lufbery.

Born in France to an American father and a French mother, Gervais Raoul Lufbery learned to fend for himself at an early age. His mother died before his first birthday, and five years later his father remarried and moved back to the US, leaving Raoul and his brothers in the care of relatives in France. Growing up, Raoul worked at a number of jobs, first in France and then in North Africa, Turkey, the Balkans, and Germany. He traveled to the US (he was a US citizen thanks to his father's citizenship) and served in the US Army. He traveled to India and the Far East, where he met a French pilot named Marc Pourpe. Raoul became Marc's mechanic and helped him give flying exhibitions in China and Egypt.

When World War I began, Marc joined the French army as a pilot. Raoul enlisted in the Foreign Legion and was assigned to Aviation as Marc's mechanic. Several months later, Marc was killed attempting a night landing in fog. Raoul blamed the Germans for Raoul's death and became a pilot so he could take out his revenge. He didn't make much of an impression when he was first assigned to the American Escadrille, but he quietly learned his craft until he became deadly in the air.

Shortly after Lufbery arrived, Clyde Balsley and Chute Johnson were assigned to the squadron. Horace Clyde Balsley was born in Pennsylvania. When he was fourteen, he moved with his family to San Antonio, Texas. In 1915 he came to France as an ambulance driver, and he transferred to aviation in September 1915. He completed his flight training at Pau about the time Jim McConnell arrived. Charles Chouteau "Chute" Johnson was born and raised in St. Louis, Missouri. He was a friend of Jim's at the University of Virginia, briefly went into business with Jim in New York and North Carolina, and came to France as an ambulance driver shortly before Jim did. He transferred to Aviation in September 1915, completing his training shortly after Jim arrived at Pau.

Kiffin Rockwell has what appears to be a difficult conversation with Capt. Thénault, possibly about the fact that Kiffin has no plane. New pilot Clyde Balsley walks in from the left, while Raoul Lufbery waits patiently on the right. *W&L Archives*

On May 28, Jim excitedly wrote Marcelle that the parts he needed to repair his plane had finally arrived. He hoped to fly to Behonne on the following day. His plan was to do more than just fly to the squadron's new air base. He wanted to fly over the Bois-le-Prêtre, the battlefield that had created the casualties he evacuated during his ambulance days, and drop a bomb with the compliments of Betty Baldwin. The only bombs they had at Luxeuil were large ones, but he calculated that if he removed the machine gun, his Nieuport could handle the weight. He rigged up a way to carry and release a bomb that he thought was practical. Much to his disappointment, though, the aviation chief didn't agree and ordered him <u>not</u> to carry a bomb.[17] Since the aviation chief didn't have a problem with Capt. Happe being an "ogre with other people's lives" by carrying bombs in antiquated Farmans, it's possible he was more worried about the bomb falling off on takeoff and exploding on the Luxeuil airfield than about any risk to Jim's life. This proved to be a doubly disappointing day for Jim, since on that same day he discovered that the parts that had finally arrived were for a different model of Nieuport.[18]

Jim gave up waiting for factory longerons and had some makeshift braces made at a nearby town. "I'm damned if I'm going to wait any longer," he told Paul. He was looking forward to going to Verdun, "but as I haven't yet had any practice you may see me coming in on a *brancard* [stretcher] one of these fine days." He asked for Paul's help in drawing up a writer's agreement, since the *Sun* newspaper wanted Jim to be their aviation correspondent. He would have to do it anonymously, since Cowdin was "thirsty for printer's ink" and didn't want any competition. He also wanted to make certain he got the "filthy lucre" [money] up front.[19] He was successful in getting his plane fixed, but bad weather prevented him from flying to Verdun until June 1.

Jim's first day at Verdun was a memorable one. He arrived late in the morning, and Capt. Thénault immediately asked him to fly with the squadron's afternoon patrol*. The patrol was scheduled for 12:30, and the first time that Jim saw a map of the Verdun sector was when one was handed to him as he was climbing into his plane.[20] He'd never seen the territory from the air, so he counted on staying with the others to keep from getting lost. "Lovebury" [*sic*] (Jim hadn't had time to learn the names of the new pilots yet) took off first, and Jim followed him.[21] Bert Hall was scheduled to take off next, followed by Norman Prince, Victor Chapman, Elliot Cowdin, and Capt. Thénault. Kiffin Rockwell, Chute Johnson, and Clyde Balsley had no planes, so they stood on the airfield and watched the others depart.[22]

Jim and Raoul Lufbery climbed to the designated assembly point, but the other planes never joined them. Then, as Jim had feared, he lost sight of Lufbery as well. Alone, he set off in what he believed was the general direction of the front lines. He saw a plane beneath him and felt relieved to find a "friend." Then he saw the black crosses on the wings. It was the first German he'd ever seen in the air. He realized he didn't have the slightest idea how he was supposed to attack an enemy plane, and he had never fired a machine gun in the air.[23] Nieuports couldn't take the stress of diving with full power, and rotary engines had very little throttle control, so "with a queer feeling," he shut off his engine, dove toward the enemy plane, and put his hand on the firing lever for his machine gun. As he got closer, he realized that the enemy plane was a two-seater. When he was about 150 feet away, the observer opened fire on him. Jim opened fire too, but with no results. He shot past the enemy plane, then pulled up and turned to make another pass. The enemy had turned also, and Jim found himself level with the enemy plane, an easy target for the observer. "It was a fool move on my part," he wrote.[24] "I found myself staring into the flames of his machine

---

* Jim wrote letters about this patrol to his mother, Paul Rockwell, and Marcelle Guerin. Several other pilots wrote about it as well. This description of that patrol is based on all of those accounts, each of which will be cited only once.

gun." Jim could hear the "tut-tut-tut" of the German's machine gun and feel the thuds as bullets slammed into his plane. Jim fired a short burst, then turned to his right and dove again. He pulled up and tried to attack from the other side, but his machine gun wouldn't fire. Jim pulled away, tried cocking the gun, but still couldn't get it to fire. He tipped the gun back to the reloading position to examine it, but then he heard a machine gun firing at him from behind. He looked and saw that the German plane was coming straight at him, with the pilot firing the forward gun. Jim dove away and finally managed to lose the German plane. He examined his gun and found that the ammunition drum had been knocked off and the cooling fins were loose, and he suspected there was more damage from German bullets. There were also nine bullet holes through his wings on both sides of the cockpit, some within a foot of his body.

Jim had escaped the German, but now he was totally lost. He followed several canals and tried to proceed in a generally southwest direction to get to or stay on the Allied side of the lines, but he could find nothing on his map that matched the countryside he was flying over. He was certain he had flown off the map, but he had no idea which way to turn to get back to the map. After searching for over two hours, his engine started missing and he decided it was time to land. He found a grassy field that "looked as if it were made for aviation." He flew over it several times until he attracted the attention of some soldiers. They were wearing blue uniforms, not gray, so he knew he was in French territory. He then made his final approach to land.

Unknown to Jim, the grass hid a line of ridges on the surface. As Jim put it, "The only way to land is from the direction I didn't take." As he touched down, he felt "a hell of a bump," bounced back into the air, nosed down, and flipped the plane over on its back. The plane was demolished. Fortunately, Jim wasn't hurt. He was given a ride back to the Behonne airfield, which was about 15 miles from where he landed. There he learned that he had already been reported as missing and believed dead.

When Jim returned to the airfield, he also learned why the rest of the planes hadn't joined him for the scheduled patrol. Just as Bert Hall was about to take off, he spotted a formation of German bombers high overhead, flying in their direction. Bert and the other remaining pilots took off and began climbing to intercept the bombers. Jim and Raoul Lufbery had flown underneath the bombers without spotting them. Clyde Balsley, Kiffin Rockwell, and Chute Johnson were left standing on the airfield, watching the Germans get closer. Balsley counted ten bombers;[25] other reports put the number at fourteen. French antiaircraft batteries began filling the air with shrapnel. Four of the Germans broke away from the formation and flew directly over the airfield. As bombs began whistling down, Balsley and company realized they were more than just spectators and dove for cover in a shallow ditch beside the field.

Being the target of a bombing raid is a terrifying experience for anyone. It's particularly galling for a fighter pilot who has no plane, since the sense of helplessness is coupled with the frustrating certainty that if he *had* a plane, he could shoot down the bastards. The three pilots huddled in a ditch while bomb fragments whistled over their heads and antiaircraft shell fragments rained down on them. Balsley wrote that as the bombs came whistling down, it seemed as if each one was going to fall right on him. One hit a hangar about 30 feet away. Kiffin wrote, "I thought I was going to be killed by the bombs, which was a very disgusting feeling."[26]

After the bombers passed over the airfield, they proceeded to bomb the town of Bar-le-Duc. Section 2 of the American Ambulance Service, Jim's old unit, had recently been stationed in the town. Walter Lovell stood in the middle of the town square, with bombs falling all around him, and directed ambulances to rescue the wounded (Walter would soon transfer to Aviation and join the American Escadrille). Several ambulances were damaged by bomb fragments, and a driver in a British ambulance unit had his arm blown off. Forty people were killed by this bombing raid, including ten children who were playing in a schoolyard. About two hundred people were injured.

The pilots who had taken off from the airfield as the bombers approached had climbed high enough to attack them as they returned from the raid, but with no success. Elliott Cowdin's machine gun jammed, and he couldn't clear the jam in the air. Norman Prince emptied a drum of ammunition into two bombers and thought he killed an observer in one and damaged the engine of another. He replaced the empty ammunition drum and was ready to attack again, but while changing drums he bumped the ignition switch with his elbow and shut off his engine. Not realizing what he had done, he thought his engine had been disabled by enemy fire (his plane had been hit by several bullets), so he glided down and landed.[27] German bullets perforated Capt. Thénault's fuel tank, and he was forced to land. He was lucky the plane didn't catch fire in the air. Victor Chapman and Bert Hall chased the retreating bombers back to the lines but could never get high enough to mount a successful attack.

It was a disappointing day for the American Escadrille. They failed to stop a bombing attack on their own airfield and on the town of Bar-le-Duc. Jim had totally demolished his airplane, and several other airplanes were damaged. To make matters worse, the pilots were convinced that the publicity surrounding their transfer to Bar-le-Duc had prompted the raid. (They later learned that General Petain, commander of all French troops at Verdun, had just moved his headquarters to Bar-le-Duc. His headquarters was probably the target of the raid.) Their frustration and disappointment are apparent in their letters and diaries. Kiffin Rockwell wrote his brother Paul, "For Christ sake let's try and shut down on the publicity about the Escadrille!"

Jim did provide a bit of hope in the postscripts to the letters he wrote about that day. He had received a letter from Betty Baldwin, written in her own handwriting, which showed she was recovering from the injuries she sustained in the torpedo attack. He tempered his optimism by telling Marcelle that it was "poor, shaky writing that would almost make one cry, the poor kid."

TEN

Death Strikes

Bad weather set in shortly after the German raid on Bar-le-Duc, and the pilots could fly only sporadically over the next few weeks. Paul Rockwell wrote that the weather was "vile, more like February than June."[1] He also mentioned a "rumor of a big British offensive in the North, within the next ten days." His timing was a little off, but the British were planning to open a major offensive in the Somme valley in late June (later postponed to July 1). The fact that Paul, a civilian reporter in Paris, had heard rumors of this offensive and was openly writing about them shows how abysmal the operational security was.

Two new pilots joined the squadron, both of whom Jim had met during flight training. Lawrence Rumsey arrived on June 4. He was born in Buffalo, New York, the son of a railroad, banking, and tannery tycoon. He studied at Harvard, then became a professional polo player. When the war started, he sailed to France and joined the American Ambulance Field Service about a month before Jim did. He transferred to Aviation about two months before Jim did, but had problems passing his cross-country flight, which delayed him earning his brevet. (He was the pilot whom Jim wrote about who got lost, violated Spain's neutrality by flying into Spanish airspace, realized his mistake, and barely made it back to France before running out of gas and smashing his plane while making an emergency landing.)

Dudley Hill joined the squadron on June 6. "Dud" Hill was born in Peekskill, New York, and began studying mechanical engineering at Cornell in the fall of 1914. He dropped out the following spring, sailing to France and joining the American Ambulance Field Service in April 1915. He transferred to Aviation and began flight training in September 1915. How he managed to get accepted into Aviation is a bit of a mystery, since he was

Escadrille aircraft at Behonne. Norman Prince's Nieuport 11 is in the foreground. Elliot Cowdin's plane is next in line. The "Texas Lone Star" plane is Clyde Balsley's, and Laurence Rumsey's "RUM" plane is at the end. *W&L Archives*

blind in one eye as the result of a high school hockey accident and deaf in one ear as the result of a childhood diving accident. He failed an eye test while in flight training but managed to earn his brevet before his discharge paperwork was received, and so was allowed to stay.

Rumsey and Hill arrived at a time when squadron morale was not at its peak. The German bombing raid on Bar-le-Duc, followed by the bad weather and consequent lack of flying and victories, seemed to have put everyone into a funk. Jim wrote that "there seems to be a split up in this outfit. Thaw & Co. v. Cowdin, Prince, et al. I don't give a damn and won't join either club." He complained there was "nothing doing" due to rain and clouds, and Bar-le-Duc had been closed to the pilots for "some fool reason," so they couldn't go to town to let off steam. He closed with an issue of concern, although apparently not one that depressed him. "Did I tell you Marcelle wrote me a 'I'll go to you if wounded' note? The net is drawing closer."[2]

Norman Prince's Uncle Charles visited the squadron and brought a phonograph, which most of the pilots appreciated. It didn't seem to cheer up Victor Chapman though. He usually saw the bright side of things, but the events of the past few days and the dreadful weather depressed even Victor. He wrote,

> Meanwhile I sit in an upper window with waves of leaden clouds drifting by, and the indefatigable graphophone* churns out some

* "Graphophone" was a brand name for phonographs made by the Columbia Phonograph Company. Sometimes it was also used as a generic name for a phonograph.

> vulgar tune below, and the other "heroes" play poker, and the Captain practices scales on the piano. It is disintegrating to mind and body, this continued *inertia.*[3]

It would be hard to imagine two pilots who were more different than the artistic Victor Chapman and the earthy Bert Hall, but their views of the squadron's musical entertainment were in agreement. Bert described the forced idleness in the villa as follows:

> We had a phonograph in our villa and a piano too. The phonograph was supplied with the most terrible old records, but we played them just the same. . . . The piano was most troublesome. The Commanding Officer thought he was a musician. He really wasn't. His musical efforts were limited to pounding out a few bad tunes, and when I say pounding, I mean just that—pounding! He used to use the same bass notes for everything he played. But he was the CO, and we had to put up with it. Now and again a Red Cross man or an ambulance driver would happen in and they could oftentimes play real music.[4]

The following day, June 9, Jim was on guard duty when a German plane was sighted over Fort Vaux, one of the forts in the Verdun complex. Jim flew out to investigate, along with Victor Chapman and Clyde Balsley. They didn't find the German, but they got a good look at the battlefield. It was Balsley's first trip over the lines. He was impressed by the smoke over Hill 304 and Mort Homme (Dead Man's Hill). He saw flashes through the smoke, like someone striking a match. "The air over the battlefields seemed to be all nervous and troubly. I was blown around way up there like a leaf. What must it be below?"[5] Jim's description to Marcelle was more poetic:

> There is a broad brown band north of Verdun which marks the territory where the fighting has taken place. It does not seem of this earth. At each side are shell holes, but in the brown band there are none to be seen. They are so numerous that they blend into each other. What trees there were have all gone, and if villages were there, there is no sign of them left. Even the broad white roads have vanished as if erased from a blackboard. Beneath one there are flashes as if one turned on a pocket lamp, and the machine rocks. Soon there is a puff of smoke when the projectile explodes. That's

> as much as we see of a battle. The motor drowns all other sounds and we see but the flash and smoke. The battle seems quiet and still. It is very weird. To see the endless fall of shells makes one wonder how men can stand in the face of such fire. There is a haze above Mort Homme—so thick is the smoke. But it's all silent.[6]

Jim sent a similar description of the battlefield to an old friend from North Carolina, Frank Page, who would later edit Jim's book *Flying for France*. In this description he referred to the brown band as a "strip of murdered Nature," a phrase he would use again in his book. His description to Frank contained a few additional details about the battlefield and went on to describe one of Jim's recent sorties:

> It looks as if shells fell by the thousand every second. There are spurts of smoke at nearly every foot of the brown areas and a thick pall of mist covers it all. There are but holes where the trenches ran, and when one thinks of the poor devils crouching in their inadequate shelters under such a hurricane of flying metal, it increases one's respect for the staying powers of modern man. It's terrible to watch, and I feel sad every time I look down. The only shooting we hear is the tut-tut-tut of our own or enemy plane's machine guns when fighting is at close quarters. The Germans shoot explosive bullets from theirs. I must admit that they have an excellent air fleet even if they do not fight decently.
>
> We made a foolish sortie this morning. Only five of us went, the others remaining in bed thinking the weather was too bad. It was. When at only 3,000 feet we hit a solid layer of clouds, and when we had passed through, we couldn't see anything but a shimmering field of white. Above were the bright sun and the blue sky, but how we were in regard to the earth no one knew. Fortunately the clouds had a big hole in them at one point and the whole mass was moving toward the lines. By circling, climbing, and dropping we stayed above the hole, and, when over the trenches, worked into it ready to fall on the Boches. It's a stunt they use, too. We finally found ourselves 20 kilometers in the German lines. In coming back I steered by compass and then when I thought I was near the field I dived and found myself not so far off, having the field in view. In the clouds it shakes terribly and one feels as if one were in a canoe on a rough sea.[7]

On June 15, Jim elaborated on his views about the pilots, probably in response to a question from Paul Rockwell:

> I don't mean I'm neutral in opinion as to the camps here but I can't see any good in putting my voice in. Here's the way I've got the outfit sized up. Kiffin, Bill, Chapman, et al. are the most serious, Lufbery included. Prince and Cowdin are in it for the sport, especially the latter and while they do their work, will never ring any gongs. Hall is minus a few cogs but runs along in the average. Johnson & Rumsey frankly dislike the game, and I believe Balsley needs a new pair of drawers whenever he goes out. Hill is a nice sort and I believe will try hard. The only ones with the really right feeling are the first named.[8]

Jim would revise his opinion of Balsley in a few days. It's surprising that his initial opinion of Chute Johnson was so negative, since they had been friends since they met at the University of Virginia. Johnson would prove to be a reliable member of the escadrille throughout its existence. When the US entered into the war in 1917 and absorbed the escadrille into the fledgling US air service, Johnson became an instructor pilot for the Americans.

Jim's opinion of Elliot Cowdin wouldn't have improved if Kiffin told him what Paul had written him. "Mr. Prince says that Cowdin imparted to him that he was very nervous, could not sleep, and had absolute need of a rest!!!! Seems that worthy is always resting."[9]

It was easy for Jim, Paul, Kiffin, or any of the new pilots to criticize Elliot Cowdin. They hadn't been flying combat missions for a year. Cowdin had. The cumulative effects of stress were only beginning to be recognized by military doctors, and then only for infantry soldiers. It was called "shell shock" at the time. Prevailing theories held that it might be caused by the concussive force of an exploding shell, or by breathing the gases expelled by exploding shells. As the war progressed, doctors observed that it affected pilots as well as people who were directly exposed to exploding shells, and they began to theorize that it was caused by mental shock or stress. Pilots noticed the problem long before doctors did, and experienced flight commanders like Capt. Thénault knew that they needed to give pilots frequent opportunities to get a break from the stress. It affected different people differently, and it took much longer for the symptoms to appear in some pilots, but no one was immune. Bill Thaw, Norman Prince, and Bert Hall had been flying combat missions for a year with no apparent ill effects, but that didn't mean Elliot Cowdin wasn't an early victim. At this remote date, it's impossible to tell.

Jim didn't limit his criticism to the other pilots. He was surprisingly critical of his own abilities, an attitude that is in sharp contrast with the stereotype of the cocksure fighter pilot:

> The general run of see-the-war boys from Amerika are going to hurt us like hell by coming in. It makes me sore for they are taking the place of good Frenchmen. In other words, hurting the cause. I feel that way about myself at times. I feel that a French pilot would do better than I am able. I do not feel that I am a good pilot, but I cheer up when I think that I'm just starting. I entered aviation after all the crowd here and so being the youngest pilot have a little more to learn. At present the only way I'm clever enough to get a Boche would be to catch him sleeping. If he's awake and shooting I can't dodge well enough to keep him from filling me with holes as the first chap did.[10]

In mid-June the weather cleared, and the long days let the pilots fly multiple patrols. Jim reported that they were in the air for six hours (probably three patrols) per day and on alert the rest of the time.[11] Kiffin Rockwell, who frequently flew voluntary patrols in addition to the squadron patrols, often flew four patrols in one day and was nearly brought down twice by Germans who caught him by surprise. The only reason he survived was because "the Boche shot poorly."[12] He was "up and down" all the time, sometimes diving from over 13,000 feet to 6,000 feet to attack a German plane. "It tires you out a lot, the change in heights and maneuvering*."

June 17 was another stressful day, particularly for Victor Chapman. Capt. Thénault led Chapman, Rockwell, de Laage, and Balsley on a morning patrol. Their orders were to patrol the right bank of the River Meuse, but not to cross the river. Chapman spotted several German planes on the left bank of the river. Capt. Thénault said that they were so numerous they looked like a swarm of bees.[13] The impetuous Chapman once again dove, against orders, across the river to attack. The others quickly followed. As Kiffin put it, "Chapman has been a little too courageous and got me into one of the mess-ups because I couldn't stand back and see him get it alone."[14] The pilots rescued Chapman from the planes he had stirred up and managed to disengage. Capt. Thénault led the patrol back to Behonne. Chapman, however, wasn't satisfied. He broke off from the patrol, landed at the nearby airfield of Vadelaincourt to refuel, and set off on his own. Jim described the result:

---

* Rapid changes in air pressure during a prolonged dive often bothered pilots' ears, breathing the thin air at high altitudes was debilitating, and of course the g-forces and stress of a dogfight were exhausting.

> Chapman was wounded. Considering the number of fights he had been in and the courage with which he attacked it was a miracle he had not been hit before. He always fought against odds and far within the enemy's country. He flew more than any of us, never missing the opportunity to go up, and never coming down until his gasoline was giving out. His machine was a sieve of patched-up bullet holes. His nerve was almost superhuman and his devotion to the cause for which he fought sublime. The day he was wounded he attacked four machines. Swooping down from behind, one of them, a Fokker, riddled Chapman's plane. One bullet cut deep into his scalp, but Chapman, a master pilot, escaped from the trap, and fired several shots to show he was still safe. A stability control had been severed by a bullet. Chapman held the broken rod in one hand*, managed his machine with the other, and succeeded in landing on a near-by aviation field.[15]

The nearby aviation field was at Froidos. Capt. Saint-Saveur, the pilot who had written Kiffin Rockwell that he didn't have enough Nieuports for the pilots he already had, was in command. Victor wanted them to make emergency repairs to his plane so he could fly back into combat, but Saint-Saveur forbade him from flying *that* plane until it had been extensively rebuilt.

Victor Chapman next to his damaged Nieuport. Note the bullet rip just behind the cockpit, the shattered windscreen, and the bandage on Victor's head. *North Carolina State Archives*

Jim McConnell was on alert at Behonne while Chapman was getting into trouble over the lines. A call came in that German planes were crossing the lines, so he pulled on his flight coveralls and climbed into his plane. The call apparently came in a bit late, since bombs began falling on the airfield as he took off. "One went off to my right as I was leaving the ground and I was glad to jump into the air."[16] By the time he could get to the bombers' altitude, they

* On the Nieuport, aileron control rods to the left and right upper wing run vertically on either side of the cockpit, just ahead of the pilot. This is probably where Victor held the broken ends together.

were diving for safety on their own side of the lines. He gave chase, but with no success. Jim flew a second sortie that day, but before he left on that sortie he saw a distressing sight:

> Two men went up in a large Breguet [a French bombing plane]. It rocks and floats as if it were not meant for the air. At fifty meters high the pilot tried a very steep turn. The big thing flopped over, made a swerve and nose down hit the earth. There was a sickening thud. Both men were killed instantly but before anyone could reach them the machine took fire and for half an hour we had to look on being unable to do a thing.[17]

Jim had no luck on his second sortie, and Kiffin Rockwell failed to score on the four sorties he flew that day. It was not a good day for the American escadrille. Worse days were to come. The following day, June 18, was one of those worse days. Jim was on guard duty, beginning at four o'clock in the morning. He took off on several calls that proved to be false alarms. Capt. Thénault led Kiffin Rockwell, Norman Prince, Elliot Cowdin, and Clyde Balsley on a morning patrol to protect several French observation planes that were directing artillery fire.[18] When they finished that job, they went on an offensive patrol. Cowdin had disappeared by that time. Jim described the fight the other four got into:

> Rockwell, Balsley, Prince, and Captain Thénault were surrounded by a large number of Germans, who circling about them, commenced firing at long range. Realizing their numerical inferiority, the Americans and their commander sought the safest way out by attacking the enemy machines nearest the French lines. Rockwell, Prince, and the captain broke through successfully, but Balsley found himself hemmed in. He attacked the German nearest him, only to receive an explosive bullet in his thigh. In trying to get away by a vertical dive his machine went into a corkscrew and swung over on its back. Extra cartridge rollers dislodged from their case hit his arms. He was tumbling straight toward the trenches, but by a supreme effort he regained control, righted the plane, and landed without disaster in a meadow just behind the firing line.[19]

Numbed by the shock of his wound, his loss of blood, and his crash landing, Balsley crawled out of his plane and onto the ground. He couldn't move his legs, but by grabbing tufts of grass with his hands, he dragged

Clyde Balsley, in front of his Nieuport with the Texas star. *W&L Archives*

himself away from the plane "like a dog with a broken back." [20] Four French soldiers came to help, crouching low to avoid snipers and the shellfire. Two grabbed him by the shoulders and two by the feet. They dragged him to safety, but as they did so the pain burst out of its stupor "like a beast unleashed." Emergency surgery saved his life, but he would be in critical condition for weeks, in hospitals for years, undergo many more surgeries, and be crippled for the rest of his life.

Clyde Balsley's injuries showed the pilots just how dangerous combat flying was, and it drove home the point that the Americans were not immune to the dangers. They had all watched their fellow student pilots crash in training, sometimes with fatal results, and they had just witnessed the deaths of the Breguet crew, but this was the first time it had happened to one of their own. The pilots visited Balsley in the hospital and saw firsthand what a bullet could do to a human body. It wasn't just victory or an instantaneous death, as young warriors like to imagine. Balsley's hip was shattered, his leg was useless, he was in constant pain, and his torment was made worse by hunger and thirst. Bullet fragments had perforated his intestines in several places, and the doctors wouldn't let him eat or drink until his intestines healed. Jim wrote, "Take back everything I said about the poor boy. He's been very brave and decent during his suffering."[21] Victor Chapman asked the doctor if there was anything Balsley could eat or drink, and the doctor said perhaps he could suck on an orange to get some relief.

The day after Balsley was wounded, Pierre Didier Masson was assigned to the squadron. Born in Asnieres, Seine, France, Masson was an experienced pilot, having flown bombing and observation missions for Mexican rebels during the Mexican Revolution, in 1913. When war broke out in Europe, he returned to France, fought in a French infantry unit, transferred to Aviation, and flew bombing missions in a Caudron and fighter missions in a Nieuport before being assigned to the American Escadrille.[22] The French obviously intended to staff the American Escadrille with American pilots, but Didier Masson appears to have been an exception to this rule. He had spent several years in the US, but there is no evidence that he ever applied for or obtained American citizenship*. He was probably assigned to the squadron because Capt. Thénault felt he needed an experienced pilot. Whatever the reason, he was immediately accepted by the Americans and proved to be a valuable addition to the squadron.

Jim wrote to Paul Rockwell on June 21, filling him in on all the latest squadron "gossip." He described Didier Masson as an "interesting, serious chap." Chute Johnson had gotten lost on a patrol on a previous day and had gotten lost on a morning patrol that day. When he wrote, they had been waiting for news of Johnson's whereabouts for five hours. Victor Chapman had borrowed Jim's machine, broken it, and left it at an airfield 45 kilometers away. And Elliot Cowdin was asking Capt. Thénault for a month's leave because the strain was "too great for his delicate nerves." (One can understand why Capt. Thénault might have asked for an experienced pilot to replace Clyde Balsley.) On a more personal note, Jim added that "my sweet smelling friend of Kodak [Yvonne] has moved to another branch. She's at 41 B[d] Rasphail as I was informed in a note this morning."[24] Apparently Jim had gotten her to drop her "never try to speak to me" attitude (the publicity given to the American Escadrille and to fighter pilots in general may have helped).

The good weather continued, and the hectic pace of activity continued. A rash of accidents forced several pilots to stop flying for a day or two. Jim flew a patrol with Lawrence Rumsey on the twenty-second, and when they

---

* Correspondence with the US Citizenship and Immigration Services produced no evidence that Masson was ever naturalized. They did find that after the war, he used a French passport to travel to the US, indicating he was still a French citizen.[23]

** Accidents like this were not uncommon. With no radios, there could be no ground control to coordinate landing and taxiing airplanes. The lower wing limited downward visibility, especially when landing, so it was hard to see if any other airplanes were beneath you.

returned to the airfield, Rumsey landed on top of Jim's plane**. Both planes were damaged and could not be flown for a few days. There was an alert late in the day, and three more planes were damaged trying to land at dusk.[25]

Victor Chapman's head was still swathed in bandages, but when his new plane arrived on the twenty-first, he immediately began adjusting it to fit his tall frame. Despite his bandages, he insisted on flying with the others on the late alert the next evening. He similarly insisted on taking part in the morning patrol the following day. The patrol was uneventful,[26] and he hit the ground hard when landing and damaged a rubber "sandow" on the landing gear. (Sandows were essentially thick rubber bungee cords wrapped around the axle and the landing gear. These absorbed the shock and provided a rudimentary suspension to the wheels and axle.[27]) Victor's mechanic, Louis Bley, had just begun removing the damaged sandow when an alert came in that German planes were headed for Bar-le-Duc. Victor rushed back to his plane, tossed Louis's tools out of the way, and insisted he was going to take off to intercept the Germans. Louis argued that it was too dangerous to take off with the damaged sandow, since it could break when he tried to land again, which would cause his plane to flip over. Victor insisted it didn't matter as long as he was able to shoot down a Boche first. The sound of the German bombers slowly faded away during this impasse, and it became obvious that they were not, in fact, headed for Bar-le-Duc. Victor relented and went to lunch, letting Louis know that he wanted to participate in a patrol that was scheduled to leave at 12:30.

Louis finished replacing the sandow, serviced the plane, and had it ready for another sortie when Victor returned from lunch. Victor was carrying a large bundle of newspapers, mail, oranges, and chocolates, which he was going to take to Clyde Balsley in the hospital. The afternoon patrol consisted of Capt. Thénault, Norman Prince, and Raoul Lufbery.[28] Victor told Capt. Thénault he would follow them for a little while and then fly to Vadelaincourt to take the oranges to Balsley. Louis stored Victor's package in his plane as the first three took off. Victor shook his hand when he had finished and said, "Goodbye; I won't stay long," and climbed into his plane. He took off a little after the other three and climbed into the sky, trying to catch them.

When Capt. Thénault got to the lines, he saw two German planes below. He, Prince, and Lufbery dove on the two planes. Three more German planes dove into the fight, and, finding themselves outnumbered, the Lafayette pilots broke off. When their patrol was over, they flew back to their base, assuming that Victor had long ago flown to Vadelaincourt with the oranges. Later that afternoon they received a report from a Maurice Farman two-seater. The pilot and observer had seen three

Nieuports attack five German machines, and then they saw a fourth Nieuport dive into the fight. The fourth Nieuport was Victor's. The other three disengaged without knowing that Victor was there. The observers saw the fourth plane fall straight down with the motor full on. No plane of that era could sustain a vertical dive with full power. The plane broke apart as it fell behind the German lines.

The loss of Victor Chapman was devastating to the American pilots. Victor was always cheerful, admired by all, and seemingly afraid of nothing. The loss of Clyde Balsley had been hard enough, but he was the "new guy," and he wasn't dead. He still had a future. Victor had been their friend since the squadron first formed, and he was gone forever. Jim described the mood in *Flying for France*:

> We talked in lowered voices after that; we could read the pain in one another's eyes. If only it could have been some one else, was what we all thought, I suppose. To lose Victor was not an irreparable loss to us merely, but to France, and to the world as well. I kept thinking of him lying over there, and of the oranges he was taking to Balsley. As I left the field I caught sight of Victor's mechanician leaning against the end of our hangar. He was looking northward into the sky where his *patron* had vanished, and his face was very sad.[29]

Jim was a little more specific in his private letters and conversation. He wrote Paul Rockwell: "If it only could have been someone else. Cowden, for instance or any like him."[30] Capt. Thénault later wrote that when Jim talked to him about Victor's death, Jim said, "It would have been better had I been killed rather than Chapman. He would have done better work than I, for he was much more clever."[31]

According to Bert Hall, "One of the most ghastly things about losing a partner in war times is rolling up his kit—packing what he left behind and sending it back to his folks."[32] That task fell to Kiffin Rockwell, since he shared a room with Victor. He wrote his brother Paul that "there is no question but that Victor had more courage than all the rest of us put together. We were all afraid that he would be killed, and I rooming with him had begged him every night to be more prudent. He would fight every Boche he saw, no matter where or what odds." He asked Paul to try to keep the news of Victor's death out of the papers until after his family was notified.[33]

Late that night, the squadron got a call from the hospital at Vadelaincourt with news that Clyde Balsley was dying. Jim woke up Capt. Thénault and Kiffin Rockwell, and the three of them drove the squadron car through pouring rain to Clyde's bedside. When they arrived he was sitting up, surprised to see them. The doctors told them Clyde had gone through a crisis, had a high fever, and was delirious, but the fever had broken and he was now recovering. None of them said anything to Clyde about Victor. On the return drive, they were delayed by tire blowouts and didn't get back to Bar-le-Duc until 5:00 a.m. They had been scheduled to fly the morning patrol at daybreak, but fortunately it was called off because of the weather.[34]

The bad weather was a mixed blessing. Certainly the three pilots who had spent the night going to see Balsley were in no shape to fly the morning patrol, but the lack of action gave all the pilots time to brood about Victor's death. Kiffin Rockwell and Norman Prince in particular had planned to spend the entire day in the air, looking to avenge Victor Chapman, but were forced to sit idle in the villa. When the weather did clear, the pilots had no luck trying to make the Germans pay for Victor's death. It was around this time that Bert Hall had "BERT" painted on one side of his plane and "TЯƎᗺ" painted on the other side, perhaps in an effort to lift the spirits of the grieving pilots. He explained that this would let the enemy know who they were fighting regardless of which side of his plane they flew past.[35]

The death of Victor Chapman may have been a factor in Elliot Cowdin's departure from the squadron. Jim obviously wasn't fond of Cowdin, and it appears that other pilots (and the squadron's historian, Paul Rockwell) were suspicious of his complaints about tiredness, ulcers, and heart problems and the way he consistently overstayed whatever leave Capt. Thénault would give him. There were rumors that he had overstayed his leave once too often, and Capt. Thénault gave him the choice of leaving or facing a court-martial. Most accounts say he departed on June 25, but concerns about him overstaying his leave and facing court-martial continued to surface in pilots' correspondence, so either he departed much later or his departure was kept quiet, and the pilots didn't know about it.

Whenever he left, it may well be that, as historian Steve Ruffin described it, "the 30-year-old Cowdin—elderly in fighter pilot years—had simply reached his limit, as nearly all combat pilots eventually did."[36] After he left the squadron, Cowdin was hospitalized for a while, tested French aircraft being delivered to the British, was medically discharged from the French army, and returned to the US, where he worked in the Bureau of Aircraft Production.[37] After the war he lived in relative obscurity. There were many impostors after the war who cashed in by writing articles, giving presentations, etc., claiming to have been a pilot with the escadrille, but to his credit, Elliot Cowdin—a founding member of the squadron—never sought to profit from his service.

Bert Hall with his "Backwards "TЯƎB" " aircraft. *World's Work*

On June 26, Bill Thaw briefly returned to the squadron for an award ceremony. His arm in a cast, he was made a Chevalier (Knight) in the Légion d'honneur (Legion of Honor). He wanted to stay after the ceremony, claiming he could fly as well one-handed as with both hands, but Capt. Thénault sent him back to Paris.[38] During the same ceremony, Kiffin Rockwell and Bert Hall received the Médaille militaire (Cross of War) and the Croix de guerre (War Cross) in recognition of their aerial victories. Jim, Lawrence Rumsey, Chute Johnson, and Clyde Balsley were promoted to sergeants.[39] Jim confessed to "a feeling of marked satisfaction at receiving that grade in the world's finest army. I was a far more important person, in my own estimation, than I had been as a second lieutenant in the militia at home."[40] Victor Chapman's promotion to sergeant was included in the same order, but, sadly, he was not there to receive the promotion.

Jim described the ceremony in a letter to Paul Rockwell. He also softened his criticism of Norman Prince a bit. "Old Norman Prince is not a bad sort at all. He's serious and works hard and tho crazy as a loon means well all the time." He also gave Paul a heads-up that the squadron might have to move north for the "coming fight,"[41] the rumored Somme offensive that Paul had mentioned early in the month. Like Verdun, the Battle of the Somme would rage for months and eventually suck the American Escadrille into its maw.

On June 28, Jim wrote to an old friend from the University of Virginia, Henry A. Johnson, who was learning to fly in the US. His letter provides a nice "snapshot" of Jim's activities and thoughts, as well as a hint about how far behind the Europeans the American aircraft industry was at the time:

> Thank you so much for your welcome letter. It is great pleasure to hear from you all and I wish you would write more. As for myself I have trouble finding the time to do so. Especially now in view of the fact that out of twelve in our escadrille three have been wounded and one killed and the rest of us have to work all the harder. I hated to see Chapman go. He was the best—and as a man he was one of those rare types who, broadened by the world, had not been disillusioned. He was a delightful sort. Even on his fatal flight he had put oranges in his machine to take to one of our comrades who had been wounded in the stomach with an explosive bullet.
>
> I hope you have good luck in your flying. Go slow and take it easy. Flying is nothing and you will get away with it all right. Don't try any stunts on American machines, however, for the wings are apt to leave you in the air.
>
> The German *Avion de Chasse* [fighter planes] are mounting higher and higher and as a result we go over the lines now at about 15,000 feet in order to have the advantage of height before attacking. We hope soon to have machine guns firing 500 rounds and then we'll be able to keep them on the move. There are about 5,000 machines mixed up in this one big battle and one has to keep a sharp look out.[42]

Bad weather limited flying as the month of June came to an end. Kiffin Rockwell wrote that Jim and Raoul Lufbery sent a German plane down out of control on the morning of June 30, but the fight occurred behind German lines and was not confirmed by ground observers.[43] Curiously, Jim did not mention this presumably memorable event in a July 1 letter to Paul Rockwell, or in any of his other surviving letters. The squadron logs that survive show operations only from August 24, 1916, onward, so this tantalizing report has to go down as one of the many things we don't know about Jim McConnell.

ELEVEN

A Hard Job

The Battle of the Somme was originally planned as a joint French and British offensive that would, with the irrational optimism that was prevalent in World War I, break through the enemy lines, turn the cavalry loose on the enemy's unprotected rear areas, and force the enemy into a massive retreat. Follow-on attacks would force the enemy to surrender. This was the plan before the Germans attacked at Verdun. By the time the battle began on July 1, 1916, the horrendous French expenditures of men and material at Verdun forced them to scale back their participation, so the Somme offensive became a primarily British effort, with the French playing a supporting role. A new objective was added to the battle's strategic plan—to relieve the German pressure on the French at Verdun.

The small professional army that the British had at the beginning of the war had been decimated by the battles of 1914 and 1915, so the army that fought on the Somme largely comprised new recruits. They had been trained and equipped, but most had no combat experience. Like the German plan at Verdun, the British plan involved a massive, weeklong bombardment that was expected to obliterate the enemy defenses and allow the attacking troops to march across no-man's-land unopposed. Unlike the German plan, the British troops had no instructions to stop, dig in, and call for artillery support when they encountered strong resistance.

The battle did not open well for the British. The bombardment succeeded in obliterating many of the German trenches, but it created shell holes and piles of debris that could effectively be used as defensive positions. The Germans had dug deep underground shelters that protected most of their troops, and the shrapnel that the British expected to cut the German barbed wire was largely ineffective. Most British troops did not leave their trenches until the bombardment stopped, which gave the Germans plenty of time to emerge from their dugouts and get their machine guns and riflemen ready to fire.

The first day of the battle is widely recognized as the bloodiest day in the history of the British army. On that day alone, the British suffered nearly sixty thousand casualties, roughly twenty thousand of whom died, with only a few scattered units capturing their initial objectives. The British commander in chief, General Douglas Haig, considered these losses "acceptable." He pressed on with the attack. Over the next five months, British troops would, with incredible bravery, determination, and losses, capture most of the territory assigned to them. They never achieved the breakthrough they dreamt of, but they did succeed in exhausting the German army and relieving pressure on the French at Verdun—but at a terrible cost.

The American pilots at Bar-le-Duc did not initially see any change in the air war over Verdun. As the summer months dragged on, they would begin to see fewer enemy aircraft on their patrols and note that the enemy pilots were less aggressive as the Germans transferred air units and their top aces to the Somme. That was not obvious in July and August, though, as the intense air fighting continued at Verdun. The initial excitement of flying in the greatest air battle the world had ever seen had long since disappeared, replaced by the exhausting realities of multiple daily patrols and the absence of familiar faces at the squadron mess. The pilots were "grinding through"—fighting with grim determination for a cause they believed in, but with very few successes to reassure them they were making a difference.

Capt. Thénault took leave in Paris at the beginning of July, leaving Lt. de Laage in charge. Jim was not particularly thrilled with the change:

> The Capt. is off on permission. Lieut is running us. He's a wild one and needs a few bullets near him to tame him down. This morning he led us 20 kilometers inside the lines and we kept diving on Boches there that were in far greater numbers. Also three new Aviatiks that went so fast we looked as if tied. Couple of Fokkers in the mix up but there was no battle. The Lieut got into a vrille [spin] and spun down from 3,000 meters to 500 feet. We thought it was all off. He'll keep this "Nach Berlin" [to Berlin] stuff up once too many times and about a half of us will stay over there. It's fool work and does no good. Kiffin's sore on him for being so wild. The outfit seems to have tamed down, anyway, having learned that there are certain precautions to follow. When we first got here no one knew anything about this aerial warfare as conducted at present and it took some while to learn.[1]

The fact that Kiffin Rockwell was upset with these tactics is surprising, since Kiffin was an aggressive pilot who often flew voluntary "hunting" expeditions behind enemy lines with Lt. de Laage. Kiffin was not, however, as aggressive as Victor Chapman. Kiffin took time to evaluate the odds before initiating an attack. Having his nose nearly shot off may have tempered his aggression a bit.

Jim also provided a bit more insight into his fellow pilots. Paul Rockwell had apparently heard that Bert Hall was trying to get out of the French air service to return to the US, and Jim thought perhaps that rumor had confused Bert with a pilot named Winslow*.

> I was greatly surprised at the developments re our boy Hall. That lemon Winslow has been pulling the same sort of line to Sayles. Are you sure it's not Winslow? . . . Norman predicted that Hall would follow in the footsteps of Cowdin and take the "cure" but it's hard to say. As we all know he's an awful liar and hot air artist, and every time he sees a fire on the ground he comes rushing back and reports bringing down a Boche, but I believe he has the where with all in a pinch.

In between patrols, the pilots had time to relax, think, and write letters. Jim commented on this in a letter to his UVA and Hot Foot Society friend Lewis Crenshaw. Jim thanked him for sending an article about the fact that the Hot Foot Society had been disbanded, then reincarnated as I.M.P. Jim sent a photo of his plane with the now-banned Hot Foot emblem boldly painted on the side. He described the life of a fighter pilot at the front as a

> funny life, this. You sit around comfortably and wait for your flights and you don't know whether you will come back or not. At this stage of aerial warfare the fighting is generally done "en escadrille." In fleet formation as it were. One or two here have no chance as the Boches are always in flocks.[2]

* Carroll Dana Winslow was an American pilot flying with a French Maurice Farman two-seater squadron at Verdun. He was granted a temporary leave of absence to return to the US when his daughter became ill with diphtheria.

Jim proudly shows off the "banned" Hot Foot emblem on his Nieuport. *NASM*

Despite Jim's comment to the contrary, some pilots still flew voluntary patrols alone, in pairs, or in small groups. Kiffin Rockwell, Lt. de Laage, and Norman Prince in particular flew many voluntary patrols. That didn't mean they were always in the air, though. On the same day that Jim wrote to Lewis Crenshaw, he told Mrs. Weeks that "this is quite the hottest part of France I have been in and all I keep thinking of is Africa. Kiffin's sitting outside the door now in a camp chair. Looks like a general waiting for reports."[3]

On July 9, the famous French ace Charles Nungesser came to Behonne for a visit.[4] Nungesser had ten victories to his credit when he arrived, which was an extraordinarily high score for that point in the war. Like Victor Chapman, he was a strong believer in the "attack whatever the odds" philosophy. In achieving his ten victories, he had been shot down or crashed multiple times, breaking both legs, suffering multiple internal injuries, breaking his jaw three times, breaking his nose, and dislocating his knee. When he visited the Americans, he was on convalescent leave from injuries suffered when he crash-landed near his tenth victim. Somehow he managed to get himself attached to the escadrille while he was there, and he spent his convalescent leave flying combat missions, although it isn't clear that he actually flew on patrols with the Americans*. Jim's assessment of him was that he "seems a nice chap but draws the long bow"[5] (i.e., exaggerates; given Nungesser's record, it's hard to believe he had any need to exaggerate).

The Americans were undoubtedly impressed that Nungesser, an old friend of Capt. Thénault's, chose to temporarily join their squadron. As excited as the pilots were to meet Nungesser, they must have been thrilled to see his airplane. Nungesser was flying the new Nieuport 17, an upgraded version of the planes they were flying. Most notably, it featured a synchronized Vickers machine gun firing through the propeller. Early versions were prone to jamming, which caused many pilots to continue to carry a Lewis gun on the top wing as a backup, but overall it was a much more stable and reliable weapon—and it fired from a five-hundred-round belt rather than a forty-seven-round drum that had to be changed in flight. Nungesser's personal plane was distinguished by a black paint job and a macabre skull-and-coffin motif on the fuselage. Capt. Thénault soon received a Nieuport 17 as well, but the rest of the pilots wouldn't get them for two months.

Sometime in early July, Jim took a brief leave (Capt. Thénault was generous with three-day passes, and he may have given one to Jim). After he returned, he wrote Marcelle an almost poetic description of flying above the clouds:

> It certainly was great to see you, even tho I did have but such a short glimpse. Since returning there has been but little going on. Most of the flying has been above the clouds and those sorties are not satisfactory even though pretty. It's more like naval work. One feels as if one were maneuvering in a sea of ice—snow covered ice. The tiny machines skirt over the glistening surface, dip down into holes, disappear behind a tall pillar cloud and show up on the horizon. It's almost as if one were at sea—I usually am. There may be enemy machines standing out against the white but they are very small and you know they are far within their lines. The other day I watched a Fokker running back and forth like a swift torpedo boat.

---

* There are no squadron logs from that period, and flights with Nungesser are not mentioned in pilots' letters or memoirs.

Charles Nungesser in front of his Nieuport 17. Note the fixed Vickers machine gun in front of the cockpit. *W&L Archives*

> He was keeping over the line of German observation balloons afraid that we were going to bother them. What we look for are the *relage* [artillery-directing] machines underneath the clouds. When one shows beneath a hole then someone dives at him. The little Nieuports turn tail up and disappear beneath the white like flying fishes falling back into the water. A couple of days ago we *picqued* [dove] several times on the Boches but couldn't bring them down. There were a lot that morning and away off across the lines I saw the black plane of the famous Capt. Boelcke*. The white crosses stand out very clearly. He went further in his lines when we went towards him."[6]

In a postscript, Jim commented that he visited Betty Baldwin while he was on leave. He said she was still quite weak but otherwise showed no sign of her injuries from the torpedoing. (Modern biographies of her father, Professor Mark Baldwin, indicate that Betty was crippled for life as a result of her injuries.[7])

---

* The American pilots believed that Boelcke flew a black Fokker with white crosses or white skull-and-crossbones insignia on the wings, but photographs and historical references indicate he flew a tan Fokker with black crosses, the standard factory color scheme.

Jim received a letter from his friend from flight school, "Skipper." Paul Pavelka, "Skipper," began training before Jim did and was breveted well ahead of Jim, but while Jim was assigned to the American Escadrille directly out of flight training, Skipper was sent to some of the newly created combat-training programs for aviators. He commented that all the guns they used in marksmanship training were made in America—not surprising, since the Allies were literally buying tons of weapons and ammunition from the US. His training included shooting a machine gun at small balloons from the observer's compartment in an airplane and shooting a machine gun at floating balloons from small motorboats. The boats were called *glisseurs* (sliders) and were propelled by a rotary engine and a propeller behind the pilot, while the pilot steered them with a rudder.[8] This was probably good training for fighter pilots, but with pilots sliding around a lake at 60 mph, shooting madly at floating balloons, the evaluators must have kept well clear.

Skipper had finished his advanced training with flying colors and was now stuck at Pau, waiting for orders. He flew whenever he could, irritating the training staff by doing loops, spins, and other "unnecessary" stunts to hone his skill for the front. Overall, morale at the school was not good. Skipper wrote,

> Oh! I tell you this is some hell hole. One fellow hung himself in the jail yesterday. Four of them smashed up and one went into a *vrille* [tailspin] and fell into the road, and is expected to die. Still another took a notion to go to Spain and was brought back to the school by gendarmes. To make things still worse, one of the pencil-pushing *embusqués* [literally "ambushers," often used in World War I to mean "shirkers"] cleared out with 1,200 francs of the payroll. Therefore, no pay this 10th for some of us.[9]

Skipper had been assured he would leave by the middle of the month, but without orders in hand he had his doubts.

The poor flying weather continued, and the pilots had much idle time. Jim commented to Paul Rockwell that the weather wasn't good enough for regular work, and when they did get out, no Boche were visible. The squadron was given July 14 off in honor of Bastille Day, and the squadron made the most of it. Jim noted that Lawrence Rumsey and Chute Johnson were in no condition to fly when the festivities ended.

Mrs. Weeks offered to give Jim a dog that a friend of hers didn't want, and Jim promised to take good care of it (the squadron pilots accumulated a menagerie of pets, dogs being the least exotic of the bunch). Marcelle's mother was feeling run down, and Marcelle took her to Évian-les-Bains, a resort town on Lake Geneva, in southeastern France. She suggested that Jim take leave and join them there. Jim regretted that he couldn't get the time off and wrote a romantic letter in response.

> I've just been thinking it over this morning, and how delightful it would be to walk around the charming country with you—we'd have the dog along, of course, to chase the golf balls you lost and then we'd sit down where we could get a glimpse of the deep blue lake and I could make love to you and drink Evian sparkling H_2O. No, but seriously it would be fine—a real rest and the best of company. However it's moonlight now and I'm afraid I might get foolish, and then afterwards feel as badly as I did for long after that night we docked at Havre which seems a few hundred years ago.[10]

Jim wrote to his mother on July 23 and, in what seems to be a universal tendency for personal correspondence, began by saying there wasn't much new to write about. He did say he'd been given a higher-powered airplane, presumably a Nieuport 16, which could climb to 6,000 feet in seven minutes and to 12,000 feet in twenty minutes. He thought that the German army was beginning to crumble and the war would end soon. His only comment about their operations was to say, "Kiffin Rockwell is a wonder at this game and its only hard luck that's kept him from bringing down four or five Boches instead of one. He's in the air all the time."[11] (Kiffin would log eighty-one hours of combat patrols that month—a record that would not be matched by any other Lafayette pilot through the end of the war. It's a particularly remarkable achievement considering the weather, the danger, and the fact that the Nieuport was an exhausting plane to fly. Jim would log thirty-three hours, which was about average for the other American pilots.[12])

Jim mentioned a new type of mission that at least one of the pilots attempted. "De Laage and Kiffin have just gone out to act as guard for Prince who, loaded down with sky rockets, is off after a Boche observation sausage."[13] Both sides used sausage-shaped observation balloons to lift an observer high above the trench lines to spy on the enemy. Using powerful binoculars and a field telephone, they could warn of enemy activities and direct artillery fire against any visible targets. They were extremely effective, and, not surprisingly, both sides tried to shoot down the other side's balloons. That was easier said than done. The balloons were surrounded by machine guns and antiaircraft artillery, which, given the fact that the balloons flew at a known altitude, could be deadly. They were often protected by enemy fighters as well. And even though they were filled with highly flammable hydrogen gas, balloons were hard to ignite. Pure hydrogen doesn't burn. Only hydrogen mixed with oxygen in the air will burn. There was always a small amount of leakage, and it was possible for a tracer to ignite the mixture around the balloon, but until special incendiary ammunition was developed, most machine gun attacks simply perforated the balloon with easily patched holes. Balloons were also tethered to high-speed winches, which could pull them down surprisingly fast if they were attacked.

In 1916, a French lieutenant named le Prieur developed a rocket with a knife-edged tip, which some pilots used to successfully down balloons. It looked like a large Fourth of July bottle rocket, and it was about as inaccurate as its firework cousin. Pilots had to fly within 100 yards of the balloon and aim carefully to have any chance of hitting it. Tough to do when you're being plastered by antiaircraft fire and diving on a rapidly descending balloon. Bert Hall claimed that Prince actually shot down a balloon on one of these patrols, but the victory was unconfirmed.[14] Jim described this attack as follows:

> He found one just where it ought to be, swooped down upon it, and let off his fireworks with all the gusto of an American boy on the Fourth of July. When he looked again, the balloon had vanished.[15]

Saying the balloon had "vanished" might have been a diplomatic way of saying the balloon had been dragged to the ground. Ignited balloons didn't just vanish; they burned brightly and left a huge smoke trail. A burning balloon would almost certainly have been confirmed by ground observers*.

German observation balloon being launched. *Wikimedia Commons*

* There's an old military adage that "if the enemy is within range, so are you." A balloon whose purpose was to observe the enemy's front lines would of necessity have been within view of those lines.

Norman Prince examining his le Prieur rockets. *W&L Archives*

The heavy pace of operations and frustration at not scoring victories was beginning to take its toll. Pilots were getting tired and making mistakes. Quarrels between pilots were common. Planes were wearing out. "Prince damn near ran into me on landing and made a swerve with the result he tipped over." Jim complained. "Lufbery had a terrible smash. We thought him dead but he hadn't a scratch. Sick now from gasoline he swallowed." Out of eleven airplanes in the squadron, only four were in commission when Jim described the situation. They were discovering just how hard it was to score a victory against a determined enemy. Jim summed it up as "God in Boston it's a hard job."[16]

On the morning of July 27, Lt. de Laage succeeded in that hard job. He shot down an Aviatik two-seater while flying a morning patrol with Kiffin.[17] This was de Laage's first victory with the squadron, and his second overall. That evening, Jim had an "adventure" while flying cover for reconnaissance planes with Norman Prince. Jim described the incident in *Flying for France*:

> Weather has been fine and we've been doing a lot of work. Our Lieutenant De Laage de Mieux brought down a Boche. I had another beautiful smash-up. Prince and I had stayed too long over the lines. Important day as an attack was going on. It was getting

> dark and we could see the tiny balls of fire the infantry light to show the low-flying observation machines their new positions. On my return, when I was over another aviation field, my motor broke. I made for [the] field. In the darkness I couldn't judge my distance well and went too far. At the edge of the field there were trees and beyond, a deep cut where a road ran. I was skimming ground at a hundred miles per hour and heading for the trees. I saw soldiers running to be in at the finish and I thought to myself that James's hash was cooked, but I went between two trees and ended up head on against the opposite bank of the road. My motor took the shock and my belt held me. As my tail went up it was cut in two by some very low "phone wires." I wasn't even bruised. Took dinner with the officers there who gave me a car to go home in afterward.[18]

Jim may not have been bruised, but he wrenched his back in the crash. It would grow worse as the month progressed.

Earlier in the month, Jim had tried to take advantage of the bad weather to earn some extra money through his writing, but with mixed results. He complained to Paul Rockwell:

> Page*, editor of *World's Work*, wanted an article on American Aviators so he wrote Eyre** and suggested getting me to do it. Eyre just wants dope and experience and says he'll write it. I felt sort of hurt that Page didn't write direct. Told Eyre I wouldn't have it run under my name unless I wrote it but he tells me it's got to appear in personal [impersonal?], and unless I wanted to conform, to turn over job to Prince, Johnson, or Cowdin. Well I need the 75 francs and so I'll conform.[19]

In the same letter, he told Paul that "my little deal with the *Sun* has proved lucrative." No matching article by Jim has been found in the *Chicago Sun*, but an article obviously written by Jim appeared in the *Chicago Daily News* a few weeks later. Attributed to "An American Aviator—Special Correspondent to the *Daily News*," the article was submitted by Paul Scott Mowrer, the *Daily News*'s correspondent in Paris. It is possible that Jim confused the two Chicago newspapers when he wrote to Paul Rockwell.

---

* Arthur W. Page, editor of *World's Work* magazine. The magazine was started by Arthur's father, Walter Hines Page, a vice president of Doubleday, Page & Co. publishing house. Arthur's brother, Frank C. Page, was a friend of Jim's from North Carolina and an editor at Doubleday, Page & Co.

** Probably Lincoln Eyre, an American correspondent for the *New York Times*.

The article, titled "American Eyes of French Army—Volunteer Aviators at Battle Front,"[20] is typical of Jim's writing but *not* typical of most aviation pieces at the time. It describes a day in the life of an American pilot at the front, not in the period stereotype of a "one-on-one duel with a German ace, machine guns rattling a staccato symphony of death," but as an honest description of the type of patrols the American Escadrille was experiencing. They dive on a flight of German planes, but the Germans see them coming and dive to safety behind their own lines. Later they see another flight of German planes. Jim writes in a second-person "you are there" manner as he describes diving on these additional planes:

> Something white with black crosses on it appears in front of you. It is a machine you did not see before. It is very close and you see the man in back crouching as he works the stovepipe looking machine gun. Sharp little sounds bite your ears as his bullets zip into your wings. You take aim at the pilot and your gun whirs out a stream of lead. You wonder why the German doesn't fall. You pull up and turn. Below are four or five Germans you did not see before. A rapid "tut-tut-tut" comes from behind. You look up and see a Fokker heading for you, firing as he comes. You are lower, so you head for your lines, making a vertical turn. The firing keeps up and you wonder if you'll be hit. Finally it ceases.

The patrol is scattered, and the pilots make their way back to their base individually and compare notes as they land. One pilot telephones from a different airfield, where he was forced to land because of a bullet hole in his gas tank. Another pilot is missing, worrying his friends, but they eventually learn that he was lightly wounded and made an emergency landing. They realize there is a chance that one or more pilots might not return from the scheduled afternoon patrol, but it's more likely they won't spot any German aircraft, no air battles will take place, and all the pilots will return safely.

In some ways the article sums up Jim's experience to date. No great victories over an evil foe, and no shame in diving for safety when you are caught by surprise by a plane that has the advantage. Long hours of patrolling in bitter cold while gasping for breath in the thin air, punctuated by moments of fear and bedlam in a battle with enemy aircraft. The article even describes the battlefield below as "a strip of murdered nature," a phrase Jim used frequently in his writing.

Raoul Lufbery quickly recovered from the crash where he swallowed gasoline, and he began to show what he was capable of. He had flown many hours since joining the squadron, with no success, but he was carefully studying his craft. On July 30, he shot down his first enemy aircraft, and he downed his second the following day. He was now tied with Bert Hall for the squadron lead. The tie wouldn't last long. On August 4, Lufbery shot down his third plane, becoming the squadron's leading scorer. He would hold that title for a long time.

The wear and tear on their airplanes continued to be a problem. Jim wrote to Marcelle on August 8 and said they had only four flyable aircraft, so they were taking turns. He had requested leave starting on August 15 and asked her to keep some time open to him. "Hope that your stay at Évian-les-Bains has resulted in the complete recovery of your mother and that you feel as fresh as a rose. . . . I certainly am looking forward with pleasure to seeing you soon."[21]

Jim was doing his share of flying, and he described one of his flights during this period in an undated account in *Flying for France*:

> De Laage (our Lieutenant) and I made a sortie at noon. When over the German lines, near Côte 304 [Hill 304], I saw two Boches under me. I picked out the rear chap and dived. Fired a few shots and then tried to get under his tail and hit him from there. I missed and bobbed up alongside of him. Fine for the Boche but rotten for me! I could see his gunner working the *mitrailleuse* [machine gun] for fair, and felt his bullets darn close. I dived, for I could not shoot from that position, and beat it. He kept plunking away and altogether put seven holes in my machine. One was only ten inches from me.[22]

On August 8, Jim flew a patrol with Raoul Lufbery. They got separated, and Jim spotted several French observation planes flying over Fort Douaumont. He decided to fly above them, providing protection and looking for any German planes that might be stalking them.

Raoul Lufbery in front of a Nieuport at Behonne. Even during the hot August weather, pilots wore insulated coveralls to keep warm at high altitudes. *W&L Archives*

High above Jim, Lufbery spotted a German two-seater. He carefully stalked it, approaching from the "blind spot" below and behind the German plane, while keeping his eye out for any German fighters that might be protecting it. When he got within range, he fired. Jim described the result:

> Just then I chanced to make a southward turn, and caught sight of an airplane falling out of the sky into the German lines. As it turned over, it showed its white belly for an instant, then seemed to straighten out, and planed downward in big zigzags. The pilot must have gripped his controls even in death, for his craft did not tumble as most do. It passed between my line of vision and a wood, into which it disappeared. Just as I was going down to find out where it landed, I saw it again skimming across a field, and heading straight for the brown band beneath me. It was outlined against the shell-racked earth like a tiny insect, until just northwest of Fort Douaumont it crashed down upon the battlefield. A sheet of flame and smoke shot up from the tangled wreckage. For a moment or two I watched it burn; then I went back to the observation machines.
>
> I thought Lufbery would show up and point to where the German had fallen. He failed to appear, and I began to be afraid it was he whom I had seen come down, instead of an enemy. I spent a worried hour before my return homeward. After getting back I learned that Lufbery was quite safe, having hurried in after the fight to report the destruction of his adversary before somebody else claimed him, which is only too frequently the case. Observation posts, however, confirmed Lufbery's story, and he was of course very much delighted. Nevertheless, at luncheon, I heard him murmuring, half to himself: "Those poor fellows."[23]

A few days later, Paul Pavelka ("Skipper") finally arrived at the squadron. He was assigned to a well-worn Nieuport 16 that the pilots referred to as the "hoodooed" plane because it had a history of bad luck. Bill Thaw had been flying that plane when he was shot in the elbow. It was then given to Elliot Cowdin, who soon left the escadrille for "medical reasons." Chouteau Johnson flew the plane for a while, apparently with no problems other than repeatedly getting lost. Norman Prince used the plane on his "balloon busting" missions until he swerved to avoid crashing into Jim while landing and flipped it over. It sported a new set of wings as a result of that crash.

On August 15, the hoodooed plane turned on Pavelka. He was flying behind the German lines at about 9,000 feet when the engine caught fire. This was the most terrifying thing that could happen to a World War I pilot. Parachutes small enough to fit into a fighter plane had not yet been developed, so the pilot had to choose between jumping to a certain death or risk burning alive in a highly flammable wood-and-fabric airplane. Pavelka was lucky. The fire was still confined to the cowling, so he immediately shut off the fuel and ignition. He put the plane into a sideslip, banking so that the plane slid sideways through the air as it descended, to keep the flames from blowing into his face. He managed to get back to friendly territory, descending as rapidly as possible because the flames had now ignited his lower wing. He crash-landed in a swamp on the French side of the lines. He slogged through the swamp, managing to get clear of the plane before the fuel tank exploded.[24]

Paul Pavelka in front of the "Hoodooed" Nieuport. *North Carolina State Archives*

The smoke attracted the attention of German artillery, and they began shelling the area. Pavelka was fortunate to escape the fire and the shelling, although he did have second-degree burns on his hands and face.[25] The hoodooed plane would never jinx another pilot. Pavelka was in the air again the following day, flying one of Bert Hall's old planes. He had that plane painted in a brown-and-white "cowhide" pattern to mark the time he had spent working as a cowhand in the American West.

On August 15, the same day that Pavelka's plane caught fire, Jim left for his much-anticipated leave in Paris. It did not go as well as he had hoped. Although he got to spend some time with Marcelle, his back was bothering him more and more. Jim blamed it on a recurrence of the rheumatism he had suffered as a child, but it's probable that his July 27 crash either triggered, aggravated, or was wholly responsible for the problem. Jim was staying with Mrs. Weeks and Paul Rockwell. Kiffin Rockwell joined them before Jim's leave was up. Paul Rockwell described the situation:

> Jim's back grew worse and worse, and often he sat up all night, unable to sleep because of the pain. Of a morning Kiffin and I had to help him put on his clothes, and he could walk only with the support of a cane. Yet, when his seven days were up, he insisted on returning to the escadrille.[26]

Friction between the pilots was smoldering, perhaps not surprising given the pace of operations and the strain everyone was under. Apparently Paul Rockwell had written something about Elliot Cowdin's departure that incurred the wrath of Norman Prince. Jim returned to the squadron with "marching orders" from Paul and soon wrote back with the results:

> I gave Norman the hell of a call down at supper last night. He denied the "Cowdin to be shot" rumor. Says all he had against you was that you wanted to send cable about Cowdin being in jail. That it hurt escadrille. I gave him the hell of a call down and put in all the details you wanted. Haven't seen Prince today. Out in morning and claims to have brought down a Boche. Acted like a wild man on landing, turned summersault [*sic*] and yelled. It was so far behind the lines no one saw it. Don't know if it will be official, but Norman immediately went off on leave.[27]

Jim's back continued to get worse. He could barely walk, let alone climb into an airplane. He tried to convince Capt. Thénault that if someone would just help him into the airplane, he could fly combat missions, but to no avail. The captain's reply was "Jimmie, go to bed."[28] Capt. Thénault also told Jim to report to the flight doctor, a major. Jim described the results to Marcelle:

> Well, I'm elected and have to leave. The Major tells me that if I do not get treatment I will be laid up and will not hear of my staying. I am being evacuated tonight but do not know to what point. Marcelle, every time I see you, you are more charming. . . .Well here's the auto to lug me to the d---- hospital so will have to end. I am very sorry. My new machine is here waiting for me and looks fine. I will be away about two weeks they tell me. Can't figure it out at all. Seems it's a recurrence of my rheumatism I had twelve years ago. It was great seeing you in Paris.[29]

The two-week prediction proved to be optimistic. It would be months before Jim could return to the squadron.

TWELVE

Depot des Éclopés

The next day Jim sent a postcard to Paul Rockwell, saying, "Well, here I am at Vitry-le-François in a Depot des Éclopés [Center for Cripples]. Am being looked out for all right, but it's hell being laid up this way."[1] Vitry-le-François was a small town between Bar-le-Duc and Paris. It was about 200 miles from Paris and 30 miles from Bar-le-Duc, so it would be difficult for Jim's friends to visit him.

Jim wrote Marcelle the next day, but in a more upbeat tone. "Here I am, an *éclopé*, whatever that is. I'm being treated like a prince and massaged enough to wear me out."[2] He sent a much-longer letter to his sister the following day, opening with "I am trying to write this while lying on my back in a *depot d'éclopés* where I was sent after my return from permission because of rheumatism*. Hope to be out in two weeks."[3] The rest of the letter focused on people whom Jim had met in France, optimism about the Allies' fortunes, an article Jim was writing for *World's Work* magazine, and other positive topics. (The article he was writing for *World's Work* was probably the one that Jim had previously complained was being "ghostwritten" for him by a reporter named Eyre. Apparently the editor wasn't happy with Eyre's work and hired Jim to write it himself.) Jim's only complaint about the hospital was that he was bored and wished he had something to read.

Adjusting to hospital life was difficult for Jim, as indeed it is for anyone. Small military units, like the pilots in a flying squadron, become a family.

---

* In his letters, Jim generally ascribed his back problems to rheumatism, but in *Flying for France* he said, "I had been sent to a hospital at the end of August, because of a lame back resulting from a smash up in landing, and couldn't follow the escadrille until later."

There may be cliques and squabbles in the unit, just like there are in many families, but there are strong bonds as well. These bonds tend to become stronger when the unit is located in a foreign country, where the only people who share a common language, background, and experiences are the members of the unit. They become stronger still in time of war, when the members are working together to protect each other and achieve a common goal. Overnight, Jim went from living, flying, and partying with the American Escadrille to lying on his back in a foreign hospital, doing nothing. As the weeks unfolded, he became frustrated because his back did not seem to be getting any better. Dr. Gros, an American doctor in Paris who played a leading role in forming the American Ambulance Service and the American Escadrille and personally examined all American pilot candidates, suspected that Jim had kidney problems as well.[4] On August 31, Jim wrote to Paul Rockwell and expressed optimism, but with the first note of concern that his back didn't seem to be getting better:

> I'm well taken care of here and on a diet of milk and eggs I am becoming young and well. Ice takes care of the annoying member. They examined my urine and find I'm in good shape. No sugar, no albumin. Was in a tent sort of ward with millions of flies . . . but the Doc moved me to the infirmary and I have a bed and good attendance. Won't be more than two weeks now. Hate to be laid up while others are working. . . . The doctors can't figure out my back but massage and dope keeps the pain down. There's no connection between it and the other trouble*.[5]

Marcelle sent him some books to read, including one by Irving Cobb that he particularly liked. He closed his "thank-you" letter to her on a sweet note, followed by a very perplexing postscript that mentioned Yvonne, the woman whom Jim had met at a Kodak shop in Paris when Jim took film there to be developed. It's *possible* that this postscript was "retribution" for a description that Marcelle had sent him of a Russian gentleman. No such letter has survived, but Jim obviously knew about a Russian suitor, since he will mention the Russian in a subsequent letter to Paul Rockwell. Jim's closing and perplexing postscript to Marcelle was

---

* Jim made a few references to the "other trouble" or "secondary illness" in his letters, but he never provided any details. It's possible it was related to a condition that caused Jim to make a second trip to a hospital later on, which will be described in a subsequent chapter.

> You're a very fine girl Marcelle. I've just been thinking you over as I lay here in bed. Too serious sometimes—with a young girl's illusion about romance, but nevertheless - - - - My best to you, Jim.
>
> P.S. My you should see the letter I got from Yvonne—very friendly. Calls me a *grand garcon bien sage* [big wise boy]. Maybe I'll cut out the *embusqué* [ambusher; presumably someone else who was vying for Yvonne's affection] yet.[6]

Paul "Skipper" Pavelka sent him what must have been a very welcome letter with the latest news from the squadron.[7] The squadron had received orders to leave Verdun, being replaced by Escadrille N.12. They were to turn over their planes to N.12 and would get their choice of aircraft to replace them. They did not know where they would be assigned next, but they assumed it would be at the Somme. Skip was taking care of Jim's things for him, sending the books, slippers, and other things he thought Jim would want immediately to the hospital. He was packing the rest of Jim's things up to move to their new assignment. Skip commented that "we all hope to see you with us soon and feel very sorry for the plight you are in," but he also cautioned that the new planes and assignment would make Jim "feel like a stranger."

Other welcome news in Skip's letter was that Skip had been recommended for promotion to sergeant, and that Bill Thaw's elbow wound had finally healed and he was back flying with the squadron. One bit of news that Skip didn't mention was that Bert Hall had shot down a German reconnaissance aircraft near Fort Douaumont on August 28.[8]

Jim wrote a long letter to Paul Rockwell on September 4, saying that his secondary illness was much better, "but my back has not improved to any marked degree. I get massages, but in spite of these the pain keeps on." Paul had invited Jim to come to Paris and stay with him and Mrs. Weeks, but Jim had to decline because the doctors wouldn't let him leave the hospital. He thought that when he was finally released, it might be possible for him to come to Paris, but cautioned Paul, "Don't mention this to our young lady friends for if I only have a day I would rather spend it with you and don't want Marcelle et al. to be offended."

Jim also told Paul that his mother was sending him "annoying letters" asking him to consent to her efforts to get him released from the French military service. She wanted Jim to cable his response to his brother-in-law (Mitchell Follansbee), and she sent him the money to pay for the reply. Since Jim couldn't send a cable from the hospital, he asked Paul to do it for him, and to say, "Letter received. Will not contemplate release. Jim."

In addition to asking Paul to send a cable to his brother-in-law, Jim brought up the mysterious "Russian" who apparently had caught Marcelle's eye. Jim asked Paul to "tell Marcelle she missed her greatest joy in life by not sleeping with the Russian. She would have have had her ecstasy, and then been disillusioned so that she would have had no regrets at not marrying him." It's doubtful that Paul was indiscreet enough to actually deliver that message.

Jim closed his letter by describing a concert that had been given at the hospital. The concert included a soldier singing a "delightful ditty about picking up a queen on his permission and getting a frightful and torturing dose," which led to him being sent to a *depot des éclopés*. "There was a surprising amount of appreciative guffaws which would lead me to infer that several of the gentlemen here have had unwise love affairs."[9]

A few days later, Jim wrote to both Marcelle and Paul Rockwell, complaining that he had been moved from the depot to a hospital downtown, where he was getting no treatment. He thanked Marcelle for sending him reading material. He had caught a cold, and when he coughed, "my back, or rather sides, feel as if they were being torn apart." Jim was also being annoyed by another patient who constantly talked to him, leaning over him and spraying as he spoke.[10]

He told Paul that he was discouraged by the fact that his back was "awfully slow" at coming around. "If they'll let me, I want to go back with it as is for I can at least sit in an aeroplane with it" (they didn't let him do that). The good news was that the *Medecin chef* (head doctor) offered him two months' convalescence leave when they did release him. Jim told him he'd need only a few days, and he told Paul he'd spend that time in Paris.[11]

Jim also wrote a letter to an old college friend, Henry A. Johnson, who was now learning to fly in the US. Jim expressed thoughts on airpower, which were very prescient:

> America will never get anywhere in aviation as long as she keeps it restricted to the army and navy. Of course those branches of the service need aeroplanes for scout, observation, photographic and artillery regulation work, but aviation, broadly speaking, is as distinct from the army and navy as they are from themselves. There should be a Secretary of Aviation as there is a Secretary of the Navy (or used to be before Daniels* got in) and a school for pilots, observers, and crew should be

* Josephus Daniels was the US secretary of the navy during World War I. His strong advocacy of segregation and government control of steel production and radio transmitters made him a controversial figure, and his prohibition of alcoholic beverages on Navy ships made him unpopular with many sailors as well. Supposedly the slang "cup of Joe" to describe a cup of coffee came from his suggestion that the traditional Navy rum ration be replaced by coffee.

> established along the lines of West Point or the Naval Academy. America comes nowhere near the proper viewpoint. She thinks in terms of hundreds of machines while she ought to figure it in thousands. From this day on control of the air will mean as much as control of the sea.[12]

On a less upbeat note, he also told Henry that "Balsley, who got hit in the stomach with an explosive bullet, was now at last out of danger, after two months of agony. He'll always limp and it would have been much better if he had been killed outright." While it's doubtful that Balsley thought he would have been better off dead, his injury did plague him for years, and he died at the relatively young age of forty-eight.[13]

On September 9, the squadron finally had some good luck, which cheered Jim up considerably when he learned about it. In the morning, Norman Prince was on a solo patrol when he spotted four enemy aircraft. A French pilot, Lt. V. Régnier of Escadrille N.112, attacked one of the aircraft at the same time Prince did, and they succeeded in bringing it down for a shared victory.[14] Later that same morning, Kiffin Rockwell, who had been frustrated several times over the previous week by gun jams as he attacked German planes, attacked a Roland C-II "Walfisch" (Whale) at about 10,000 feet. His gun jammed three times during this attack, but he managed to clear each jam and continue attacking until he was driven off by two other German planes. Observers reported that the plane crashed behind enemy lines, and Kiffin was given credit for the victory.[15] (German records indicate that the crew survived the crash, although the observer was badly wounded by Kiffin's fire.[16])

Two days after Prince's and Rockwell's victories, the squadron turned their planes over to N.12 and left Bar-le-Duc. Capt. Thénault had managed to arrange a special treat—the entire squadron would be given a week's leave in Paris. While the pilots had been able to visit Paris individually in the past, having the entire squadron there was like taking a vacation with family and friends versus traveling alone. They found places to stay individually or in small groups but met as a group for lunches, cocktails, and other adventures. While in Paris, the pilots acquired one of the most famous members of the squadron, a lion cub named Whiskey. When Jim finally got to see him, he described Whiskey as such: "He was a cute, bright-eyed baby lion who tried to roar in a most threatening manner but who was blissfully content the moment one gave him one's finger to suck."[17] He also explained why they didn't keep him in a cage. "Why put him behind bars? He'll see all the bars he needs traveling with this mob."[18]

Whiskey. *W&L Archives*

Kiffin Rockwell (*left*), Whiskey, Bill Thaw, and Paul Pavelka. *North Carolina State Archives*

The good news about the squadron victories and the new lion mascot cheered Jim up, but it didn't help his back. He wrote Marcelle, "Nothing new with me except that I'm getting mighty sick of this place with the prayers and music of soup eating etc. Yet the Major tells me I'm in for ten days more."[19] The Somme offensive was still raging, and Jim was afraid he was going to miss that. He told Paul Rockwell that his back was getting better, but he was getting fed up with the hospital. The doctors were going to have him try a new "elixir," but the only thing he knew about it was that he'd be laid out for twenty-four hours.[20] He'd been moved to a ward where the orderlies were overworked, and he was no longer getting massages or other therapy. He displayed his gift for words in describing another irritant:

> The crapper's stopped up and the contents remain to permeate the *salle* [hall] with their Mephitic redolence. The outer one is always occupied so I have to go to town to perform the function.[21]

A few days later, he wrote Marcelle to say that his back was feeling better, and he was arguing with the major to let him go. He was afraid the major would keep him in the hospital for another week. They were treating his back with hot pads. His back hurt the most when he got up after writing or sitting in a chair for a while, but it didn't hurt enough to keep him from doing his job. He was anxious to get back to the squadron and see the lion cub, speculating that when the cub got big enough, they could turn him loose on the Boche.[22]

The squadron's leave in Paris came to an end, and, to their great surprise, they were not sent to the Somme. Instead, they were sent back to Luxeuil-les-Bains. They did not know it yet, but the reason for this assignment was to escort a joint French and British long-range-bombing mission against the Mauser arms factory at Oberndorf. This was to be one of the first major strategic bombing raids of the war—a raid not aimed at tactical targets such as enemy troops, ammunition dumps, or transportation centers near the battlefield but instead intended to cripple the enemy's ability to manufacture critical materials. It foreshadowed the strategic bombing campaigns of World War II.

When they returned to Luxeuil, the pilots stayed at the Grand Hôtel de la Pomme d'Or (Golden Apple Hotel), an elegant family business run by a man named Auguste Groscolas.[23] Once again the pilots enjoyed fine quarters and excellent food. Also once again, the pilots had no airplanes. They had turned their old planes over to N.12 before leaving Bar-le-Duc and were promised Nieuport 17s as a replacement, but once again the demand for Nieuports was far outstripping the supply. There was nothing the pilots could do except entertain themselves in Luxeuil. Jim wrote, "I received a letter written at this time from one of the boys. I opened it expecting to read of an air combat. It informed me that Thaw had caught a trout three feet long, and that Lufbery had picked two baskets of mushrooms."[24]

Jim was still being frustrated by his back. Some days it seemed better; other days it was worse. In 1916 there were no medical tools to diagnose soft-tissue damage such as strained muscles, torn ligaments, or herniated discs. Doctors could only guess and try to treat the symptoms. Jim desperately wanted to leave the hospital and return to the squadron, and it is possible he was trying to convince himself and the doctors that his back was better than it was. Bert Hall visited him in the hospital and wrote, "September 18. I visited Jimmy McConnell today. He's worse off than he thought at first. It'll be next spring before he gets out."[25] Jim told Mrs. Weeks, "I am getting discouraged about my back. It seems to be getting well and then flop, she drops back to first condition. If it doesn't build up soon, I am going to tell them I am well anyway."[26]

Jim also vented his frustration to Paul Rockwell. Apparently, the elixir that was going to "lay him out" for twenty-four hours was not a success. His back problems hadn't dampened his spirit, though, since he finished his note in classic McConnell style:

> Am getting damned discouraged about my back. Thank God the experiments are over. . . . Can't get 'em to make my bed up, tho, and I can't do it 'cause of my back. So I lie midst the bread crumbs. Great! . . . Am freezing my balls off here. All my clothes with escadrille—even coat. Have sent for it. . . . Wrote Yvonne that I lay awake at night thinking about her and then after that I was afraid to go to sleep. Wonder if she'll catch on, and if so will stand for it? Thought it time to play first card.

The promised Nieuports finally began to arrive at Luxeuil. They were Nieuport 17s, with a belt-fed Vickers machine gun mounted in front of the pilot. As before, the planes arrived disassembled, so the mechanics and pilots began assembling them. While assembling them, they discovered that the planes did not come with ammunition belts for the machine guns. Kiffin described the situation at Luxeuil to Jim:

> I would have written you before this but you know how I am about writing. Received your card the other day and thank you. On arriving here found everyone surprised but glad to see me and they have all asked about you and send their best regards. I have not as yet seen Rosa but if I do will tell her you are on the way here. All the same old girls are here but some a little worked out after the summer. We are living at this hotel [letterhead from Pomme d'Or] where the food is better and cheaper than at the Lion Vert. So far we have six machines for the escadrille all of them Vickers but we haven't the cartridge bands for them. . . . Now the machines make no difference for from now on here it will be bad weather and no flying, so take your time and get fixed up right. Hope you are getting about alright [*sic*] by now. Sincerely, Kiffin.[27]

The following day, the mechanics had two Nieuports ready to fly, and they had somehow scrounged two ammunition belts. Capt. Thénault assigned these first two planes to Raoul Lufbery and Kiffin Rockwell. Capt. Happe, the French bombing-squadron commander, had asked him not to let his pilots fly over the front, for fear the new planes would make the Germans suspicious, but Capt. Thénault demurred. "How could two such ardent souls like Lufbery and Rockwell be held in restraint when they had at their disposal superb machines, fitted with the latest devices?"[28] Lufbery and Rockwell made two uneventful patrols that day and planned a sortie for the following morning. Kiffin's mechanic, Michel Plaa-Porte, took a picture of

Kiffin standing beside his plane. Four months of combat made him look much older than when they came to Luxeuil the first time, but he was obviously happy to be in the air again.

Kiffin Rockwell in front of his Nieuport 17. This was the last photo ever taken of Kiffin. *North Carolina State Archives*

The following morning, Kiffin and Raoul went hunting for Germans. They attacked a patrol of three Fokker fighters near Hartmannswillerkopf. During the ensuing dogfight, Lufbery's gun jammed and a German bullet broke one of his wing spars. They successfully disengaged from the Fokkers (not always an easy thing to do), and Kiffin escorted Raoul back to a French airfield at Fontaine. Raoul landed for repairs, and Kiffin went off on his own, searching for German planes. He spotted an Albatros two-seat observation plane flying over Roderen, very close to where Kiffin had scored his first victory in May. He used the same tactic that had proved successful in May to attack this plane. He dove toward the Albatros, ignoring the fire from the observer, and waited until he was within point-blank range to open fire. This time it was the German plane that jerked out of the way to avoid a collision, and the Nieuport that plunged toward the earth. Kiffin's lifeless hands no longer controlled its flight. One wing ripped off at about 10,000 feet, and the rest of the plane spun into the ground just behind the French lines.[29]

Like the death of Victor Chapman, the death of Kiffin Rockwell stunned the squadron. Capt. Thénault broke the news to the other pilots, saying, "The best and bravest of us all is no longer here."[30] Jim wrote, "No greater blow could have befallen the escadrille. Kiffin was its soul. He was loved and looked up to by not only every man in our flying corps but by every one who knew him."[31]

Kiffin's death was especially devastating to Paul Rockwell. The two brothers had been inseparable growing up, sharing the same interests and attending the same university. Although Kiffin was younger than Paul, their mother described Kiffin as the "directing head" of the partnership.[32] Kiffin was the one who suggested the two travel to France and join the Foreign

Legion. Kiffin was the one who discouraged Paul from returning to the Legion after Paul was wounded, indirectly leading to Paul's becoming a war correspondent. Paul's role as historian of the Lafayette Escadrille was entirely due to Kiffin's position as a founding member of the unit. Capt. Thénault sent Bill Thaw to Paris to break the news to Paul. Bill brought Paul back to Luxeuil to attend Kiffin's funeral and to view the place where Kiffin fell.

Kiffin's death was a terrible blow to Jim McConnell as well, and Jim was especially worried about how it would affect Mrs. Weeks and Paul Rockwell. He learned about Kiffin's death from a newspaper article on September 25 and received a letter from Mrs. Weeks telling him about it shortly afterward. He immediately wrote back to express his sympathy and to tell her that he felt he should be with her during this terrible time. He had previously told the doctors he did not want a long convalescent leave after they released him from the hospital, but now he was going to see if he could reclaim it. Kiffin's death made him more determined than ever to rejoin the squadron, but he felt that he would recover faster at Mrs. Weeks's apartment than he would at the hospital.[33] Later that day, he wrote her another letter to say he would be arriving on the twenty-seventh:

> I have seen the *medicine chef* and everything is arranged. He is letting rules and regulations go by the board and although I am not cured, he is letting me leave for treatment under your direction on a convalescence. I will leave here Wednesday night at six something, arriving in Paris at 9:30. I will go straight to your apartment. I feel a great hesitancy about arriving as an invalid, but I feel that you and Paul want me for a while and I know I want you. This new sorrow makes it hard for me to be alone.[34]

THIRTEEN

Writing for France

Paul Rockwell was still at Luxeuil, attending Kiffin's funeral and gathering Kiffin's personal effects, when Jim arrived at the apartment that Mrs. Weeks shared with Paul and with any "motherless" pilot or Legionnaire who happened to be in Paris. While there, Jim worked on the manuscript for his book *Flying for France*. The inspiration to write the book undoubtedly came from the article "Flying for France" he had recently written for *World's Work* magazine. *World's Work* was an influential news magazine, with a circulation of 100,000. The magazine was edited by a son of one of the founders of Doubleday, Page, & Co. publishers, so it seems likely the publisher asked Jim to expand the article into a book.

Most of the surviving correspondence we have from Jim McConnell's time in France was written to Paul Rockwell or Marcelle Guerin. During his recuperation, Jim was living in the same apartment as Paul and could regularly visit Marcelle, who also lived in Paris, so there was little need for Jim to write to them. Jim normally wrote to several other people, but he seems to have curtailed his correspondence while he was focusing on his book. (When he was working on a subsequent magazine article, he commented that seventy-five unanswered letters piled up while he was writing.[1]) The net result is that we have very little information about Jim's day-to-day activities while he was recuperating in Paris. He did write a few letters, however, and both he and Paul got regular updates and occasional visits from the American Escadrille pilots, so the period isn't a complete mystery.

When Jim first arrived in Paris, he received a letter from Paul Pavelka:

> God almighty! Jim I feel terribly broken up about Kiffin's death. Today Paul, the Captain, and I went down to where he fell, and looked at that sacred piece of earth. He saw this Boche bastard in our lines and attacked him at a height of about 3,000 meters [9,800 feet]. Everything went fine in the fight, and it was a case of one or the other, and the Boche mitrailleur hit poor Kiffin in the breast, but the dirty son-of-a-bitch used an explosive ball for the poor boy had a hole as big as your fist in his breast. The major who picked him up said that he was killed instantly. . . . I am all the wilder because we have no machines, nor cartridges. Lufbery is the only one who has cartridges, he only having about 100 for his Vickers. How in hell can we avenge Kiffin under such circumstances? Five machines for twelve pilots, and only a few cartridges. We can only be patient and wait until the opportunity presents itself, which I earnestly trust will be very soon.[2]

Paul Pavelka wrote another letter to Jim the following day, giving Jim an update on Paul Rockwell's visit to the squadron:

> I certainly shall heed what you say, and remember that it is for France that I am fighting. I pray to God that I may be able some day to square a few accounts with the Boche. For the present our prospects are not very bright, as we still have no machines. Furthermore there is no talk or any signs of any coming to us.
>
> Paul is still with us and we all wish he could remain with us. Norman Prince apologized, and Paul's kind heart forgave him for all the injustice that he had done. Masson took Paul up in a twenty-three meter Nieuport [probably a Nieuport 12 two-seater] but only remained up for about ten minutes and came down on account of a leaky reservoir*.[3]

Paul Rockwell returned from Luxeuil on September 29. Jim wrote to Marcelle that night:

> Paul returned shortly after you left last night. The poor boy is very despondent and all interest in life seems to have left him. Kiffin attacked the German at an altitude of 3,500 meters [11,500 feet].

---

* Possibly an oil reservoir, since castor oil was injected into the intake air of rotary engines to lubricate the bearings.

> The Boche was one of their new ones which carries a pilot and two machine gunners*. It is very fast and deadly. Two other French machines had been brought down near where Kiffin fell in the same hour. . . . He fell into a field of flowers just back of the trenches. An explosive bullet had hit him in the chest. An ordinary one, so a Major who examined him said, would have given him an even chance for life**.
>
> I have never appreciated you so much as I did last night. I felt how wonderful you are."[4]

The lack of aircraft and ammunition continued to plague the pilots at Luxeuil. Capt. Happe's bombing squadron was also waiting for new planes, so there was no date set for the bombing raid on the Mauser works at Oberndorf. Paul Pavelka told Jim how the squadron was managing:

> Everything is quiet here with us and we pass our time away by hunting mushrooms and fishing, in which we are very successful. Lufbery and I brought home about 5 kilos of mushrooms. Thaw caught a mountain trout weighing 6 pounds 200 grams. This the absolute truth. We are having him for dinner this evening. . . . Masson is going to Bar to get an apparatus [airplane] for himself, and is going via Paris so he is mailing this in that city for me. Yesterday I saw your Rosa. She is some girl and I do not blame you at all for being friendly with her.
>
> P.S. The lion is some pet. Johnson had him in bed with him all night. Some brave man, that boy.[5]

Moving to Paris didn't result in any dramatic improvement in Jim's back. He told Marcelle that

> I was getting on much better, but today after not being able to sleep during the night, I am only able to move with two canes. Queer sort of trouble—I can't figure it out. It goes and then comes back.[6]

---

* Differing altitudes are often cited for this flight, since the altitude was estimated by ground observers, and different observers might give different estimates. Also, most accounts identified the enemy plane as an Albatros, which had only one gunner.

** It's difficult to imagine how a pilot who was flying at 11,500 feet when struck in the chest by a machine gun fired at extremely close range could land the plane and survive, whether or not the bullet was explosive.

Paul Pavelka wrote several letters to Jim and to Paul Rockwell, keeping them up to date on what was happening in the escadrille. Jim used these letters and information he gathered when he later returned to the squadron to flesh out the narrative of *Flying for France*, providing a continuous account of the squadron's activities, with no apparent "gap" during Jim's absence. For example, Paul Pavelka described a fight that Norman Prince got into as follows:

> Yesterday Norman Prince returned in a most miraculous manner. His lower right wing was shot to pieces by an explosive ball, as well as one of the supports of the cabin, which is steel, cut in two. His story of it was that he attacked a Boche, at the same time another one fell on him from behind. He was greatly shaken up and stuttered a great deal when explaining things.[7]

In his book, Jim described this dogfight as

> Prince was out in search of a combat at this time. He got it. . . . Bullets cut into his machine and one exploding on the front edge of a lower wing broke it. Another shattered a supporting mast. It was a miracle that the machine did not give way. As badly battered as it was Prince succeeded in bringing it back.[8]

Jim similarly "jazzed up" a description of a battle that Lufbery had a few days later:

> Lufbery whirred off to chase the other representative of Kultur [German culture]. He caught up with him and dove to attack, but he was surprised by a German he had not seen. Before he could escape, three bullets entered his motor, two passed through the fur-lined combination he wore, another ripped open one of his woolen flying boots, his airplane was riddled from wing tip to wing tip, and other bullets cut the elevating plane. Had he not been an exceptional aviator he never would have brought safely to earth so badly damaged a machine. It was so thoroughly shot up that it was junked as being beyond repairs. Fortunately Lufbery was over French territory or his forced descent would have resulted in his being made prisoner.[9]

The excitement of Prince's and Lufbery's miraculous escapes notwithstanding, there was little activity for the escadrille at Luxeuil. The squadron still had only six airplanes[10] (five after Lufbery's plane was junked), and bad weather often kept those planes on the ground. There was still no scheduled date for the bombing raid on Oberndorf, the mission that had brought the squadron to Luxeuil. Capt. Thénault went on leave, after Capt. Happe assured him he didn't expect the bombing raid would take place anytime soon.[11] Paul Pavelka, Chouteau Johnson, Dudley Hill, and Bert Hall went to Bar-le-Duc to try to scrounge some more airplanes.[12] Then, to everyone's surprise, orders were received on October 11 that the raid would take place the following day. Lt. de Laage, Raoul Lufbery, Norman Prince, and Didier Masson were the only escadrille pilots who could escort the bombers that day. Lufbery, Prince, and Masson were credited with victories during the raid.[13] This was Lufbery's fifth victory, making him the squadron's first "ace." Fifteen of the attacking bombers were lost during the raid, which claimed to have dropped 4 tons of bombs on the Mauser plant at Oberndorf. German reports admitted that sixty bombs fell on or near Oberndorf, but said damage was light and operations at the Mauser plant were not affected.[14]

Of more importance to the Americans was what happened after the raid. As Jim described it,

> Darkness was coming rapidly on but Prince and Lufbery remained in the air to protect the bombardment fleet. Just at nightfall Lufbery made for a small aviation field near the lines, known as Corcieux. Slow-moving machines, with great planing [gliding] capacity, can be landed in the dark, but to try and feel for the ground in a Nieuport, which comes down at about a hundred miles an hour, is to court disaster. Ten minutes after Lufbery landed Prince decided to make for the field. He spiraled down through the night air and skimmed rapidly over the trees bordering the Corcieux field. In the dark he did not see a high tension electric cable that was stretched just above the tree tops. The landing gear of his airplane struck it. The machine snapped forward and hit the ground on its nose. It turned over and over. The belt holding Prince broke and he was thrown far from the wrecked plane.[15]

Both of Prince's legs were broken, and he suffered serious internal injuries. Despite these injuries, he initially seemed to be doing well, but a blood clot lodged in his brain and he died two days later. At the age of twenty-nine years, Prince became the third founding member of the escadrille to die for France.

With the Oberdorf raid over, there was no need for the escadrille to stay at Luxeuil. They received orders to move to an airfield near Cachy Wood, about 325 miles northwest of Luxeuil. There they would provide air support for the Battle of the Somme. The days of luxury accommodations were over. The pilots were billeted in a drafty, wood-and-tar-paper barrack, and there was no *popote* (squadron mess) or other arrangement for eating. The squadron also lost some of its independence, being assigned to Groupe de Combat 13 under Commandant Phillipe Féquante.[16] "Skipper" (Paul Pavelka) wrote to Jim:

> We are in Cachy at last, and have a hard time of it. Quartered in a woods and no *popote*. We have to go pan handling to the other escadrilles for something to eat. Never have been up against a proposition like this before. Same as infantry, just one door away from the trenches. Take my advice and remain in Paris.[17]

About a week later, Skip updated Jim[18] and Paul Rockwell[19] on the conditions at Cachy. Bill Thaw and Didier Masson had just returned from Paris, where they had scrounged enough cooking supplies to set up a squadron mess. The pilots were doing what they could to fix up their barracks and were anxiously awaiting blankets that Mrs. Weeks was sending. They had done very little flying, not only because of the atrocious weather but, more importantly, because they lacked airplanes. Skip had been up only twice since they moved to Cachy, both times in aircraft borrowed from other squadrons. New aircraft were on the way, and they were hoping to receive a few Spads*. Bert Hall was leaving the squadron to join escadrille N.103, the unit he had flown with before joining N.124. N.103 was also stationed at Cachy.

The winter of 1916–17 was to prove exceptionally cold. Mrs. Weeks wrote to her surviving son, Allen:

> The weather here is very cold for this time of year and we have no heat yet, only a little fire in the grate. I can't write long it is so cold here where I am writing. Jim has just run in and out again, saying, "How can you write in here?"[20]

---

* Spad 7 airplanes, with water-cooled, in-line Hispano-Suiza V-8 engines, were faster and more rugged than the Nieuport 17s the squadron was flying, but they were also heavier and not as maneuverable.

Presumably, the temperature was a little warmer in Jim's room, since he was busy writing his book. The article "Flying for France" was published in the November 1916 issue of the *World's Work* magazine. The first half of Jim's book is basically an updated version of that article. Not surprisingly, the last squadron activities described in the article occurred in late August 1916, just before Jim left the squadron to go to the hospital. An editor's note said that the article was written before Kiffin Rockwell was killed, which means that Jim had finished the article before he left the hospital, so he was free to focus on his book in Paris.

The *World's Work* magazine was founded by Walter Hines Page and published by Doubleday, Page & Co. When Jim's article was published, the magazine was being edited by Walter's son Arthur Page, and, probably not coincidentally, another son of Walter's—Frank C. Page —was an editor at Doubleday, Page & Co. Frank had met Jim while Jim was working as an agent for the railroad in Carthage, North Carolina, and Frank became the editor of Jim's book.

It's not hard to imagine why the editors wanted Jim to write a book. Aviation was still so new that many Americans had never even seen an airplane, much less flown in one. The idea of fighting in the air seemed almost like science fiction. Also, in 1916, air combat was one of the few "colorful" aspects of a war dominated by mud and misery. Rightly or wrongly, fighter pilots were regarded as "knights of the air," jousting with chivalry in the clear blue sky. Given these circumstances, the air war was a subject that attracted thousands of readers. Reporters had written hundreds of articles about the American pilots, but they weren't written from a pilot's perspective. Jim was a pilot, one of the handful of heroes idolized in the press, and he could provide the inside story of the men and adventures that fascinated readers.

The fact that Jim was an accomplished writer could not have escaped the editors' attention. His article about the ambulance service had been so impressive that Teddy Roosevelt wrote the introduction. His informal, easy-to-read style and wonderfully descriptive writing made readers feel as though they were actually present for the events he wrote about. Both the magazine article and the book open with a present-tense description of life on an airfield:

> Suddenly there is the distant hum of a motor. One of the pilots emerges from the tent and gazes fixedly up into the blue sky. He points, and one glimpses a black speck against the blue, high overhead. The sound of the motor ceases, and the speck grows larger. It moves earthward in steep dives and circles, and as it swoops closer, takes on the shape of an airplane. Now one can make out the red, white,

> and blue circles under the wings which mark a French war-plane, and the distinctive insignia of the pilot on its sides.[21]

Jim didn't limit himself to writing in present tense. When describing the exploits of the first Americans who volunteered to fly for France, he wrote in past tense:

> Going to the assistance of a companion who had broken down in landing a spy in the German lines, Bach smashed his machine against a tree. Both he and his French comrade were captured, and Bach was twice court-martialed by the Germans on suspicion of being an American *franc-tireur* [mercenary]—the penalty for which is death! He was acquitted but of course still languishes in a prison camp "somewhere in Germany."[22]

When describing his own experiences, Jim naturally used a first-person point of view:

> Rooms were assigned to us in a villa adjoining the famous hot baths of Luxeuil, where Caesar's cohorts were wont to besport themselves. We messed with our officers, Captain Thénault and Lieutenant de Laage de Mux [*sic*] at the best hotel in town. An automobile was always on hand to carry us to the field. I began to wonder whether I was a summer resorter instead of a soldier.[23]

But when he described what it was like to fly a mission over Verdun, he made the reader a part of the action by writing in second person:

> *Contact!* he shrieks, and *Contact!* you reply. You snap on the switch, he spins the propeller, and the motor takes. Drawing forward out of line, you put on full power, race across the grass and take the air. The ground drops as the hood slants up before you and you seem to be going more and more slowly as you rise. At a great height you hardly realize you are moving. You glance at the clock to note the time of your departure, and at the oil gauge to see its throb*. The altimeter registers 650 feet. You turn and look back at the field below and see others leaving.[24]

---

* Oil was injected into the engine's intake air, so this wouldn't have been an oil pressure gauge. It was probably a "blinker" gauge with an indicator that moved every time a pulse of oil entered the engine.

His description of the battlefield "you" are flying over powerfully captures the destruction of the war:

> Peaceful fields and farms and villages adorned that landscape a few months ago—when there was no Battle of Verdun. Now there is only that sinister brown belt, a strip of murdered Nature. It seems to belong to another world. Every sign of humanity has been swept away. The woods and roads have vanished like chalk wiped from a blackboard; of the villages nothing remains but gray smears where stone walls have tumbled together. The great forts of Douaumont and Vaux are outlined faintly, like the tracings of a finger in wet sand.[25]

Unlike the "memoirs" written by many other pilots during or shortly after the war, *Flying for France* sticks to the facts and is not filled with wildly exaggerated descriptions of dogfights, pilots pitting their skills against a vicious foe in a duel to the death, and amazing but unverifiable feats of skill and luck. Jim got a few details wrong, occasionally placed events in the wrong order, and sometimes deliberately ignored complications such as not having airplanes when they first arrived at Luxeuil. That's not surprising. He wasn't writing a reference for historians—he was writing for his contemporaries in the US. He wanted to let them know what their fellow Americans were doing in a war that was then raging on the other side of the Atlantic. While it's clear from his letters that Jim was interested in the money he could earn through his articles and the book, that wasn't his only motivation. By describing the war as he saw it, avoiding the exaggerations, stereotypes, and outright lies that characterized propaganda of the period, Jim undoubtedly hoped his writing would convince Americans to support the cause of France.

Jim was not able to finish his manuscript before his convalescent leave came to an end. He was faced with a decision—should he go back to the squadron or admit to the doctors that his back was still bothering him.

Back problems were more than just a painful irritant to a combat pilot. Although Jim had tried to convince Capt. Thénault that even though he had trouble walking, he could still fly, both Jim and the captain knew that wasn't true. Single-seat fighters were vulnerable to attacks from behind. If a pilot could get on the tail of another fighter, he could fire with no fear of the other plane firing back, and he could follow the other plane's maneuvers to stay behind it. For that reason, World War I fighter pilots would frequently twist and turn to look behind them, searching the sky for enemy planes that might be trying to get on their tail. Jim couldn't do that.

The pilots at Cachy were living in cold, drafty barracks. Cold weather causes muscles to tighten, which often makes back problems worse. Paul Pavelka had already warned Jim of the conditions at Cachy and told him not to be in any hurry to leave Paris. The weather would only get colder as winter approached, and flying at high altitudes would expose Jim's back to arctic conditions.

When Jim went to the squadron's first duty station at Luxeuil, he traveled with Victor Chapman, Kiffin Rockwell, and Norman Prince. Jim told Capt. Thénault that Victor was a better pilot than he (Jim) was. Victor had been killed in combat. Jim wrote that "Kiffin Rockwell is a wonder at this game." Kiffin had been killed in combat. The nicest thing Jim ever said about Norman Prince might have been that he was "serious and works hard, tho crazy as a loon," but Norman had been flying in combat for a year when Jim joined the squadron, and Norman had four confirmed victories. Jim must have realized that Prince was a much more experienced pilot than he was, and yet, Prince had been killed in a landing accident. Jim couldn't have had any illusions as to what his chances were, especially flying with a bad back.

Fellow Lafayette Escadrille pilot Ted Parsons described the situation all the pilots were in as "We had hold of the bear's tail and no one to help us let go. With few exceptions, I believe most of us would have welcomed an opportunity to bow out gracefully."[26] Jim McConnell had the opportunity to bow out gracefully. If he had been honest with his doctors and told them how bad his back was, he would have been transferred to a nonflying job. He could have served France, finished his book, and been safe. None of his fellow pilots would have blamed him for that. They knew how dangerous it was to fly with a bad back. Paul Pavelka had advised him to stay in Paris.

There is no evidence that Jim even considered this option. On November 11, 1916, Mrs. Weeks wrote to her son Allen:

> Jim McConnell left this morning for the front. I got up early to see him off. He has been here six weeks and I am so sorry to see him go, especially as he is not well yet.[27]

FOURTEEN

End of the De Luxe War

Jim had been gone from the squadron for two and a half months. When he left, it was a hot August day, and the pilots were living in an elegant chateau near Verdun. He returned on a cold, rainy day in November, and he described their quarters as follows:

> Before its arrival in the Somme the escadrille had always been quartered in towns and the life of the pilots was all that could be desired in the way of comforts. We had, as a result, come to believe that we would wage only a de luxe war, and were unprepared for any other sort of campaign. The introduction to the Somme was a rude awakening. Instead of being quartered in a villa or hotel, the pilots were directed to a portable barracks newly erected in a sea of mud. It was set in a cluster of similar barns nine miles from the nearest town. A sieve was a watertight compartment in comparison with that elongated shed. The damp cold penetrated through every crack, chilling one to the bone. There were no blankets and until they were procured the pilots had to curl up in their flying clothes.[1]

Paul Pavelka had warned Jim that when he returned to the squadron, he would "feel like a stranger." In addition to the new quarters, there were several new faces to greet him. Robert "Doc" Rockwell of Cincinnati, Ohio, had joined the squadron in September as a replacement for Victor Chapman. He had been studying to become a doctor when the war broke out, and in 1915 he dropped out of med school so he could go to France and take care of wounded soldiers. He transferred to aviation in early 1916. He was a solid, reliable pilot who flew with the escadrille until it was absorbed into the US Air Service, then flew with that service until the war ended.[2]

Emil Marshall of Brooklyn, New York, was assigned to the squadron in mid-October. He traveled to France and joined the French army in 1914, somehow using his French ancestry to join the regular army instead of the Foreign Legion. He served with distinction in the French army and survived the murderous conditions in the Bois-le-Prêtre and Verdun. After two years of infantry combat, he transferred to aviation but, due to a bureaucratic mix-up, was sent directly to the squadron without ever having learned to fly. He provided a variety of nonflying services to the squadron while Capt. Thénault worked to get him assigned to flight school. Eventually, the captain succeeded, but doctors at the flight school discovered that Marshall had been blind in one eye since birth. Prohibited from flying, he requested a transfer back to the infantry so he could once again take an active role in hostilities. All this took several months, during which he was warmly accepted by the pilots. After the war, he and Paul Rockwell were the two nonflying members welcomed into the Lafayette Escadrille veteran's group.[3]

Robert Soubiran, Willis Haviland, and Frederick Prince joined the squadron on October 22. Soubiran had been born in France but moved to the US at the age of four and grew up in New York City. He became a naturalized US citizen but returned to France in August 1914 and joined the Foreign Legion. After recovering from combat wounds, he transferred to Aviation. He would prove to be a valuable member of the squadron, transferring to the US Air Service with the squadron and flying with the US until the end of the war.[4]

Willis Haviland of Minneapolis, Minnesota, had served with Jim in the ambulance service at Pont-à-Mousson. Willis transferred to Aviation shortly after Jim did. He would be an active and successful member of the squadron, achieving one confirmed victory. In September 1917, he left the squadron to fly with a French unit for a few months before transferring to the US Naval Air Service and flying with them for the rest of the war.[5]

Frederick Prince was Norman Prince's older brother. With Norman's encouragement, "Freddie" joined the Foreign Legion in January 1916 and applied for an assignment in aviation. He completed his training shortly before Norman was killed.[6] His wealthy and influential father strongly opposed Freddie's combat assignment, especially after Norman's death, and he may have pressured Capt. Thénault to keep him grounded. The squadron log shows no flights for Freddie, although he apparently flew one or more patrols with a neighboring escadrille at Cachy. When Jim rejoined the squadron, Freddie left on emergency leave to the US because his father was seriously ill. He returned in late January, but his father, now recovered, soon succeeded in getting him removed from the front and sent to Pau as an instructor.

Jim met one other member who had joined the squadron since Jim was sent to the hospital—their lion cub, Whiskey. Offsetting these new faces, several familiar faces were absent from the squadron mess. Kiffin Rockwell and Norman Prince had been killed in combat, as had Victor Chapman before Jim was hospitalized. Elliot Cowdin left the squadron for medical and perhaps other reasons. Bert Hall left the squadron also, but he was flying with N.103 at the same airfield.

Another new development since the squadron moved to Cachy—they now had a squadron emblem. Insignias for flying units were coming into widespread use, and in particular the French Groupe de Combat 12, which also flew out of Cachy, painted a stork on the sides of their planes and were known as Les Cigognes (the Storks). Inspired by the trademark on a case of ammunition* from the Savage Arms Company,[7] Caporal Suchet, an artistic French mechanic, painted the head of a Seminole warrior on the American pilots' airplanes.[8] Suchet used red, white, and blue on the headdress and feathers to feature the colors of the US and French flags. (Months later, the insignia was updated to a fiercer-looking Sioux warrior by pilots Harold Willis and Edward Hinkle.[9])

The exact date when the squadron began using this insignia is unknown, but on November 1, Paul Pavelka wrote to Paul Rockwell that "for a mark of the escadrille, we all have a North American Indian painted on our machines. And a darned pretty one too."

A reporter from the *New York Sun* visited the squadron on November 9, just two days before Jim returned. He was there on one of the few days with good flying weather, and he described squadron activities as well as the new insignia:

> After several days of rain Thursday [November 9] was gloriously fine, with a blue sky and little wind, although it may be said that this group hardly allows the wind to interfere with its activities. Hence it was not surprising to find in the next day's French communiqué there had been seventy-seven air engagements during the day on the Somme front. When I reached the American escadrille Thursday I found almost every one of them had been over the lines

* Squadron lore says it was copied from an ammunition case, but it's more likely it was copied from a catalog or other Savage document.

1906 Savage Arms catalog (*left*) and N.124 insignia (*right*). *Public domain (left) and Steve Ruffin* (right)

> during the morning. Several reported they had had fights, but were unable to state the results until the official observers' reports were received. Paul Pavelka dived from a height of 9,000 feet to 6,500 feet upon his adversary, and fired. The German dropped as if hit, but Pavelka thought he might have recovered. Raoul Lufbery returned from a fight he had volunteered to make during the afternoon with a bullet hole through his machine, saying he believed he had forced his enemy to descend. Bert Hall, who has now exchanged into a French escadrille forming a part of the same group, visited the Americans' quarters and reported he had downed one. Dudley Hill of Peekskill, NY, formerly a student at New York University; Ralph Sobiran [*sic*], Willis Haviland, and Didier Masson all reported that scraps were plenty, as the German aviators were out. "You have to go to Germany to find them, however," they said. The only inactive members were McConnell, who is rejoining on Saturday after having been on sick leave because of rheumatism, and Lawrence Rumsey, who had been laid off by an attack of bat, an Egyptian plague of boils. William Thaw and Chouteau Johnson are absent on leave, on their way to New York. Fred Prince sails on Sunday for a fortnight's leave.
>
> The American machines now bear as the escadrille's mark the profile of a North American Indian with war feathers. . . . The Americans live in a wooden barrack built in the forest around the aviation field. Each man has his own cubicle, with a common living room at the end of the building.[10]

The article was remarkably accurate and restrained for the time. None of the planes the Americans attacked were listed as confirmed victories, but Pavelka, Lufbery, and Hall were given credit for "probable" victories that day.[11] Two or three pilots shared each cubicle in the barracks rather than each man having their own cubicle, but other than that, the article accurately summed up the situation when Jim arrived.

Jim wrote to Paul Rockwell on November 15, providing an update on local conditions as well as squadron news and gossip.

> This is some climate—mist and rain most of the time. I have no machine as yet but haven't missed anything. . . . I feel on the bum for fair in this climate. . . . I have Bill's bunk in the shed with Havi [Bill Thaw was on leave in the US]. We all motored over and saw a tank the other day. Very interesting . . . Boches come over on clear nights and drop bombs. Pretty close last time. Skip [Paul Pavelka] is to try night flying in Nieuport. A couple of Frenchmen here do it when there's a moon. . . . Lots of my old friends have gone since I was at the front last.[12]

Jim also commented that he was looking forward to seeing Paul for the "big event." Paul's wedding to Mademoiselle Marie Francois Jeanne Leygues was fast approaching, and Jim was going to be his witness and best man. Jim also thanked Paul for sending him copies of the *World's Work* magazine with his article. The fact that copies of an article that Jim wrote in September made it to France in early November shows how anxious the publisher must have been to run Jim's story. The manuscript and the magazines had to travel to and from the US by steamship, so a two-month turnaround was exceptional.

Jim wrote to Mrs. Weeks that night, but in a more despondent mood:

> It is always damp and misty and the Escadrille has not been out since my arrival. I miss you deeply and would give anything this night to be at home. I am quite lonely. It doesn't seem like the Escadrille now that Kiffin has gone. It has a very different atmosphere, if I can use the word. The old Skipper is fine. He and I are going to fix up a shed together. I have Bill Thaw's bunk now. The wind and mist come in through the chinks, but the place is much better than I thought, with electric lights and a floor. It is cold, though, as the deuce.[13]

He was in a cheerier mood when he wrote to Marcelle the following day. The weather had finally cleared enough for the squadron to fly, although Jim's flights weren't trouble-free:

> This is quite an interesting tho rotten place. The climate is fierce. My back is stiffer and it isn't easy to fly, tho with the usual weather we do not do much. I've only been out twice. It's fearfully cold at 4,000 meters [13,000 feet] now. The main thing that bothers me is that I can't turn to look back.
>
> In our barracks it's so cold that one can hardly hold a pen and I'm afraid I won't be able to fill up the book. We just hug the stove and cuss the quarters.
>
> The Boches come over nearly every night for this is a big aviation center. Last night bombs hit a hangar fifty meters from our barracks and burnt up eight machines, killing a mechanic who burnt to death, and wounding others. Guess they will be over again tonight.
>
> I feel the lack of all the delightful sweetness you gave to my life in Paris. It was wonderful Marcelle. Letters will help, you know.[14]

As Jim mentioned, Cachy was a large aviation center. The French had sent their top pilots to the Somme as the battle of Verdun began winding down, and the Americans flew out of the same airfield as Georges Guynemer, Charles Nungesser, Rene Dorme, Albert Duellin, and others (René Fonck, who finished the war as the top Allied Ace with seventy-five confirmed victories, would arrive in April). This, plus conversations with British airmen stationed nearby, gave the Americans an opportunity to discuss strategy and tactics with some of the best pilots in the war, topics that were not yet being taught at flying schools. Albert Duellin created a "code of fighting tactics," somewhat comparable to the "Dicta Boelcke," which the top German ace was distributing on the other side of the lines. Duellin's code was as follows:

> 1. Never attack without looking behind you.
> 2. Attack a single-seater from behind and above, then break the combat by a "chandelle" (vertical climb) to always maintain a superior altitude.
> 3. Attack a two-seater by getting under its tail in the "dead angle" formed by the fuselage and stabilizer, and stay there to prevent him from taking you unaware.
> 4. Never fly in a straight line, and break combat when expedient by a quick renversement [a vertical climb followed by a wingover and half roll].[15]

While obviously not complete, rules like these were a valuable first step toward developing tactics for air combat. (Rule number 3, for example, might have saved Kiffin Rockwell's life. With Jim's back problems, he couldn't follow rule number 1.)

Although the bad weather meant the pilots made few flights during this period, the widespread press coverage given the squadron during its previous assignments led the German government to claim that the mere existence of the Escadrille Américaine was a violation of US neutrality. The US secretary of state dutifully passed this complaint on to the French government, and on November 16, 1916, the squadron received orders that they would henceforth be known as the Escadrille de Volantaires (Squadron of Volunteers). This was a name that pleased no one. There are varying accounts as to who suggested a new name for the squadron, but the net result was that on December 6, 1916, France's minister of war officially changed the name to L'Escadrille Lafayette—the Lafayette Escadrille.[16] The name honored the Marquis de Lafayette, a French volunteer who helped the US win the Revolutionary War. This was the name that became famous.

Jim and his Nieuport, ready to fly from Cachy. *W&L Archives*

At 5:00 a.m. on the morning after the unit became the "Squadron of Volunteers," Paul Pavelka got his chance to try the night flight that Jim wrote about. He took off to intercept German bombers that were attacking the airfield. It was still pitch black at that hour, but Paul had fitted his Nieuport with electric lights for his instruments, and lights to signal the airfield to light flares so he could land. Unfortunately, shortly after he took off, his electrical system failed. He had no way to navigate, and although he could see the airfield because a hangar was still burning, when he approached without signal lights the ground gunners fired at the sound of his engine, mistaking him for another German bomber. He tried to overtake the retreating German bombers but failed, leaving him lost in the dark. By reducing power as much as possible, he was able to stay aloft until the first light of dawn.[17] Jim described what happened next:

> "I found myself over a fairly good sized town and made up my mind to land," said Pavelka. "I spotted a promising looking château with a field near it and landed there. From the khaki uniformed troops about I knew I was in the British lines. Just as I was walking up to the château, out came a British colonel. 'Hello, good morning, had breakfast?' he asked."[18]

Pavelka sent a brief description of this flight to Mrs. Weeks, commenting that when he landed, "my fuel was exhausted, and I felt a little that way."[19] Two days later (November 19), Jim wrote to Paul Rockwell with details of the bombing raid that prompted Pavelka's night flight:

> The Boches came over the other night and dropped bombs all over us. One hitting the tank of a machine set fire to it and 8 planes went up. All together 16 were destroyed. One fellow burnt to death and 9 wounded. Skip [Paul Pavelka] tried his first night flight and landed down near the sea. He's still there on account of weather. . . . Bert Hall is in N.103 and is cleaning up on poker. . . . The lines here are hard to pick out and at 4,000 [13,000 feet] it's cold as the devil—gets to my back for fair. Rumsey is going to Paris to get cured of boils. I am afraid I can't do the work for Page out here [finish the book manuscript]. It's so cold that a short letter is about one's limit. Haven't heard from Hélène or Marcelle as yet. Strikes me as peculiar—considering.[20]

Jim's concern about finishing the manuscript for his book took on new urgency when he learned that Mrs. Weeks was going back to the US in late December. He hoped to finish the manuscript before she left, so she could hand-carry it to the publisher. (In the days before copiers, the handwritten draft of a book was often the only copy an author had. Dropping it in the mail after months of work was a scary proposition.) Finding time to write wasn't a problem, since bad weather severely limited flying. The main obstacle to Jim's writing was weather so cold that his fingers cramped and he couldn't hold a pen. Capt. Thénault described this period as follows:

> The Somme region in winter is a very foggy neighborhood; the large valley consists of marshes where only ducks and hunters were used to congregate. From the 15th of November up to the 15th of January, there were not, at the outside, more than one dozen days suitable for flying*. Low fog and rain kept us continually shut up in our wretched shed, hidden in the relatively high lands of Cachy wood. What mud![21]

Outside of occasional visits to the nearby town of Amiens, the pilots sat in their barracks, read their mail, read old magazines, read newspapers when they could get them, and played poker. They also listened to their phonograph. Capt. Thénault said,

> But I don't know what would have become of us without the phonograph. . . . The strains of the fox-trot or rag-time alternated with airs from French or Italian operas. Lufbery preferred strange, haunting tunes, often melancholic in character, which were, my boys told me, very popular in America. This was Hawaiian music, played on a "ukulele." Later I saw one of these instruments with the queer name and was a little disappointed.[22]

Lawrence Rumsey's trip to Paris "to get cured of boils" probably marked the end of his tenure with the squadron. As historian Steve Ruffin put it, his heart was in the right place, but he simply was not cut out to be a fighter pilot.[23] Older than most of the other pilots, he no longer felt the invulnerability of youth. Having seen several pilots killed or seriously wounded in training and in combat, he used alcohol to steady his nerves. When the squadron flew what planes they had from Luxeuil to Cachy, Rumsey got lost. He eventually landed at the wrong French airfield and, believing himself to be behind German lines, set fire to his plane so it wouldn't fall into the hands of the enemy.[24] On November 25, his name was removed from the squadron roster.

Paul Rockwell's wedding to Jeanne Leygues on December 4 brought Jim a welcome relief from the weather, the drafty barracks, the interminable days when flying was not possible, and the agonizing cold when flying was possible. It also brought hope and a sense of a "new beginning" to Paul and Mrs. Weeks, both of whom were still grieving over the death of Kiffin

---

* Squadron logs show more than a dozen days, but in general there was little flying from December 1916 through February 1917.

Jim McConnell (*left*) and Paul Rockwell at Paul's wedding. *UVA Archives*

Rockwell. Paul would mourn the loss of his brother for the rest of his life (he would later name one of his sons Kiffin, in memory of his brother, and name another son Kenneth James in honor of Kenneth Weeks and Jim McConnell[25]). Jim sent short notes to Paul, Marcelle, and Mrs. Weeks, letting them know how much he was looking forward to seeing them at the wedding.

After the wedding, Jim wrote to Marcelle to say that the time he got to spend with her was "short but sweet," and he was glad that the wedding gave him a chance to be with her. He was excited because the squadron was going to leave Cachy soon and move to a base closer to Paris. He hoped to get leave in January and wanted to coordinate his leave with her schedule so they could see each other.[26] He wrote a short note to Mrs. Weeks the same day, letting her know that Paul Pavelka would soon leave for Paris with a few sheets of Jim's manuscript, and he would be sending the rest of the manuscript later.[27] Less than a week later, he told her he would not be able to finish the manuscript before she left for the US, and would instead send it with Dudley Hill, who was scheduled to go to the US on leave*. Jim wished her a safe trip, admitting that he was worried about U-boat activity.[28] (The fact that Jim's friend Betty Baldwin had been seriously injured by a U-boat attack undoubtedly heightened his concern.)

On December 11, Jim wrote to Paul Rockwell, who by that time had returned from his honeymoon and moved into a new apartment with his new wife. The opening was unusually warm, expressing feelings that are often felt but seldom written.

---

* The pages that Mrs. Weeks did take with her constituted the second main chapter of Jim's book and were also published as the second installment of "Flying for France" in the March issue of the *World's Work* magazine.

Dear old Paul: I was very happy to receive your fine letter this morning, old pal, and I want you to know how deeply I appreciate all you said. You know how honored I felt at your wanting me to be witness, and how much your friendship means to me. I'm glad you are comfortably fixed up, but for some reason I can't picture you in another place than old 80 Rue B [Mrs. Weeks's apartment]. Some of the happiest days of my life were passed there.

I have done but little extra on the article for I've felt on the bum and then Whiskey chewed my fingers so it's hard to hold a pen. I'll send rest of it by Dudley. Have only flown once since my return—this a.m. Nothing doing, fortunately, as my map case came off and I couldn't shoot as I had to hold it. . . . Believe I'll ask for leave to take baths when the rest of the boys get back [Bill Thaw and Chute Johnson were on leave in the US; presumably the "baths" were therapy for Jim's back]. We expect Hoskier and Genet soon [new pilots being assigned to the squadron]. . . . We pull out of here sometime next month but the place we're going isn't any improvement. . . . Give my very best regards to your wife. Yours to a cinder, Jim."[29]

Jim wasn't in quite such a mellow mood when he wrote to Marcelle a few days later, on December 14:

Some fool general has sent orders that a few machines must be over the lines no matter what the weather. Only two machines from each escadrille go out at a time when the clouds are low or it's raining. We alternate among ourselves. The Captain sent Lufbery and Pavelka out today. They had to fly so low in the rain that they could see the soldiers in the trenches. Lufbery waved to the upturned faces and the *poilus* replied. The two pilots were in front of the artillery and in the path of the projectiles which they could see bursting in the German lines beyond. A rotten job flying like that.[30]

Jim flew his share of these miserable sorties. The squadron log shows he flew seven sorties in December in spite of his back problems. This was well above the squadron average during the atrocious December weather—only Lt. De Laage flew more, and he flew only nine sorties. If the flights served no other purpose, Jim at least gained some good material for his writing. He described one of these flights in a magazine article published a few months later:

> I know of sorties being ordered when the sea of mist was so thick that a woods only a few hundred yards distant was curtained by the veil of vapor. In a few seconds after leaving the ground you plunge into the clammy clouds. Nothing can be seen but a gray-white. You throttle down your motor and dive until the ground again comes into view. . . . One sees plainly directly underneath, but ahead and on both sides the landscape is dissolved in the thick fog. . . . Speed is reduced to a minimum, and the plane is apt to slip on a wing. You are flying at but 400 feet, and should it do so, it would be hard to recover before striking the ground. . . . It is difficult to tell which are the French and which the German trenches, but you see a handful of blue-uniformed men crouched in a shell hole, and know they are beyond the organized positions. Then you must be careful, for the enemy is dug in only a few meters away and his machine guns might find you an easy mark. . . . Dropping low, you see the soldiers' upturned faces, and, forcing an arm out into the powerful rush of air, you wave to the miserable but brave and patient *poilus*. They reply, and you feel complimented. . . . You are in the trajectory of the smaller shells and your machine rocks as they hurtle by. . . . Squalls of stinging rain sweep by. The glass windshield close to your face is streaked with water. Your goggles are curtained. To keep from getting lost, you head in the general direction of the road you use as a landmark.[31]

Jim's letter to Marcelle also noted that "a new boy, named Hoskier, has just joined the escadrille" and closed with a curious postscript about Lawrence Rumsey:

> Can you get me any information regarding Rumsey? He has been fooling around Paris and we fear that he'll get into really serious trouble. Something has been said here by our Capt. which makes the outlook black for him.[32]

November 25 is typically cited as the day that Rumsey was dropped from the squadron roster, and the squadron log shows he stopped flying sorties long before that, but Jim was still asking about him three weeks later. His departure for "medical reasons" was handled very quietly, behind the scenes, and it appears his fellow pilots didn't know what was going on.

The "new boy" Jim mentioned was Ronald Wood Hoskier from South Orange, New Jersey. He enrolled in Harvard in 1914 but left college in February 1916 because he wanted to fly for France. He drove an ambulance for a few months while waiting for his application to French aviation to be approved. (His parents had helped form the Norton-Harjes Ambulance Corps, a volunteer organization similar to the American Ambulance Service.) Hoskier joined the Escadrille Lafayette on December 11, 1916.

Jim wrote to Marcelle again on December 15, still concerned about the fact that generals who knew nothing about flying were ordering them to fly. He hoped they would be under the command of a different army at the base they were moving to, "for the orders we get now are wild. Two Frenchmen flying in the rain this a.m. fired on each other." He regretted that he would not be able to go to Paris for Christmas and promised to drink to her health. She was going to mail a Christmas present to him, and he replied in a vein that would sound familiar to young lovers today. "I'm sending you a *petite chose** [little thing] that will do me more good than you—or at least I hope so."[33]

He also wrote to Mrs. Weeks on the fifteenth, sending the letter by way of Paul Rockwell in case Mrs. Weeks left for the US before it arrived. He enclosed four pages of his manuscript for her to take with her and described how he and "Skip" (Paul Pavelka) had rigged up a stove to keep their cubicle warm:

> The stove is a great success and Skip & I are better off than anyone else in the outfit. It's quite a simple matter to fake a few minutes on flying time to account for the gasoline. Five minutes of fuel consumption in the air runs the stove 24 hours.[34]

The rotten weather continued, and the pilots were ordered to continue flying. Accidents and illnesses were the result:

> We had to go out in the rain today. It was rotten. Couldn't see a thing. . . . Poor old Pavelka is sick. He shouldn't have flown, but did, and smashed up on landing. Lufbery is laid up with rheumatism in the back. We're a great aggregation of cripples. A shell en route to the trenches went thru a Nieuport the day before yesterday. Shortly after another fellow got killed by running into a Boche. It was his first trip over the lines. [35] [The Nieuport hit by the artillery shell and the pilot who was killed were from other squadrons.]

---

* The *petite chose* Jim teased Marcelle about turned out to be a fountain pen, which he hoped she would use to write him.

Jim wrote that Lt. de Laage and Dudley Hill were sick as well. A few days before Christmas, Capt. Thénault and a few of the pilots who weren't sick spent an evening cheering their souls at a bar in Amiens. Upon leaving, they found a kilt-clad Scottish soldier passed out under a lamppost in a drizzling rain. Not wanting to let him freeze to death, they loaded him into their car and took him back to the air base. There was a bit of confusion when he woke up the next day, since he didn't recognize the Americans and feared he'd been captured by Germans. Eventually things got sorted out, and they gave him a ride back to his unit. The Scotsman sent them a case of scotch whisky as a thank-you. After seeing the results of giving a case of whiskey to a bunch of American pilots, the captain wondered if they might have been better off leaving the Scot to freeze beneath the lamppost.[36]

The American pilots invited some British pilots to join them for Christmas dinner and the case of scotch. Capt. Thénault spent the evening with Capt. Henri Saint-Saveur, the commander of N.67, which was also stationed at Cachy. Capt. Thénault described the situation he found when he returned:

> That night it was quite late when I returned home, after a bridge game at Saint-Sauveur's quarters. As I was nearing our shack, feeling my way in the darkness through the labyrinth of duckboards, I heard a wild commotion followed by some pistol shots in rapid succession. A bullet whizzed by my ears. Fearing the worst, I hurriedly opened the door. At one end of the room, a man was standing pointing a gun with a none too steady hand; at the other end, the tall MacConnell was holding, at arm's length, a wash bowl. This was the target at which each pilot in turn was taking pot shots in rapid fire. Everybody seemed in very good spirits. We happened to be in the Somme, however, not in the Wild West; and so, to their great disappointment, I stopped this dangerous game by disarming the gunner, and sent them all to bed.[37]

With so much scotch involved, it's not surprising that Jim's memory of the event was a little different. He wrote Marcelle:

> We had a big Christmas dinner last night and as a result Lufbery and "Skipper" formed a salvation army and tried to save us for God. It ended by Luff holding a wash basin and I shooting holes in it with a revolver. The Captain took the gun from me. Oh well.[38]

And Jim recalled an additional detail when he wrote Paul Rockwell a few days later:

> Nothing exciting save that Christmas Lufbery and I got lit and pulled off a Wild West show. He held a basin while I shot holes in it. Fortunately the Captain took the revolver from me as I was to essay knocking a shaving brush out of our "ace's" mouth.[39]

Regardless of who was doing the shooting or what the targets were, it was a night to remember. One other memorable event happened that night. During the dinner with their Christmas guests, Jim suddenly realized there were thirteen people at the table. He pointed this out to Lt. de Laage, who was sitting next to him. The lieutenant wasn't familiar with the American superstition concerning the number thirteen, so Jim explained that it was bad luck, and it meant that someone in the group would die within a year. Lt. de Laage laughed and said, "Well, it will hold good with this crowd, but unfortunately there will probably be more than one."[40]

Christmas with British friends, 1916. *Front row*: Jim McConnell (*left*), Willis Haviland, Dudley Hill. *Seated*: Paul Pavelka, unknown, Lt. de Laage, Raoul Lufbery, unknown, unknown, unknown, unknown, unknown (*only left arm showing*). *Standing*: Robert Rockwell. *W&L Archives*

FIFTEEN

Cold Misery

The weather cleared after Christmas, and the pilots managed to conduct a flurry of patrols on December 26, 27, and 28. Jim flew two patrols during this period, and Lufbery scored his sixth victory—shooting down an Aviatik southeast of Chaulnes.[1] Despite his status as the squadron's leading ace, things didn't always go Lufbery's way. On December 29, Jim wrote a short note to Paul Rockwell:

> "Luff" got shot up yesterday by some Boche "As" [Ace]. This is a more dangerous front than Verdun. One queer thing is that a bunch got killed landing—and it's a good field.[2]

Then the weather socked in again, and there were no more flights until the coming year.

The stove that Jim and Paul Pavelka installed in their cubicle apparently allowed Jim to hold a pen long enough to write more than just a short note. The bad weather gave him time to finish a twelve-thousand-word article about flying over the Somme. He had hoped to include this in his book *Flying for France*, but his editor told him it was too late. The book would include the article he wrote for the *World's Work* magazine, the manuscript he wrote while recuperating in Paris, and the additional pages that Mrs. Weeks hand-carried to the US, but they didn't want to delay publication to include this new material. They intended to publish that in a future issue of the *World's Work**.

* It would eventually be published as "The Day's Work of an American Airman on the Somme" in a new magazine, *National Service*, possibly in an effort to generate interest in that publication. Nelson Doubleday was on the managing board, as was former president Theodore Roosevelt.

Jim was disappointed, since he felt that the new material was ten times as interesting as what he'd already written.[3] He sent the new material back with Dudley Hill, who left to spend leave in the US on the first of January.[4]

The year 1917 didn't start any better, weatherwise. There was no flying at all for the first several days. The squadron log shows that the escadrille would fly only sixty-eight sorties the entire month, only a slight increase from December. Jim would fly more than his share of these, but that would still total only six patrols. He wrote Marcelle on January 2:

> Bill [Thaw] and [Chouteau] Johnson arrived last night. It's good to see them back. [Dudley] Hill and [Robert] Rockwell left for the States just as they came. They seem to have given up sending us out in bad weather. It has been covered [cloud cover] for a few days, and we have done no flying at all. Bill tells me the Escadrille has a rotten reputation in Paris for drinking. I don't know why for there's been none of it except on Thanksgiving and Christmas. . . . "Whiskey" gets more gentle every day. He's a big chap now.[5]

Jim's relief at having finished the manuscript for his book and sent it to the publishers was short lived. Carroll David Winslow was an American who came to France in 1915 to work with the American Ambulance Hospital in Paris, entered French aviation, and flew Maurice Farman bombers over Verdun for a short period. He then returned to the US on emergency leave because his daughter had become dangerously ill. Winslow had also just finished writing a book. Jim addressed his concerns to Paul Rockwell in a January 6 letter:

> Paul, that g– d– s– of a b– Winslow, who Thaw brought back by the nose, is getting out a book (Chas Scribners & Sons) called *Flying for France*. My title, and you can bet it's some !!!! story. It will come out ahead of my book and make me look sick.[6]

As it turned out, Jim's concern was groundless. When published, the book's title was *With the French Flying Corps* (possibly because Doubleday, Page & Co. already owned the copyright to *Flying for France* via the article published in the *World's Work* magazine). Dana's book was not "some story"; it was an honest and unembellished account of his experiences, primarily in flight training. Publishing figures are not available, but it's doubtful that the book sold anywhere near the number of copies that Jim's book did, and it is not as well remembered today. After Winslow's daughter recovered, he returned to France and flew for the French until the US entered the war, then he transferred to the US Air Service and served honorably through the end of the war.[7]

The weather cleared for five days, and Jim wrote to Marcelle on January 7. He opened with a surprisingly frank description of Bill Thaw and "Chute" Johnson's experiences during their leave in the US, possibly to remind her that pilots had "other options":

> Have I told you that Thaw and Johnson are back and they report a marvelous time in the States? All the women in New York—married and debutantes—will sleep with one, and as a whole Babylon looks like a Sunday School alongside. I'm tempted to take my permission [leave] over there.

He then described the action they were seeing now that the weather permitted flying:

> Today was the first flying day in a long time. We went out ten strong—more than ever before*. I went down on two Boches with Bill & "Havi" but my machine gun jammed. One Nieuport was brought down by French cannon—another a Boche dropped and poor Sauvage** was hit by German shrapnel [antiaircraft fire]. Lt. de la Tour, who was next to him, said he fell from 3,000 meters in 10 seconds, but that's not possible. Anyway he was to come to dinner with us tomorrow night with four others, and now there will be only four guests. I never have been so shot at as today, save one time over Douaumont. My mirror showed all black from the shells bursting near my tail.[8]

Sgt. Sauvage and the other pilots brought down that day were not Lafayette Escadrille pilots. They were assigned to other French escadrilles based at Cachy, but the Lafayette pilots were exposed to the same dangers—antiaircraft fire, being struck by artillery shells, and an increasingly aggressive German air force. When the Battle of the Somme began in the summer of 1916, Britain's Royal Flying Corps dominated the sky above the battlefield.

---

* The squadron log shows that de Laage, Haviland, Hoskier, Johnson, Lufbery, McConnell, Masson, Pavelka, Soubiron, and Thaw flew in that patrol.

** Sgt. Paul Johannes Sauvage of N.65, credited with six confirmed victories.

Flying planes that were equal or superior to Germany's aging Fokker Eindekers, they clearly gained air superiority. In September 1916, however, German Albatros single-seat fighters began to change this situation. Powered by a Mercedes in-line engine* and armed with twin machine guns, the Albatros was as fast or faster than anything the Allies had in the air at the time, and it outgunned all Allied planes. As the Germans transferred experienced pilots from Verdun to the Somme, the opposition facing the Lafayette Escadrille grew in numbers as well as capabilities. The top German ace, Oswald Boelcke, began flying over the Somme in September, accompanied by a group of promising young pilots who formed a Jagdstaffel, or "hunting squadron." Boelcke himself was killed in late October, in a collision with one of his fellow pilots, but his students bloomed into aces themselves and became mentors to other German pilots. One of Boelcke's students, Baron Manfred von Richthofen, would become the war's top ace, with eighty victories. When Jim flew his January 7 patrol and had his gun jam, Richthofen had already amassed sixteen victories over the Somme battlefield.[9]

Bad weather set in on January 11, and the squadron did no flying for a dozen days. Jim wrote to Paul on the fourteenth to update him on what little was happening in the squadron. They were expecting three new pilots, but none of them had arrived yet. Freddie Prince had returned to France after his emergency leave in the US but hadn't come back to the squadron. He was staying at a hotel in Paris (probably the work of his father, who was pulling strings to keep Freddie out of combat). Jim was hoping that Freddie would arrive soon, since he couldn't take leave until Freddie arrived and Jim had some "scandal" to pour into Paul's ear (no idea what the scandal was, since he didn't disclose it in the letter). Chouteau Johnson was credited with a "probable" before the weather socked in, but the victory was never confirmed. And Jim was still worried that Winslow's book would be titled *Flying for France.*

Jim described the effects of the cold, the lack of action, winter flying, and squadron life in a magazine article:

> For me it [Jim's canvas bunk] is the only warm spot in the entire region. On mornings when there is no flying most of us stay in our cots until after ten o'clock. There's nothing else to do, and it's the sole method of obtaining comfort. . . . The longer one stays on the

* A traditional, stationary engine with the cylinders in a straight line, like many car engines. In-line engines were heavier than rotary engines, took up more space, and required a water-cooling system, but they were more reliable and could develop more power. They also didn't have the throttling problems and gyroscopic effects of rotary engines.

> ground the less one likes to fly, and I've noticed as a consequence that our morale is not up to its standard of last summer. I know mine isn't. For one thing, flying is far from agreeable in winter because of the extreme cold. The sound of a motor turning over in the morning seems to waft a current of freezing air into my blankets as I contemplate going aloft. . . . We walk out in the half frozen mud to the waiting machines, and are helped into our fur combinations and boots by our mechanicians. As a protection from the cold, some of us wear face masks, and the rest are so bundled up with hood, muffler, and goggles as to be equally difficult to recognize. . . . You are flying at more than 14,000 feet and the cold begins to make itself felt. Looking up into the round mirror you see that your face is red as a beet. Sometimes there is a white line under the goggles and you know that the skin over the cheek bone is frozen. . . . At twelve we gather at the table for our noonday meal. We have a rule that only English is permitted at lunch and only French at dinner. A slip costs two *sous* [pennies]. Some of the men are strangely silent at night. When the meat is brought on, "Whiskey" starts loping around the table. He finds an opening and bounds up on the bench. "Whiskey-man, get down!" One large paw reaches out on the table, but before he upsets anything a hand takes a hold of the scruff of his neck and pushes him to the floor. He gives a long-drawn-out roar and tries again. "*Oh, le plus beau des lions*" [Oh, the most beautiful of lions], says a special friend of the cub. "Yes, and that just cost you two cents," calls his neighbor, mindful of the tin for fines.[10]

Conditions were made worse by the fact that the winter of 1916–17 was one of the coldest winters France had ever seen. From mid-November to mid-March, the daily high temperatures in Amiens averaged well below freezing. And the temperature dropped significantly at the altitude where most patrols were flown. If the ground temperature was 20°F, not unusual when pilots began a morning patrol, at 12,000 feet it would probably be −20°F. With 100+ mph winds whipping around the open cockpit, avoiding frostbite was a major concern.

On January 19, the first of the new pilots the squadron was expecting arrived. Edmond Genet, the great-great-grandson of Citizen Genet, France's first minister to the newly independent Unites States of America, was born in Ossining, New York. His youthful appearance hid a surprisingly strong spirit and adventurous background. He enlisted in the US Navy at the age of seventeen, served two years with the Navy, and then sailed to France and joined the Foreign Legion. He survived murderous shell and machine gun fire during the Battle of Champagne, being one of 60 uninjured survivors out of a company of 250. He went on to endure over a year of frontline duty, rain, blizzards, and shellfire on numerous fronts, including Verdun, before transferring to Aviation. He carried a dark secret with him when he joined the Lafayette Escadrille—he had deserted his US Navy ship to go to France and join the Legion. After the war, an understanding US government would dismiss the charge of desertion and remove all mention of it from his records.[11]

The squadron gained another new member on January 24—Edwin "Ted" Parsons. Ted was born in Springfield, Massachusetts, but, like several other Escadrille members, became a wandering adventurer. He learned to fly in 1912 and at one point flew reconnaissance missions for Pancho Villa's Mexican Revolution. When he heard that France was considering creating an American volunteer squadron, he earned his passage to France, working as an "assistant veterinarian" on a boat loaded with horses. Like Jim, he worked for a while as an ambulance driver before transferring to Aviation.[12] In addition to being an excellent pilot (by the end of the war, he had eight confirmed victories), he proved to be an excellent writer. After the war he worked on Hollywood screenplays, wrote flying stories for pulp magazines, and wrote a book about the Lafayette Escadrille titled *The Great Adventure*, later republished as *I Flew with the Lafayette Escadrille*. That book is one of the most readable and frequently quoted histories of the squadron, providing exciting and humorous anecdotes as well as honest descriptions of subjects such as fear, alcohol, and physical misery, which are "glossed over" in many memoirs. Parsons was the only American pilot who elected not to transfer to the US Air Service, and he flew with French escadrilles until the end of the war. He joined the US Navy Reserves in 1934 and served throughout World War II, eventually becoming a rear admiral.

The squadron also lost a pilot on January 24, but the loss was due to a transfer, not enemy action. Paul "Skipper" Pavelka left the escadrille to fly with France's Army of the Orient in Salonika, Greece. The Allies had established a large military presence in northern Greece in 1916 to assist the Serbian army, which had been forced to retreat south by the Austrian army. This presence was controversial, since Greece was a neutral country. The king of Greece favored the Germans, while the prime minister favored the Allies. Welcomed or not, the Allied troops in Greece needed air support, and there was aerial combat between Allied and Austrian aircraft. In December 1916 the Escadrille received a letter asking pilots to volunteer for assignment to Salonika, and "Skip" jumped at the chance to see a different part of the world (the fact that Salonika was considerably warmer than Cachy undoubtedly influenced this decision).

January 24 was a significant day for Raoul Lufbery, as he shot down an Aviatik to score his seventh victory. Lt. de Laage scored a "probable" that day, and Jim had another frustrating combat. "My machine gun went on the bum today," he wrote Paul Rockwell, "and I had a Boche 5 kilometers in our lines. I could have cried*."[13]

Two days later, the squadron moved to the south, as Jim had predicted. Capt. Thénault described it as follows:

> On January 26, we moved to Ravenel, near Saint-Just-en-Chausée. This was in preparation for a new offensive which the High Command planned for the Spring. We had instructions to show ourselves as little as possible in this sector, so as not to attract the attention of the enemy. Besides, the Boches being just as much hampered by the cold as we were, nothing special happened during the month of February. Calm prevailed everywhere.[14]

The "new offensive" being planned would become known as the Nivelle Offensive, named after the French commander in chief General Robert Nivelle, who planned the attack. General Nivelle had been placed in command of the French forces at Verdun during the closing months of that battle, and he successfully recaptured several key points from the Germans. Convinced that his formula of a "creeping barrage**" followed by a massive attack was the key to success, he convinced French politicians and his own troops that he could break through the German lines and cause a massive retreat within forty-eight hours, while suffering fewer than ten thousand French casualties. Nivelle pledged to call off the attack if it did not result in a quick success. The French would play a leading role, attacking along the Aisne front, while a smaller British attack near Arras would envelop the German defenders in a pincher movement. When the attack was eventually launched, in mid-April, it quickly became apparent that it would not succeed within forty-eight hours and that casualties were much higher than predicted. Nevertheless, Nivelle was encouraged by early reports and continued the offensive. The attack dragged on until mid-May and pushed the German lines back 3 or 4 miles in some places, but it resulted in over 180,000 French

---

* Pilots liked to bring down enemy planes within their own lines, since that virtually guaranteed that the victory would be confirmed. Planes that fell or were forced down behind enemy lines were less likely to be confirmed.

** An artillery bombardment that slowly lifted from the enemy's frontline trenches to the rear, allowing the attacking troops to stay just behind the bombardment and rush the enemy before they had time to emerge from their dugouts.

casualties. Nivelle was sacked and, in a move that stunned everyone, large numbers of French troops mutinied and refused to attack. They would defend their existing trenches, but they would not participate in any more attacks until major changes were made.

All of this was in the future when the Lafayette pilots moved to Ravenel. Jim flew his plane there and then left for a long-planned leave in Paris. It turned out to be a good time to leave. Ravenel was a new base, and the barracks weren't finished when the pilots arrived. For the first week, the pilots had to sleep on the dirt floor of covered slit trenches, which served as bomb shelters. Ted Parsons wrote,

> Then it was no war de luxe, as we suffered agonies in the arctic temperature. It was so cold that when Genet tried to wet his hair with his lukewarm wash water to slick it back, it froze straight up in little individual icicles before he could put a comb to it. Despite three pairs of socks and fur-lined boots, I froze a toe and was unable to walk for a week.[15]

By the time Jim returned from leave, the pilots had moved into barracks. Jim wrote,

> We are fixed up pretty well here. Much better than at Cachy. It's fearfully cold, tho. Whiskey ate up my Kepi last night. . . . Lufbery was evacuated with rheumatism last night [cold aggravates rheumatism]. . . . Made a flight this noon over our new sector. Very cold—some of our machines are frozen up. I got mixed up and found myself over Noyon. Seems orders were issued today forbidding us to cross lines for a certain period so I got a call down on my return. The authorities don't want the Boches to know there is a group of *chasse* [*avions des chasse*; fighter planes] at this part of the front.[16]

In a possible reference to activities Jim engaged in while on leave, he closed by saying, "Am on a water and *tilluel* [a French herbal tea] regime now. Ho, ho for the water wagon."

Jim wrote to Mrs. Weeks, who was still in the US, the same day:

> I have just returned from a most enjoyable leave in Paris, though the place wasn't at all the same without you there. Ten days ago we moved from where we were and are now further south. We have

> much better barracks but just now it is fearfully cold. The machines freeze up while one is flying. I suppose you know that our old friend Skipper has gone to Salonika. He and Haviland volunteered, but the latter wasn't sent. I was awfully sorry to see the old boy go and think he is foolish for having done so. . . . I have never seen such a spell in France before. Worst winter since 1870. Whiskey ate up my fatigue cap and last night my kepi. Yes, Page got the manuscript. Book will be out the 10th of this month.[17]

The fact that Jim's publisher expected to publish his book by the tenth of February after having received the manuscript in late December probably indicated that they expected an immediate and robust market for the book. That's a very fast turnaround, especially in the days before computerized typesetting and publishing.

Ted Parsons provided a vivid description of how "the machines freeze up while one is flying."

> During the next two months our regular patrols were carried on under the most harrowing of weather conditions. All the oil had to be heated before each patrol so that it wouldn't congeal before the motors were started. With such temperatures on the ground, flying above ten thousand feet was pure agony. With four others on a patrol over the lines, we got caught in a snow storm. My compass plate cracked, and the liquid in which it floated froze. For over an hour, with a failing motor I flew absolutely blind.[18]

Jim wrote a long, newsy letter to Marcelle on February 10:

> There hasn't been much doing since my return, tho we've flown every day. We have orders, for some reason or another, not to cross the lines, and naturally there are not many fights. The other day I went over and took a look at Noyon, however.
>
> Lieut. de Laage and I have volunteered to go "sausage" chasing [attacking observation balloons] in case of call. They asked for two men from each escadrille, and as de Laage offered his services I followed, for I'd do anything for him.
>
> Bigelow is out here now, and as he is a wonder on a piano we have acquired one of those instruments. The trouble is that the Captain thinks he can play and he drives us all crazy.

> I had a wonderful time in Paris, Marcelle, and I have you to thank for a great part of it. I appreciate immensely all you did for me and the time you gave me. I've never enjoyed any leave as much.
>
> Mrs. Weeks writes that she's coming over soon. I hope so. Pavelka sent me a letter from Malta saying he was having a great trip. Fred Prince, who's [*sic*] family objects to his being at the front, is going to Paris to take Cowden's old job. Flying French machines to British camps when one feels like it and for which one gets 260 francs a trip—*filon*—but *embusque* [a bonanza, but shirking].[19]

The "Bigelow" whom Jim referred to was Stephen Bigelow of Boston, Massachusetts. A graduate of Groton and Harvard, he traveled to France in 1916 and enlisted in French aviation by way of the Foreign Legion. He flew briefly with a French squadron, N.102, before being assigned to the Lafayette Escadrille on February 8.[20]

A few days after Jim wrote to Marcelle, he wound up back in the hospital. While most sources say his back was acting up again, he described his problem as being a *galle* (gall), which is a type of skin condition. While it's possible he was hospitalized for a skin condition, comments he made in his letters to Paul Rockwell make it appear that was a cover story to disguise the real problem—he was suffering from a sexually transmitted infection (STI), most likely gonorrhea.

Jim's condition was by no means an isolated case. By 1917, when Jim entered the hospital, the French army had treated one million soldiers for STIs since the beginning of the war.[21] Roughly three-quarters of the cases were for gonorrhea. Most of the rest were for syphilis. The problem was not limited to French troops. In 1916, one in five of all admissions of British and Dominion troops to hospitals in France were for STIs.[22] In some theaters, over 13 percent of all Australian troops were hospitalized for STIs each year.[23] Troops who stood knee deep in water and mud for weeks on end, with little or no protection from the weather, were at high risk of developing frostbite or trench foot. Statistically, however, their risk of contracting an STI was over five times greater.[24]

It's not hard to understand why the problem was so widespread. When the soldiers weren't standing knee deep in mud (or freezing in an open cockpit at 15,000 feet), they wanted to forget the war. They were young men who had a well-founded fear of being killed within the next week or two. The possibility of medical problems months or years in the future did not worry them. The French, British, German, and many other armies tried to reduce the rate of infection by sanctioning medically inspected brothels behind the lines. The inspections were often cursory, as were the twice-a-month "shortarm inspections" of troops conducted by the American army,[25] but they may have prevented some infections. Infections did not always cause immediate symptoms, though, so it was quite possible for infected men and women to pass the inspections and unintentionally spread the infections.

The brothels were not the only source of STI cases, however, and may not even have been the primary source. Wartime romances were very common, with both parties fearing they might never see one another again. Australian records show that troops stationed in England, far from the sanctioned brothels, contracted STIs at twice the rate of troops stationed in France.[26] And, of course, STIs were not just a wartime phenomenon. They had plagued society long before the war began. A study of American troops in stateside training camps, before they deployed to France, showed that over 80 percent of the troops treated for STIs had contracted the infection before they enlisted. Less than 20 percent of the cases were related to their military service.[27]

In the days before penicillin and other antibiotics, treatments for STIs were prolonged, risky, painful, and of questionable efficacy. Still, the treatments were better than no treatment at all. Untreated gonorrhea could lead to infertility, chronic pain, and chronic inflammation. Untreated syphilis could lead to gross disfigurement, insanity, and death. During World War I, syphilis was treated with injections of toxic mercury or arsenic compounds. A six-week regimen of injections was typical. Side effects could be severe, and a 1 percent fatality rate was considered good. Treatment continued until all symptoms disappeared, but this did not guarantee the patient was cured. A common saying at the time was "an afternoon with Bacchus, an evening with Venus, and a lifetime with Mercury."

Treatment of gonorrhea required twice-daily irrigation of the urethra and bladder with caustic antiseptics. This irrigation had to be retained for several hours, and in some cases infected tissue was scraped from the urethra. Treatment lasted until the patient was free of symptoms, typically five to seven weeks.[28]

Jim obviously was not happy to be back in the hospital, but he naively believed it would be for only a week or two. He wrote to Paul Rockwell on February 14:

> Well, here I am in a rotten dump not far from Amiens. Have no hope that they'll be able to fix me up here. Am telling the girls I have the *galle*, a sort of itch—so if anyone wants to know what I

> have tell them that. Big place, this is about 50 barracks. Most are for wounded. It's so damn cold that I can hardly hold a pen.
>
> Skip sent me a letter from Malta. He was having a big time and pleased with the trip.
>
> Great crowd of sergeants in my barrack and some are very interesting. There's another pilot, who comes from Zinn's escadrille*. Queer, but most of the chaps come from the artillery—suppose they get more of a chance to get in trouble than the infantry.[29]

Jim wrote to Marcelle the same day, providing a few additional details about the hospital:

> Well, here I am again in the hospital—this time with the itch so I won't be here long—week or ten days. . . . There are about fifty barracks. I'm in one with other "sous—offs" [under officers; i.e., sergeants and other noncommissioned officers]. Some of them are great chaps and mighty nice to me. Of course the food is very ordinary but sufficient. The main trouble is the cold. It's hard to write and nothing else to do. Walking is uninteresting for one cannot leave the confines.
>
> You certainly were nice to me while I was on permission Marcelle and I'm very grateful to you. I still enjoy in recollection the play, and of your presence I guard the most delightful souvenir, as one says in French.
>
> Everyone seems to get this itch at this time. The captain, Rumsey, Hill & Masson have all had it, and about a fourth of the men. It's tough luck to leave the front at this time but it's for only a short time, I hope.[30]

A few days later, Jim wrote to an old friend from the University of Virginia, Littleton W. Tazewell Jr. After apologizing for taking so long to respond to a letter that Littleton sent him (this is the letter where he said that seventy-five unanswered letters stacked up while he was writing his article on the Somme), Jim described winter flying in France:

> It was rotten in the Somme. Our barracks were in a wood and it rained most of the time. We flew in it. One time I had to cross the

---

* Frederick Zinn, who joined the Foreign Legion with Paul and Kiffin Rockwell, later transferred to aviation as an observer and aerial photographer. After the war, he would pioneer methods to locate, identify, and repatriate the remains of American airman shot down over enemy territory.

> lines at 150 meters [500 feet]. I could see the poor poilus crouched in shell holes beyond the first line. Boche machine guns opened up, but they only hit me once. After the bad weather, snow and a cold wave set in. Our poor little lion 'Whiskey' nearly froze stiff and we had to wrap him in coats. He ate the coats and then we froze.[31]

He closed with the surprising statement "I'd like to get in the land war for a time, it's so damned uninteresting up in the sky."

Jim wrote to Marcelle again on February 20. He'd been in the hospital for a week and was obviously getting bored, although he had met an interesting group of NCOs who had lived for years in French Indochina (Vietnam), Algeria, Morocco, and various Arab regions:

> Have just received your letter. It was like water to a man dying of thirst. When I arrived I sent Johnson a card giving him my address, but he's an irresponsible cuss and as yet I've not received a letter from the Escadrille, tho it is but a few kilometers from here. I could choke him. You're a dear to volunteer to send me anything but really there's nothing I want—save letters and I'll appreciate those. I don't even want anything to read for I'm trying to answer fifty letters that have piled up on me since last September.
>
> So, Captain Hall* is in town—well, well, I suppose when I get down again you and Hélène won't notice me. He's quite a wonder from all I hear.
>
> I am feeling in fine shape save for the itch. I let it go too long, and it will take longer to cure.[32]

It would be easy to assume that Chouteau Johnson, a friend of Jim's since their days together at the University of Virginia, and the other Lafayette pilots hadn't written or visited Jim because they were busy fighting a war, but the squadron log shows that, except for a few patrols on the day after Jim went to the hospital, the weather did not allow flying until the end of February.

Jim seemed cheerier when he wrote to Paul Rockwell on February 25, although he was obviously frustrated that his medical problems were still lingering on:

---

* It is not known who "Captain Hall" was, but references to Hélène du Bouchet appear in several of Jim's letters.

> Mighty glad to get your letter tonight. Ah, I'm feeling in good spirits all right, old boy, but damned anxious to get out of here. I felt cured two days ago. Nothing showed at all, even in morning, but this a.m. there was the damned reminder. I want to get fixed right for if I do this sausage work [attacking observation balloons] during the next attack and get taken prisoner, I don't want to land with trouble aboard me.
>
> I wrote Doc. Gros asking him if he knew where I could get better treatment. He suggested my going to American Hospital. Can't you see me there! With Hélène, Marcelle, et al.! I guess not.
>
> Mighty interesting crowd here and I'm getting lots of side lights [insights into interesting people, possibly for future writing]. World's Work London is using a new article of mine as well as W.W. New York. It's the copy I sent over by Mrs. Weeks, unfinished. Tell 'em about the book in Paris for I get a royalty, you know.
>
> I'm sorry, old pal you're feeling so blue. I'm glad the spring is most here. It will give you a change of mind I'm sure.[33]

The new article in the *World's Work* magazine was part 2 of their serialization of his book *Flying for France*. It appeared in the March 1917 issue. Essentially a slightly revised version of chapter 2 of Jim's book, it described the Escadrille's activities from late September to early November 1916. This was the period that Jim spent in the hospital, suffering from back problems, and his convalescent leave at Mrs. Weeks's apartment in Paris. Reading the article, however, it's not obvious that Jim was not with the squadron during this time. The squadron leave in Paris, the Oberndorf raid, the deaths of Kiffin Rockwell and Norman Prince, and the move to Cachy all are covered in the article*. Jim was anxiously awaiting the release of his book *Flying for France* as well, which is why he wanted Paul to make certain that Paul's friends and fellow war correspondents in Paris knew about it. It was supposed to have been published on February 20, but copies wouldn't reach Jim until mid-March.

Jim wrote to Marcelle on February 26, gently reminding her that he was still in the hospital, and it seemed like ages since he'd heard from her. Her mother had sent him cake and chocolates (implied but left unsaid was that Marcelle could at least send him a letter). Jim then began describing a most welcome softening of the weather:

---

*Jim's subsequent article, "The Day's Work of an American Airman on the Somme," would logically have been published as part 3 of this series, but as mentioned previously, Doubleday, Page & Co. decided to publish that in *National Service* magazine instead.

> It's been beautiful the last two days—just like spring. It's warm and there is that indefinable sweet smell in the air that goes with the rebirth of growing things. The soft caress of the gentle breeze fills one with a lively joy and makes one forget *la crise du charbon* [the coal crisis]. Here's a good "trade" for you. Excerpt from letter of one Betty Baldwin, date of Feb. 23: "Yesterday Marcelle had a tea party to which she very kindly asked me—I was simply overcome at the charm of that girl in her own home. She was delightful. No one who hasn't seen her as hostess knows how very charming she is, I think. Then too, she has such glorious hair. She looked ravishingly pretty and her manner was cordiality itself." Endorsed by J. R. McConnell.[34]

The relationship between the US and Germany was not enjoying "the soft caress of a gentle breeze" at this time. In 1915, Germany had declared a "war zone" around the British Isles, announcing that any ship sailing in those waters was subject to being sunk without warning by German U-boats. U-boats in use at that time were relatively slow and limited in range, but they still proved to be capable of significantly reducing the shipment of food and war materials to England. In the process, they also sank neutral ships, killed seamen from neutral nations, killed innocent passengers, and destroyed cargo that had no connection to the war. The US and other neutral nations protested, especially after the passenger liner *Lusitania* was sunk. Over a thousand passengers and crew were lost in that tragedy, including 128 Americans. Fearful of bringing the US into the war, the German kaiser imposed severe restrictions on U-boat operations. U-boat captains were supposed to surface beside unarmed merchant ships, use the threat of their deck gun to force the ship to stop, search the ship, and, if it was carrying contraband, allow the crew to leave on lifeboats before sinking the ship.

This restricted U-boat warfare proved to be ineffective. Merchant ships could often outrun the submarines. British and many neutral countries began arming merchant ships so they could sink any U-boat that surfaced, to warn them. The British also began using "Q-ships," armed navy ships disguised to look like unarmed merchants, which they sailed in known U-boat waters, hoping to sink any sub that surfaced. The failure of restricted submarine warfare showed itself in many ways. The Germans suffered huge losses at Verdun and the Somme, many of which were inflicted by munitions shipped from the US to the Allies. German troops were underfed, and civilians were facing starvation due to the British blockade, while Allied troops were well fed with food from around the world. The German military pressured the kaiser and the civilian government to resume unrestricted U-boat warfare, and the resumption was announced on February 1, 1917. On February 3, President Wilson broke off diplomatic relations with Germany.

Jim and many others hoped that the break in diplomatic relations meant the US was about to declare war on Germany. President Wilson wasn't ready to go that far, but Jim didn't know that. He hoped the US would soon enter the war and transfer the Lafayette pilots to the American Air Service. He wrote to Frank Page on February 23, thanking him for a royalty check of 861 francs* for *Flying for France.* Jim also said he hoped to soon transfer to the US Air Service, believing that since he and Bill Thaw were the most-senior pilots, they would receive high ranks.[35]

By the end of the month, however, President Wilson had taken no further action. Disappointed, Jim vented his feelings in a letter to his University of Virginia friend Henry A. Johnson:

> I was very pleased to get your letter of November 9th and to know that some of you at home realize the deplorable condition of the States, as well as we do over here. It is easier for us to judge for we have the comparisons to go by. I had hopes for the revival of the spirit of '76 after the break in diplomatic relations but I over estimated the country again. Its present attitude is pitifully childish. Why in hell doesn't it act instead of talk? . . . We look for hard fighting in the air this spring and summer. I've volunteered to bring down observation balloons during the next attack and I sure hope I can get away with it. During the winter they had us flying in all weather for a short period—even in rain. Crossed trenches at 400 feet, but was only hit once by the machine guns. The cinch days of aviation are over, alas![36]

The Germans had another surprise for the Allies in February. Since the war's opening battles of 1914, the Western Front had stagnated into trenches that ran from the North Sea to the Swiss border. The heavy fighting and huge losses in battles such as Verdun and the Somme had barely nudged these lines. Gains of a mile or two by either side were considered tremendous victories. The Germans knew that the Allies were planning another major offensive in the spring, and they were afraid that their exhausted troops, spread across a front that twisted and turned its way across France, couldn't withstand another bloodletting like the Somme.

---

* $150 in 1917 dollars, or $3,700 in 2024 dollars.

Their solution was to straighten out a huge salient or "bulge" that extended into the Allied lines between Arras and Soissons. It was about 70 miles wide at its base, and straightening this salient required German troops to retreat up to 25 miles in some places. Considering how hard they'd fought to advance a few yards at Verdun, or to keep the British from advancing a few yards at the Somme, a retreat of this magnitude seemed incomprehensible. But by shortening their lines, they freed roughly ten divisions of troops for use elsewhere, and the troops that remained fought from new, well-designed and heavily fortified positions.

The Germans staged a few small, limited withdrawals in mid-February, often to limit casualties from local Allied attacks. While Jim and others were hopeful that this was a sign of German weakness, Allied intelligence soon learned the truth. The Germans were falling back to a tremendously strong defensive position known as the Hindenburg Line. The Germans had spent months constructing multiple lines of trenches with concrete-reinforced underground shelters, strategically placed machine gun nests, and miles of barbed wire. In early March they began conducting a scorched-earth withdrawal. Even before this major retreat began, by late February the Lafayette pilots knew that the Germans would soon retreat to the Hindenburg Line. The pilots were asked to look for signs of the German retreat during their flights.[37]

Jim couldn't stand sitting in a hospital doing nothing while his buddies were monitoring a German retreat and preparing for a major French offensive. Once again there were sound medical reasons why he should stay in the hospital. His back still wasn't right, his new medical problem was unresolved, and his knees were beginning to bother him as well. Nevertheless, Jim left the hospital and returned to his squadron. Historian Philip Flammer, who worked directly with Paul Rockwell when writing a history of the Lafayette Escadrille and interviewed several of the pilots, said Jim left the hospital in March without permission.[38] Paul Rockwell wrote that "against orders and virtually deserting from the hospital, Jim rejoined the Lafayette Escadrille." Paul also wrote that "his back was so bad that his comrades had to help him dress."[39] Nordhoff and Hall, who had access to Jim's diary, wrote that "with a good deal of difficulty he persuaded the *Médicin Major* to let him go, and returned to the squadron on March 12."[40] Whether he left with permission or simply walked out of the hospital, Edmond Genet saw Jim in Paris on March 10,[41] and the squadron log shows that Jim was back in the air on the thirteenth.

SIXTEEN

Vive la France!

Jim wasted no time getting back into action. There was no flying on the day he returned to the squadron, but on the following day, March 13, he flew a lengthy patrol. That was a memorable day for Jim, since the author's copies of his books arrived in the morning. He wrote to Paul Rockwell after his patrol, enclosing 200 francs to repay a loan (a repayment that was probably enabled by his having received a royalty check from the publisher). Jim described the book and the events of the day:

> The books arrived a.m.—that is author's copies and I'm sending you one when I get your address. Not a bad set up, but of course one or two mistakes—and Frank Page got off nutty stuff in the introduction. . . . Lovell et al. doing well, but we have some queer specimens now. [Pilots Walter Lovell, Edward Hinkle, and Harold Willis had arrived while Jim was enduring his most recent hospital stay. He had served with Lovell and Willis in the Ambulance service at Pont-à-Mousson.]
>
> I'm worse off than when I went to hospital and feel damned discouraged. Don't know what to do about it. Seems hopeless. I'm trying to take care of myself as well as I can out here. Feel the old rheumatism in my knee. Have a little partition room all to myself now and like it immensely better than rooming with someone. There was a fire while I was away and I lost some of my stuff but not much of value, thank God.
>
> The Boches are going to drop back all along the front from Arras to Soissons. The line will approximate Cambrai–St. Quentin-

> Soissons. They are now tearing up railroads and burning villages thru all that territory. Noyon has been flooded. The clouds were at only 600 meters [2,000 feet] today and over the lines it was funk, for a big bombardment was going on and one was in the trajectory of the shells. Our guys were giving the Boches hell. I could feel the shells go by, and now and then I'd cut my motor, slip on a wing and listen to the exploding projectiles. It was very interesting but just at that time my motor went on the bum and I stretched out for home. Half way there the motor went completely and I landed in a field near Crèvecœur-le-Petit. Several men used my buss [airplane] in my absence and have put it on the bum. A new motor will be put on tomorrow and I'll go over and get it. Capt. offered me a Spad but I want the Nieuport for a while longer.[1]

Jim had good reason to be proud of his book. It's always exciting for an author to get the first copies of a new book, and it was obvious that this book was going to be a hit. Publishing figures for the book are not available, but on the basis of the advance royalties that Doubleday, Page, & Company gave to Jim, they must have expected healthy sales. The *New York Sun* "Books of the Week" called it "one of the most intimate and remarkable books of its kind that the war has brought forth."[2] American novelist Henry Sydnor Harrison wrote an article about Jim in *Collier's* magazine in which he said, "Why hang it, the fellow can write! . . . If I find a fault with Sergeant McConnell's book, it is that it says so little about Sergeant McConnell."[3] The book went into its second printing within a year, so sales must have been impressive. After the war, Nordhoff & Hall wrote, "His book *Flying for France* did genuine patriotic service in shaping public opinion before the US entered the war."[4] Paul Rockwell, who was the Lafayette Escadrille historian as well as a good friend of Jim's, said, "The first, and by far the best book, written by a pilot of the Escadrille Lafayette, was *Flying for France*, by James Rogers McConnell."[5]

Jim's comment to Paul that he was now suffering from rheumatism was yet another difficulty he had while flying. Paul Rockwell noted that Jim's back was still so stiff that his comrades had to help him dress,[6] he had to be helped in and out of his plane by two mechanics, and he couldn't turn around to see danger from behind.[7] But that didn't stop him from flying. The German retreat to the Hindenburg Line covered a huge amount of territory, and German fighters made it extremely difficult for slow-moving observation planes to cover the retreat. French fighter pilots were asked to look for signs of retreat during their patrols and report what they saw. Jim flew every day but one during his first week back, and on one of those days he flew two patrols.

Jim was in a reflective mood that night, when he wrote in his diary. The next day would be his thirtieth birthday, and it was natural to think about where he was and how he got there. He wrote, "This war may kill me, but I have it to thank for much."[8]

Bad weather prevented morning patrols for several days, but on the afternoon of March 16, Jim led a patrol of five planes over the lines.[9] Their initial objective was to shoot down enemy observation balloons, but none were spotted. Apparently, the Germans had already withdrawn their balloons. The patrol climbed to 8,000 feet, and Jim led them into what had been German territory, searching for the retreating enemy.

The "front lines" that Jim was used to seeing no longer existed, since the Germans had abandoned their trenches in their retreat to the Hindenburg Line. He was looking for the rear guard—improvised positions in cellars or behind walls, and similar natural defensive points where they could protect the retreating troops from Allied attacks. It was essential to report these ever-changing positions as quickly as possible, since the advancing French patrols tried to harass the retreating enemy but didn't want to walk into a trap.

Normally, pilots could tell when they crossed the lines because antiaircraft batteries would immediately open fire on them, but the Germans had withdrawn their artillery too. Only one battery fired on Jim's patrol, and he couldn't be certain that was located near the front line. What he could see were tracer rounds from German machine guns. The streams of luminous rounds flashing past reminded him of "water falling in the sunlight," although these drops were deadly and were falling up. The tracers let him know where the Germans were, and the utter destruction on the ground let him know where the Germans had been. As they braved the bone-numbing slipstream to survey the ground beneath them, they saw mile after mile of utter desolation. Smoke was rising from the burned ashes of many villages—Écuvilly, Beaulieu-les-Fontaines—and the town of Ham was still in flames. Orchards had been cut down, railroads were torn up, telephone and electric lines were torn down, and bridges had been dynamited. Some of the trees that lined the roads had been cut down so they blocked the road. The barren ground beneath them looked uninhabited, as indeed it was. The Germans had rounded up the able-bodied inhabitants and taken them with them, so they couldn't help the Allies when they moved into the abandoned territory.

What they couldn't see from the air was that some of the trees that were still standing beside the roads had been cut halfway through, so it wouldn't be safe to use the road until the Allies finished cutting the trees down and hauled them off. Wells were poisoned. Delayed-fuse mines were buried and booby traps were set. Choice souvenirs such as a seemingly abandoned spiked helmet or Luger pistol on the floor of an abandoned German dugout could trigger a deadly explosion when moved. The Germans were making it as difficult as possible for the Allies to make use of the abandoned territory. When they abandoned their headquarters in Péronne, 35 miles northeast of Ravenel, they burned the town to the ground and left a sign on the ruins of the town hall that read "Don't be angry, be amazed."[10]

Jim described the mission to Marcelle:

> The season for flying has now opened and a lot of new things have been assigned us such as observation work too far in the lines for slow machines. Today Lovell, Willis, two others [Genet and Soubiran] and I went 35 kilometers inside to do reconnaissance. We flew low and saw many ground details. You know that the Boches are preparing to withdraw all along this front and will retire to what is known as the Hindenburg line roughly approximated by Cambrai, St. Quentin, Chauny, and Soissons. They, by so doing, evacuate a fifth of the ground they hold in France. They are tearing up railroads, burning towns and destroying everything in the area.
>
> Have a little partition room to myself and like it much better than rooming with someone. It's just the size of a steamer cabin, and has been lots of fun fixing up.[11]

Jim would never get a chance to finish fixing up his room. On the nineteenth, he, Ted Parsons, and Edmond Genet took off on a morning patrol to protect a French reconnaissance machine. The ground temperature was hovering around freezing when they took off, but it quickly dropped to subzero (Fahrenheit) as they gained altitude. The oil in Parsons's plane almost immediately turned sludgy, clogged an oil line, and forced him to land with a dead engine. Jim and Edmond Genet continued on their own. Genet recorded the flight in his diary:

> Cloudy windy day. Escadrille on duty this a.m. MacConnell [*sic*], I and Parsons went out for 3rd Patrol at 9 o'clock to protect French reconnaissance machine around Ham. Parsons had to return before we reached the lines on account of motor trouble. "Mac" and I kept on—he leading. We stayed under 2,000 metres [6,500 feet] and patrolled around Ham over the French *relage avions* [reconnaissance planes] until about 10 o'clock. Then "Mac" headed north towards St. Quentin and I followed to the rear and above him. North of Ham I discovered two German machines much higher than we coming towards us to attack. One was much nearer than the other

> and began to come towards "Mac." I immediately started up towards it and met it at 2,200 metres [7,200 feet]—leaving Mac to take care of the end. The German Avion was a biplace [two-seater] and his gunner opened fire on me at 200 yds. As the pilot began to circle around me, I opened fire with my incendiary bullets and headed directly for them. The German's first few shots cut one main wing support in half and an explosive bullet hit the guiding rod of the left aileron and cut open a nice hole in my left cheek. I scarcely noticed it and kept on firing until we were scarcely 25 yds apart. We passed close and I peaked [piqued; i.e., dove] down. The Germans didn't follow but an anti-aircraft battery shelled me for quite awhile. At 1,000 metres I stopped and circled around for 15 minutes in search of Mac and the second Boche but the clouds were thick and I saw nothing. I was afraid my supports would break entirely and my wound was hurting some so I headed for St. Just at a low altitude reaching there at 10:45 hoping all the way back that Mac had preceded me but when I arrived I found he had not and tho Lufberry [*sic*] and Lt. de Laage have been out over the region north of Ham with their Spads this afternoon to look for him. (de Laage also landed to ask the troops if they saw him brought down.) They found nothing and the chances are Mac was either brought down by the German machine or else wounded in combat and forced to land in their territory and so is a prisoner. It's the best we can hope for—that he is at least alive. I feel dreadfully—my wound, tho a bit painful, is nothing compared with my grief for poor "Mac's" loss. The Commandant told me, when I described the combat to him this morning, that I fought bravely. I wish I had been able to do more for MacConnell. The French and English forces are advancing beyond Nesle, Ham, and Noyon and with few losses. Perhaps to-morrow will bring forth better news of "Mac." . . . My machine has been nearly repaired this afternoon, and as my wound is scarcely grave enough to bother over I hope I shall be out on service again either to-morrow afternoon or at least the following day. Thank God I escaped so luckily to-day but I do wish I had brought down that damned Boche machine and that poor MacConnell was back safely with us to-night. If he was killed I know he met his end bravely fighting. God grant he isn't dead![12]

The weather didn't allow flying for the next two days. On March 22, Genet flew two patrols in the morning, along with several other members of the squadron, but nobody saw any sign of Jim's plane. Cold weather and clouds interfered with the flights. Several pilots had to return, and a few were forced to land at other airfields because of cold-induced engine and machine gun problems. Harold Willis suffered frostbite on his face. Afternoon patrols were canceled because of high winds and snow.[13]

Jim's disappearance made headlines across the US. Most correctly reported he was missing. Less careful editors reported he was "killed in battle."[14] Jim's editor Frank Page wrote to Mrs. Weeks, who was still in the US, on the twenty-second, letting her know that he read in the *New York World* that Jim had fallen behind German lines. "I have known Jim for a good many years, have known him very well as one of the best men I have ever met in my life, and I cannot tell you how much of a shock to me it was to hear of his bad luck."[15] He said Jim had told him on several occasions how much Mrs. Weeks had done for the men in France, and he was sending her a copy of Jim's book at Jim's request. When she received the book, she saw that it was dedicated to "Mrs. Alice S. Weeks—Who having lost a splendid son in the French Army has given to a great number of us other Americans in the war the tender sympathy and help of a mother."

In France, the squadron continued searching for signs of Jim's plane. On March 23, they received word from a group of French cavalry that had witnessed Genet's battle with the German two-seater. They said they also saw two German planes attack the other French plane and bring it down. They couldn't tell whether that plane came down safely or crashed. Genet wrote to Paul Rockwell to give him this news, adding that if he'd known there were three German planes instead of two, he wouldn't have strayed so far from Jim. Genet was still hopeful that Jim had survived and been taken prisoner.[16]

On March 23, at about 10:00 p.m., the news everyone feared was confirmed. The squadron received a message that advancing French troops had found the wreckage of Nieuport #2055 near the Bois l'Abbé. The pilot, a sergeant, was found lying dead beside the plane. German soldiers had apparently taken all identifying papers from the body and had also taken his boots*.[17] A doctor estimated he had been dead for three days.[18]

The next day, Capt. Thénault flew to an airfield near Ham, recently abandoned by the Germans, and found someone to drive him to the wreckage. It was in a field beside the road from Bois l'Abbé to Petit-Détroit, about a

---

* Germany was running short of leather, and warm, fur-lined aviator boots were highly prized by German soldiers. The soldiers also took a silver Lafayette Escadrille pin from his uniform, but this detail wasn't known until a nephew of one of the soldiers sold the pin to an antique dealer 105 years later.

mile and a half south of Jussey. Jim's "Hot Foot" emblem was still visible amid the wreckage of the plane. A nearby battalion of *chasseurs* [light infantry or cavalry] made a coffin out of wood from a wrecked house and buried Jim's body, with a simple wooden cross over the grave.[19] (Chouteau Johnson would later salvage the canvas from Jim's plane with the Hot Foot emblem on it and mail it to Lewis Crenshaw, who, like Jim, had once been elected King of the Hot Foot Society.[20])

Groupe de Combat 13 commandant Phillipe Féquant, at Jim's grave, April 14, 1917. The machine gun and other parts of Jim's plane can be seen on top of the grave. *Photo courtesy of Jean-Marc Simon*

While the *chasseurs* were arranging for Jim's burial, a peasant woman told them she had witnessed Jim's last fight. She said the French plane was battling a German plane when another German plane dove from above, got behind the French plane, and shot it down. The victory was credited to Leutnant Heinrich Kämmerer of Jasta 20.[21]

Capt. Thénault returned to the squadron with a heavy heart. He looked at the photo of Jim, Victor Chapman, Kiffin Rockwell, Norman Prince, and himself standing in front of a Nieuport. That photo was taken in Luxeuil less than a year previously. The first four Americans to report to N.124—and now all four were dead. Capt. Thénault was the only survivor. After Jim's death, he always referred to that picture as the "tragic photograph."[22] He wrote to Jim's sister Julia Follansbee in Chicago, saying that Jim "loved France and had faced with *sang froid* the thought of giving his life for her. His last wish must have been a cry of '*Vive la France!*'"[23]

Paul Rockwell was devastated by Jim's death. He wrote, "The announcement of the death of the best comrade I had turns a knife in the cruel wound caused by the death of my own brother, Kiffin, which had not healed and never can heal."[24] Jim's mother, Sarah, poured out her grief in a letter to Paul. She had lived in fear for months, with a premonition of his death, but now felt that his love for France and his brave fight for human rights were lifting her frail spirit to meet his in pride and love.[25] Mrs. Weeks did not write of her grief, but one can only imagine how she felt. She had lost her son Kenneth in the war. She had become very fond of Kiffin, who called

Leutnant Heinrich Kämmerer, seated on the wheel of his Albatros D.III. *Public domain photo provided by Jean-Marc Simon*

her "my dear second mother," and he had been killed. And now Jim, who stayed with her whenever he was in Paris and who dedicated his book to her, had joined Kenneth and Kiffin.

Jim's death also hit Edmond Genet hard. He blamed himself for leaving the dogfight in which Jim was killed, even though he himself was wounded and his plane was seriously damaged. Already a reckless pilot, he vowed to do whatever it took to shoot down at least one German to avenge Jim's death.[26]

Chouteau Johnson, who'd been a friend of Jim's since their days together at the University of Virginia, grieved over Jim's death. He wrote their mutual friend Lewis Crenshaw that Jim "died for the cause he loved and chose as being for freedom and liberty against a tyrant. He died as he fought all the way through, game to the core and without a hesitation against odds. I take my hat off to old Jim and hope to mess up a few Huns to avenge him."[27]

Jim's "should I not return" letter provided a few instructions for the disposition of his worldly possessions. Most of his clothes, shoes, etc. were to be given away. His diary, photos, medals, best uniform, and similar personal items were to be sent to Paul Rockwell.[28] (Jim had previously asked Paul to sort through his belongings if anything happened to him, and to forward items to his sister Julia Follensbee.) He left his sleeping bag to Ted Parsons, who couldn't afford to buy one himself and suffered terribly from the cold weather as a result.[29]

Jim closed his instructions in classic McConnell style:

My burial is of no import. Make it as easy as possible for yourselves. I have no religion and do not care for any service. If the omission would embarrass you I presume I could stand the performance.

Good luck to the rest of you. God damn Germany and *Vive la France.*[30]

EPILOGUE

The Lafayette Escadrille pilots honored Jim's request and did not conduct a religious burial service. His American and French friends did, however, organize a memorial service for him in Paris, which was attended by many pilots, ambulance drivers, and other friends. Jim was posthumously awarded the Medaille Militaire (Military Medal) and a palm indicating a second award for the Croix de Guerre (War Cross) he earned as an ambulance driver. He was also given a Volunteer Combatants Cross, the Battle of Verdun Medal, and other military decorations. A French engineering unit later erected a handsome tomb over his grave, and the landowner deeded the site in perpetuity to Judge McConnell and his family.[1]

Another memorial service for Jim was held in Carthage, North Carolina, on April 1, 1917. On April 5, a special edition of the Carthage newspaper was devoted to Jim McConnell, printing speeches made at the memorial service as well as letters and articles paying tribute to Jim. The town erected a granite obelisk to the memory of Jim on the courthouse square, and later that year the first public hospital in Moore County was named after him. The government of France donated a bronze plaque that was placed at the entrance to that hospital.

There were also memorial services for Jim at the University of Virginia, and the university commissioned the internationally renowned sculptor Gutzon Borglum to produce a statue of McConnell (Gutzon was the sculptor who later created the Mount Rushmore National Memorial). The sculpture was unveiled in 1919 and depicts Jim as Icarus, a tragic winged youth from Greek mythology who died when he flew too close to the sun. The sculpture bears the inscription "Soaring like an eagle into new heavens of valor and devotion."

In 1928, Jim's body was moved to a crypt in the newly constructed Lafayette Escadrille Memorial near Paris. The Seven Society, a secret philanthropic fraternity that Jim joined while at the University of Virginia, donated 7,777.77 francs (about $2,000 US then, worth $37,000 in 2024) to the construction of this memorial.[2] Members of the Seven Society are revealed only after their death, and a Seven Society emblem next to Jim's crypt marks his membership. The citizens of the French village of Flavyle-Martel, near where Jim was shot down, still maintain a memorial on the site of his original grave. They refer to it as *l'entroit de l'aviateur* (place of the aviator).[3]

Jim is still well remembered in the town of Carthage, North Carolina. The memorial obelisk still stands beside the courthouse, and a giant mural depicts Jim's ambulance and flying service. The hospital has long since been replaced by more-modern medical facilities, but the plaque is now proudly displayed at the Gilliam-McConnell Airport. The airport also hosts a small museum to Jim McConnell.

It may seem ironic that in a war where millions of men died with no memorial, where hundreds of thousands disappeared with no known grave, and where the deaths of millions were mourned only by their families and friends, one man should receive so many tributes. There are several reasons why Jim's life and death were memorialized then and are still remembered today. Jim was an American, a citizen of a country that was not at war and whose president actively discouraged Americans from having anything to do with the war. When Jim defied the president and sailed to France to join the American Ambulance Service, he was probably motivated as much by a sense of adventure as by a desire to do humanitarian service, but when he saw what was happening to the soldiers and civilians in the war zone, he quickly became committed to the cause of France. He saw the war as a fight to save civilization from a barbaric horde. No longer content to serve as a noncombatant, he decided to take an active role in the war.

Jim became a pilot, one of the pioneers of military aviation, at a time when only a few hundred pilots flew combat missions. Only a handful of those pilots were Americans. Aviation was so new, and the brutal fighting that killed thousands of men to capture a few yards of trench was so grim, that the public focused its attention on pilots. The reality of fighting in the air might have been grim, but to the public it appeared to be clean, chivalrous, and glamorous. Pilots were idolized in the way that movie stars, rock stars, and sports stars would be idolized by succeeding generations.

Jim wasn't just any pilot; he was a pilot who could and did write about this fascinating new concept of aerial warfare. His articles and his book about flying in combat, and his previous articles about driving an ambulance, caught the public's attention and helped make the Lafayette Escadrille famous. More importantly, they helped sway US public opinion away from neutrality and toward supporting France. In the process, they also made Jim McConnell famous. His writings were certainly not the only thing that changed public opinion, but they played a part. A little over two weeks after Jim was shot down, the United States declared war on Germany. Had he lived to see that, he would have been overjoyed.

It may also seem surprising that so much attention was paid to a fighter pilot who never shot down an enemy plane. This did not mean that Jim was a bad pilot. Shooting down an aircraft that was maneuvering and shooting back was extremely difficult. As Jim put it, "God in Boston it's a hard job!" Twenty-five of the thirty-eight pilots who flew with the Lafayette Escadrille never shot down an enemy plane while they flew with the escadrille, and in fact most pilots in World War I failed to score a confirmed victory.[4] The ability to maneuver in three dimensions, anticipate which way the enemy plane will turn next, and calculate how much to "lead" a fast-moving opponent when aiming was a skill that defied prediction. Some pilots developed this skill, but most did not. Only a few perfected the skill to the point where they became famous aces. Jim was doing very well to have survived combat as long as he did. Estimates as to the average life expectancy of a World War I pilot at the front vary greatly. Two weeks, eleven days, fifteen hours over the front—the one thing they all have in common is that it wasn't very long. Many pilots, such as poor Clyde Balsley, were shot down during their first or second flight over the lines. Jim survived for ten months, and he survived flying over the Battle of Verdun and the Battle of the Somme—two of the deadliest battles in the air war.

The fact that Jim never succeeded in shooting down an enemy plane doesn't mean he didn't help win the war. Confirmed victories are a convenient "scorecard" for fighter pilots, but the real purpose of fighter pilots is to enable friendly aircraft to carry out their missions and to prevent enemy aircraft from carrying out theirs. Reconnaissance, artillery spotting, bombing, and close air support are the air missions that win wars. World War I was the biggest artillery duel in history, which made reconnaissance and artillery spotting critically important. Every time Jim flew cover for French reconnaissance and artillery spotting aircraft, he was helping to win the war. And every time he attacked an enemy two-seater, even if he didn't succeed in shooting it down, he was diverting it from its mission. One World War I fighter pilot described his role as that of a "flying policeman." Most of the time he wasn't fighting; he was merely patrolling his beat, protecting the good citizens, and intimidating evildoers into staying on their side of the lines. Jim was a good policeman.

Sadly, Jim's Christmas night superstition about thirteen men at the table came true. So did Lt. de Laage's prediction that there would be more than one man who would die during the coming year. It probably would not have surprised Jim to learn that he would be the first. Marcelle later wrote that

> I wistfully recall the last time we entertained dear Jim McConnell. We were about to be served coffee in the Salon & as he stood with

> his back to the fireplace, he said in a quiet voice: "Well I suppose I'm the next one to go." Those prophetic words wrenched our hearts & alas! Came true the 19th of March 1917.[5]

Jim McConnell was the last American pilot to be killed before the US declared war on Germany. His death began a streak of "Bad-Luck Mondays" for the squadron. Before the year was out, four more American pilots would meet their fate on a Monday. The first to fall was Edmund Genet, the pilot who accompanied Jim on his final flight. He fell a few weeks after Jim, and he became the first American pilot to be killed after the US entered the war. He was followed by Ronald Hoskier, Douglas MacMonagle, and Courtney Campbell, all of whom were shot down and killed on Mondays. Caporal (corporal) Jean Dressy, Lt. de Laage's orderly, was flying with Ronald Hoskier in a two-seater when Hoskier was shot down, adding a French victim to the Monday curse. None of these men were at the Christmas dinner where Jim and Lt. de Laage made their predictions, and most hadn't even joined the escadrille yet, but that didn't save them. Paul "Skipper" Pavelka, who was at the dinner, was also killed on a Monday, but he didn't die in combat. He was killed in a freak horseback-riding incident in Salonika. Lt. de Laage, who made the prediction that there would be more than one death, was also killed during that fateful year. He died in a flying accident, but his death occurred on a Wednesday.

Despite Jim's fame, there is still much that we do not know about him. At his memorial service in Paris, three women showed up dressed in black, each believing they were his intended bride.[6] Jim's mother, Sarah McConnell, and Paul Rockwell both thought that Jim was engaged, but they each thought he was engaged to a different person. Paul thought he was engaged to Marcelle Guerin, while Sarah thought he was engaged to Hélène du Bouchet. The identity of the third woman is not known, but she *may* have been Betty Baldwin. Reportedly, two more women showed up dressed in black at the memorial service in Carthage, North Carolina, but there is nothing to indicate who they might have been.

Paul and Jim were very close friends. Paul knew more about Jim's activities in France than Jim's mother did, so it seems probable that Paul was correct and Marcelle Guerin was Jim's intended. Paul Rockwell said that Jim was the "great and lasting romance" of Marcelle's life, although she eventually married twice—"first to a highly distinguished Belgian diplomat, then to a White Russian nobleman refugee from the Red Terror."[7] (Hélène du Bouchet eventually married Lafayette Escadrille pilot Walter Lovell[8]). Jim's letters to Marcelle certainly indicate they were very close, but we have those letters only because Paul Rockwell convinced Marcelle to donate them to the University of Virginia. We do not have any letters he may have written to Hélène, or Betty, or any other contenders (a quick perusal of his letters to Paul reveals twelve possible romantic interests, but there may have been more). Jim kept a diary, which was presumably given to Paul after his death. Nordhoff and Hall quoted from this diary in their 1920 history of the Lafayette Flying Corps, but its whereabouts today is unknown. If it is ever found, it might answer a lot of questions.

Speculation about Jim's social life should not obscure the fact that Jim was a hero. He may have been seeking adventure when he came to France, but he stayed out of a sense of duty. He risked his life to save others as an ambulance driver. He saw the carnage of war firsthand, and he saw what bullets and shells could do to the human body, but he did not run to safety. He volunteered to take a direct part in the war as a fighter pilot. He fought in the deadly skies over Verdun and the Somme, and he saw friends and fellow pilots killed and seriously wounded. He experienced several landing accidents that totally destroyed his plane, one of which left him with a permanent back injury. Many fighter pilots relied upon psychological "crutches" to keep flying—believing that it couldn't happen to them, the bullet with their name on it hadn't been made, "I'm too good of a pilot to be shot down," etc. Jim had no such illusions. His accidents, and the bullets that riddled his plane when he engaged other aircraft, proved that it could happen to him. He said himself that he was not a great fighter pilot, but he continued flying. He had enough experience to know that his back injury made him more likely to be a victim than a victor. He had multiple opportunities to back out, but he would not desert France or his buddies. France needed fighter pilots to protect observation machines, to observe enemy troop movements, and to chase German aircraft from the skies. Jim did his duty to the end. Perhaps the best summary of his life is written on the memorial to him in Carthage North Carolina:

He fought for humanity, liberty, and democracy.

The Aviator statue at UVA. *Photo courtesy of Daniel Kieth Addison*

ACKNOWLEDGMENTS

I could not have written this book without a great deal of help from many people, and I am deeply indebted to everyone who helped me do it. My friend and noted World War I historian Steve Ruffin has been especially helpful. In addition to supplying me with photos and documents, he proofread every chapter for technical accuracy and literary content. He saved me from making several embarrassing errors, and many times he steered me back to the primary focus of the book when I began to wander off into some side issue that interested me but no one else. I am similarly indebted to historian Dennis Gordon. His incredible work *The Lafayette Flying Corps* was a treasure trove of facts about the pilots Jim McConnell flew with, and on the rare occasions when I had a question that wasn't answered by his book, he was quick to respond by email and set me straight. French historian Jean-Marc Simon of Muille-Villette France was also very helpful, sending me photos and information about Jim while encouraging me with his infectious enthusiasm.

I am very much indebted to the University of Virginia, and to Barbie Selby of the library staff, for sharing their Jim McConnell collection with me. (Barbie has since retired, and I hope she's enjoying her retirement. She's earned it!) My work with UVA was made more difficult by the COVID pandemic, which struck in the middle of my research and pretty much shut down all the libraries in the country. The librarians at UVA worked with me through this difficult period, providing what material they could via email, and when things began to open up a little, they found a way to send a large microfiche collection of McConnell documents to a library near me that had a microfiche reader. They also provided me with many photographs and put me in touch with a former UVA library employee, Mr. Douglas Tanner, who had worked with Paul Rockwell during the donation of these materials. Mr. Tanner graciously answered many questions via email and shared his own thoughts and writings about Jim McConnell with me.

Ms. Alice Thomas of the Moore County Library in Carthage, North Carolina, was also very helpful during the pandemic, sending me photocopies of Jim McConnell materials that they had on file. She shared even more material with me when I was finally able to visit Carthage in person, as did Joanna King of the Carthage Museum and Roland Gilliam of the James McConnell Museum.

Mr. Thomas Camden, Seth McCormick-Goodhart, and Lisa McCown of the Washington and Lee University Library contributed to this book, although they may not know it. They were extremely helpful to me when I was researching Kiffin Rockwell for my previous book. Jim McConnell and Kiffin flew together and were good friends, and many of the letters they shared for that book and especially the unpublished draft of Capt. Thénault's memoir were very helpful for this book. I am also indebted to them for providing many photos, along with the National Air and Space Museum, the State Archives of North Carolina, and the Virginia Military Institute.

Jim McConnell's niece, Janeice McConnell, shared many interesting stories with me during a long telephone interview, and she shared many documents with me following that interview. Jim's relatives Alexandra Truitt and Julie von Erfa also aided me in my research.

And last, but certainly not least, my wife, Betsy, made invaluable contributions to this book. I was constantly bouncing ideas off her, she proofread every word of the manuscript (including many that didn't make it into the final draft, thanks to her keen insight and feedback), and she never complained about the thousands of hours I spent researching and writing. Thank you, Betsy—I love you.

In closing, I would like to say this to everyone who helped me with this book: Thank you. You did your best. Any errors or shortcomings in the final product are entirely my own.

CAST OF CHARACTERS

Andrew, A. Piatt: Director of the American Ambulance Field Service.

Bach, James: An American pilot who was captured landing agents behind enemy lines before the Lafayette Escadrille was formed. He was accused of being a mercenary, and his trial and acquittal established the precedent that volunteers in the French Foreign Legion were not mercenaries and should be treated as prisoners of war instead of being executed.

Baldwin, Betty: A 1914 graduate of Bryn Mawr, and a possible romantic interest of Jim's. The daughter of Professor and Mrs. James Mark Baldwin, who were living in Paris, Betty was permanently injured when the ship she was crossing the English Channel in was torpedoed by a German U-boat.

Balsley, Clyde: An American pilot from Texas who flew with Jim in the Lafayette Escadrille. He was seriously wounded in a dogfight shortly after his arrival, having fired only one bullet in combat.

Bigelow, Stephen: An American who volunteered to fly for France after graduating from Harvard. He flew briefly with a French unit before joining the Lafayette Escadrille in February 1917.

Buswell, Leslie: A British volunteer ambulance driver assigned to the same ambulance team as Jim. He wrote a book titled *Ambulance No. 10: Personal Letters from the Front.*

Chapman, Victor: An American who joined the Foreign Legion, fought in the trenches, and then became a pilot. A good friend of Kiffin Rockwell's, Victor was probably the most idealistic pilot in the Lafayette Escadrille.

Cowdin, Elliot: An American pilot who flew with the French before the Lafayette Escadrille was formed, and then flew with that unit. Older than most of the other pilots, he suffered from the strain of combat and was eventually invalided out of the squadron.

Crenshaw, Lewis D.: One of Jim's classmates at the University of Virginia and a frequent correspondent. He succeeded Jim as "King of the Hot Foot Society" and later became the first secretary of the UVA Alumni Association.

Decker, A. R.: Newspaper correspondent at Pont-à-Mousson. Mr. Decker managed an ironworks in the city before the war, stayed after the war began, and wrote articles for the *Chicago Daily News*.

de Laage de Meux, Lt. Alfred: A French executive officer, second in command of the Lafayette Escadrille.

du Bouchet, Hélène: The daughter of an American surgeon, Dr. August du Bouchet, who lived in Paris during the war. A possible romantic interest of Jim's; her name appears in several of his letters.

Eyre, Lincoln: An American war correspondent for the *New York Times*. Eyre asked Jim McConnell to provide him with information so Eyre could write an article about the American aviators. That collaboration failed, and Jim eventually wrote the article himself. After the war, Eyre was granted an exclusive interview with Vladimir Lenin that gained worldwide attention.

Follansbee, Julia Rogers McConnell: Paul's older sister and frequent correspondent.

Genet, Edmond: An American who joined the Foreign Legion and fought in the trenches before transferring to aviation. A great-great-grandson of Citizen Genet, Edmond joined the Lafayette Escadrille in January 1917.

Gros, Dr. Edmund L.: An American physician who spent many years in France. Dr. Gros worked closely with the American Ambulance Corps and helped form the Lafayette Escadrille. He also gave physical exams to Americans who volunteered to fly for France.

Guerin, Marcelle: Jim's girlfriend and steady correspondent during his time in France. She was born in France but studied nursing in the US when war broke out. They met on board a ship that took both of them to France.

Hall, Bert: An American pilot who flew with Jim in the Lafayette Escadrille. Bert joined the Foreign Legion at the beginning of the war and fought in the trenches with Kiffin Rockwell and Bill Thaw before transferring to aviation. Unpopular with some of his fellow pilots, Bert scored several victories, told some very tall tales, and won more than his fair share in poker games.

Happe, Capt. Felix: Commander of a French bombing squadron. Nicknamed "the Red Pirate," he was famous for being careless with his own and his pilots' lives.

Haviland, Willis: An American ambulance driver who served with Jim in Section 2 and later transferred to aviation. He joined the Lafayette Escadrille in October 1916.

Hill, Dudley: An American pilot who flew with Jim in the Lafayette Escadrille. "Dud" Hill managed to sneak through the medical exams and flight training despite the fact that he was blind in one eye.

Hoskier, Ronald Wood: An American from South Orange, New Jersey, who dropped out of Harvard to drive ambulances and fly for France. He joined the Lafayette Escadrille in December 1916.

Johnson, Charles Chouteau "Chute": One of Jim's classmates at the University of Virginia, briefly a business partner, and later a fellow pilot in the Lafayette Escadrille.

Johnson, Henry A.: A friend and occasional correspondent of Jim's. Jim met Henry when they were both students at the University of Virginia. Henry was learning to fly in the US while Jim served in the Lafayette Escadrille.

Leygues, Marie Francoise Jeanne: Paul Rockwell's fiancée, later his wife. She was the daughter of Monsieur Georges Leygues, an influential politician who after the war would become the prime minister of France.

Lovell, Walter: An American volunteer ambulance driver who became a pilot. He served with Jim in the Ambulance Service and later joined Jim in the Lafayette Escadrille.

Lufbery, Gervais Raoul: The leading ace of the Lafayette Escadrille. Born in France to an American father, Raoul was American by birth who traveled extensively before the war, often serving as a mechanic to a French exhibition pilot Marc Pourpe.

Marshall, Emil: An American volunteer who was mistakenly transferred from the French army to the Lafayette Escadrille without going through flight training. He served the escadrille in an administrative role while waiting to attend flight school and voluntarily went back to the infantry when he failed to pass the medical exam to become a pilot.

Masson, Pierre Didier: A French pilot assigned to the Lafayette Escadrille. Often assumed to be an American, Didier had lived for several years in the US, but there is no evidence he ever became an American citizen. Before World War I started, Didier flew for Mexican rebels in 1913 during the Mexican Revolution.

McConnell, Mayo Methot: Jim's stepmother. Judge McConnell married Mayo Methot when Jim was fifteen. Sometimes confused with her niece, Mayo Methot, who married Humphrey Bogart.

McConnell, Samuel Parsons: Jim McConnell's father. Often referred to as Judge McConnell because he served several years as a Cook County, Illinois, circuit court judge.

McConnell, Sarah Rogers: Jim McConnell's mother and frequent correspondent. She suffered a nervous breakdown after the death of Jim's older brother and eventually separated from her husband.

Mowrer, Paul Scott: A newspaper correspondent for the *Chicago Daily News*, living in Paris. Jim sold some articles to him.

Page, Arthur: Editor of the *World's Work* magazine and brother of Jim's friend Frank Page.

Page, Frank: A friend of Jim's in North Carolina. The son of a cofounder of the Doubleday, Page & Co. publishing house (and US ambassador to England), Frank would become the editor of Jim's book *Flying for France.*

Page, Walter Hines: Founder of the *World's Work* magazine, cofounder of the Doubleday, Page & Co. publishing house, US ambassador to England, and father of Jim's friend Frank Page.

Parsons, Edwin "Ted": An American pilot who flew for Pancho Villa during the Mexican Revolution, drove an ambulance in France, and joined the Lafayette Escadrille in January 1917. Ted flew several missions with Jim and wrote a very entertaining book about the escadrille after the war.

Pavelka, Paul "Skipper": An American pilot who flew with Jim in the Lafayette Escadrille. Paul served in the trenches with Kiffin Rockwell before he became a pilot and had several harrowing adventures in the air, including having his engine catch fire over the German lines and having his electrical system fail, leaving him totally in the dark during a night flight.

Prince, Frederick: Norman Prince's older brother. He followed in his brother's footsteps and learned to fly in France, completing his training just shortly before Norman was killed. He was briefly assigned to the squadron in October 1916, but his influential father soon had him transferred to a noncombat position.

Prince, Norman: An American prewar pilot who sailed to France and voluntarily joined French aviation. Working with Bill Thaw and others, he helped form the Lafayette Escadrille.

Rockwell, Kiffin: A friend of Jim's and the brother of Paul Rockwell. An idealistic pilot in the Lafayette Escadrille, Kiffin left for France during the first week of the war. He joined the Foreign Legion, was wounded during a bayonet attack, and became a pilot after recovering.

Rockwell, Paul: Jim's best friend in France. Paul joined the Foreign Legion with his brother Kiffin early in the war. Paul was wounded by shellfire and invalided out of the legion, but he stayed in France as a war correspondent.

Rockwell, Robert "Doc": A distant relative of Kiffin and Paul who left medical school and joined the Lafayette Escadrille in September 1916.

Rosa (last name unknown): A young woman whom Jim met in Luxeuil-les-Baines, and a probable romantic interest.

Rumsey, Laurence: An American pilot who flew with Jim in the Lafayette Escadrille. A professional polo player before the war, Rumsey volunteered with the ambulance service and later enlisted in Aviation. Rumsey was cursed with an addiction to alcohol.

Salisbury, Ned: Head of Jim's ambulance team, Section 2. Ned was from Chicago.

Slade, Mrs. Laurence: Bill Thaw's sister, who lived in Paris. The Slades were friends with Marcelle Guerin and Mrs. Weeks. Jim "distinguished" himself at a party given by the Slades.

Soubiran, Robert: A naturalized American citizen, born in France, who joined the Foreign Legion in 1914, was wounded in battle, and transferred to Aviation upon recovery. He joined the Lafayette Escadrille in October 1916.

Tazewell, Littleton W.: A friend and occasional correspondent of Jim's from the University of Virginia. Littleton graduated in 1910 and was president of the engineering class.

Thaw, William "Bill": An American pilot who flew with Jim in the Lafayette Escadrille. Bill was in France for an air race when the war started. He donated his plane to the French army and served as an infantryman in the Foreign Legion, with Kiffin Rockwell and Bert Hall, before transferring to the French air service.

Thénault, Capt. Georges: The French pilot who commanded the Lafayette Escadrille.

Tupper, Frank B.: A friend and correspondent of Jim's. How Jim met him is unknown. He moved to Boston during the period of this book, and Jim owed him $15.

Weeks, Alice: The wife of a Harvard professor, Mrs. Weeks moved into an apartment in Paris when her son Kenneth joined the Foreign Legion. Her plan was to give him a place to stay when he got leave, but she wound up serving as a "mother" to dozens of American volunteers who had no home in France. Jim stayed at her apartment whenever he could get leave.

Willis, Harold Buckley: One of Jim's fellow ambulance drivers at Pont-à-Mousson, and later a fellow pilot in the Lafayette Escadrille. Willis was from Boston, Massachusetts.

Winslow, Carol Dana: An American pilot who volunteered to fly for the French and was assigned to a French squadron rather than to the Lafayette Escadrille. (Many more Americans flew with the French than could be assigned to a single squadron. Those who flew with French squadrons were collectively known as the "Lafayette Flying Corps.") Winslow wrote a book titled *With the French Flying Corps* that was published shortly before Jim's book *Flying for France* was published.

Yvonne (last name unknown): A young French woman whom Jim met in Paris when he took film to a Kodak shop to be developed. No known correspondence with Yvonne has survived, but Jim referred to her often in his correspondence with Paul.

ENDNOTES

Introduction: The Aviator

1. Arlen J. Hansen, *Gentlemen Volunteers: The Story of the American Ambulance Drivers in the First World War* (New York: Arcade, 1996), vi.

2. https://en.wikipedia.org/wiki/IMP_Society.

3. Undated letter from Jim McConnell to Marcelle Guerin. Content places it in early September 1915, UVA archives.

4. Steven A. Ruffin, "Flying in the Great War: Rx for Misery," *Over the Front* 14, no. 2 (1999) and 17, no. 2 (2002).

5. Edwin C. Parsons, *I Flew with the Lafayette Escadrille* (Indianapolis, IN: E. C. Seale, 1963), 8.

6. Dennis Gordon, *The Lafayette Flying Corps: The American Volunteers in the French Air Service in World War I* (Atglen, PA: Schiffer, 2000), 7.

7. Paul A. Rockwell, "Writings of the American Pilots in the Lafayette Escadrille," *Ex. Libris* 1, no. 5 (November 1923): 131.

8. Harry Sydnor Harrison, "Pilots of the Skies," *Collier's*, August 4, 1917, 7, 29.

Chapter 1: Son of a Judge

1. Paul A. Rockwell, "Jim McConnell for France," *The State*, February 1979, 8.

2. Ibid.

3. Gordon, *The Lafayette Flying Corps*, 298.

4. Samuel P. McConnell, "The Chicago Bomb Case," *Harper's*, May 1934, 730–39.

5. Gordon, *The Lafayette Flying Corps*, 298.

6. Henry E. Mattox, "Chariots of Wrath: North Carolinians Who Flew for France in World War I," *North Carolina Historical Review* 73, no. 3 (July 1996): 292.

7. Gordon, *The Lafayette Flying Corps*, 298.

8. "Judge McConnell Is Out," *Chicago Daily News*, October 6, 1894, 1.

9. "Wedding of Miss Stein," *Chicago Daily News*, March 9, 1900, 3.

10. "George A. Fuller is Dead," *Chicago Daily News*, December 14, 1900, 1.

11. "Colossal Construction Company," *The Sun* (New York), March 30, 1901, 1.

12. "Mayo Methot's Career Told," *Sunday Oregonian*, June 13, 1915, 11.

13. "Boys End Long Auto Trip," *Chicago Tribune*, August 1, 1902, 3.

14. "Boy Autoist Here From East," *Chicago Daily News*, July 31, 1902, 1.

15. Various, *Official Automobile Blue Book 1901* (New York: Official Automobile Blue Book, 1901), 207–08.

16. John T. Baur, "The Official Automobile Blue Book, 1901–1929: Precursor to the American Road Map," *Cartographic Perspectives* 62 (Winter 2009): 11.

17. Rick Britton, "The Aviator," *MHQ: The Quarterly Journal of Military History* 31, no. 3 (Spring 2019).

18. "Boy Nears End of Long Trip on Auto," *Chicago Tribune*, July 29, 1902, 7.

19. "Ethics and the Unions, Part 1," Industrial Workers of the World, https://archive.iww.org/history/library/Dolgoff/newbeginning/1/.

20. "Delegate Sam Parks in Jail," *The Sun* (New York), June 9, 1903, 1.

21. "Owning a Walking Delegate," *The Sun* (New York), July 2, 1903, 2.

22. "I Never Saw Plenty–Parks," *The Sun* (New York), August 21, 1903, 3.

23. "Cockran Flusters Tammany," *The Sun* (New York), October 23, 1903, 3.

24. "Sam Parks Is Found Guilty of Extortion," *New York World*, October 30, 1903, 3.

25. "Judge M'Connell Resigns," *The Sun* (New York), January 5, 1904, 9.

26. Gordon, *The Lafayette Flying Corps*, 298.

27. February 2, 2022, email to the author from Sheryl Kaufmann, associate director of advancement services, Haverford School, 450 Lancaster Avenue, Haverford, PA.

28. UVA Library website, https://explore.lib.virginia.edu/exhibits/show/mcconnell/introduction.

29. "Seven Society," Wikipedia, https://en.wikipedia.org/wiki/Seven_Society.

30. "The Imp Society at the University of Virginia," https://aig.alumni.virginia.edu/imp/about/history/.

31. Bob (?) to Lewis Crenshaw, March 26, 1917, UVA microfiche.

32. Douglas W. Tanner, "Soaring Like an Eagle: James McConnell, American Aviator for France" unpublished article, UVA Archives, 3.

33. May 7, 2020, email to the author from Anna Tserelova, academic records coordinator, Office of the University Registrar, University of Virginia.

34. "IMP Society," Wikipedia, https://en.wikipedia.org/wiki/IMP_Society.

35. "Jefferson Statue Unveiled," *Free Lance* (Fredericksburg, VA), June 18, 1910, 1.

36. "Now Owns Lake and Mountain," *New York Daily Tribune*, September 28, 1909, 11.

37. "Randolph and Cumberland Railway," *The Courier* (Asheboro, NC), November 30, 1911, 4.

38. Meade Seawell, *Tale of a Tarheel Town* (Raleigh, NC: Edgeworth & Broughton, 1970), 251.

39. "May Vote Bonds to Build New Railroad," *State Dispatch* (Burlington, NC), March 29, 1911, 1.

40. Seawell, *Tale of a Tarheel Town*, 252.

41. James R. McConnell, *Carthage, North Carolina* (Carthage Board of Trade, 1914), 29-page booklet, UVA microfiche.

42. James R. McConnell, *The Select Section of the South* (Randolph & Cumberland Railroad, n.d.), 22-page booklet, UVA microfiche.

43. Jim McConnell to Julia Follansbee (?), August 25, 1913, UVA microfiche.

44. Gordon, *The Lafayette Flying Corps*, 257.

45. Charles Chouteau Johnson to Paul Rockwell, March 27, 1917, UVA microfiche.

46. Tanner, "Soaring Like an Eagle," UVA Archives, 3.

47. James R. McConnell, *Flying for France: With the American Escadrille at Verdun* (New York: Doubleday, Page, 1917), xi.

Chapter 2: The American Ambulance Field Service

1. "The Ambulance," *WWI Centennial News* (podcast), episode 82, September 7, 2018.

2. Leslie Buswell, *Ambulance No. 10: Personal Letters from the Front* (Boston and New York: Houghton Mifflin, 1916 (US National Library of Medicine digitized copy), xvi.

3. Hansen, *Gentlemen Volunteers*, 40.

4. Ibid., 43.

5. "History of US Army Medical Service Corps–the Ambulance Service," https://history.amedd.army.mil/booksdocs/HistoryofUSArmyMSC/chapter2.html.

6. Marcelle Guerin, handwritten autobiography, UVA Archives.

7. Jim McConnell to Julia Follansbee (?), February 8, 1915, UVA microfiche.

8. Jim McConnell to Sarah McConnell, undated, UVA microfiche.

9. Jim McConnell to Marcelle Guerin, February 20, 1915, UVA Archives.

10. Jim McConnell to Julia Follansbee (?), February 23, 1915, UVA microfiche.

11. Jim McConnell to Sarah McConnell, March 31, 1915, UVA microfiche.

12. "Americans Meet on French Front for First Time in Seven Years," *The Sun* (New York) July 12, 1915, 3.

13. Jim McConnell to Sarah McConnell, May 15, 1915, UVA microfiche

14. Hansen, *Gentlemen Volunteers*, 44.

15. Ibid.

16. "History of US Army Medical Service Corps–the Ambulance Service."

17. Jim McConnell to Marcelle Guerin, undated letter from early April 1915, UVA Archives.

18. Jim McConnell to Marcelle Guerin, postcard dated April 9, 1915, UVA Archives.

19. Hansen, *Gentlemen Volunteers*, 98.

20. E. B. White, *Essays of E. B. White* (New York: Harper Colophon, 1977), 163.

21. Ibid.

22. Various, *Friends of France / The Field Service of the American Ambulance: Described by Its Members* (Boston and New York: Houghton Mifflin, 1916), Project Gutenberg ebook, Kindle location 2175.

23. White, *Essays of E. B. White*, 165.

24. Buswell, *Ambulance No. 10*, 26.

25. Hansen, *Gentlemen Volunteers*, 101.

26. Various, *Diary of Section VIII: American Ambulance Field Service*, printed only for private distribution, 1917 (US National Library of Medicine digitized copy), 3.

27. Various, *Friends of France*, Kindle location 1859.

28. Hansen, *Gentlemen Volunteers*, 109.

29. Ibid., vi.
30. Julien H. Bryan, *Ambulance 464: "Encore des Blessés"* (New York: Macmillan, 1918), Google Books copy, 21.
31. Various, *Friends of France*, Kindle location 1692.
32. "History of US Army Medical Service Corps–the Ambulance Service."
33. Hansen, *Gentlemen Volunteers*, 113.
34. Various, *Friends of France*, Kindle location 2483.
35. Jim McConnell to Marcelle Guerin, April 19, 1915, UVA Archives.

Chapter 3: Pont-à-Mousson

1. "St. Mihiel Salient—Bois le Prêtre," https://www.pierreswesternfront.nl/st-mihiel-salient-bois-le-pretre-priesterwald-fey-en-haye-destroyed-village-kuehlewein-brunnen-vilcey-sur-trey (French website).
2. "Priest's Woods," https://www.lieux-insolites.fr/cicatrice/14-18/bois/bois.htm (French website).
3. "Decker's Story of the Fighting," *Chicago Daily News*, April 16, 1915, 10.
4. "Commonplace of War," *Chicago Daily News*, September 29, 1915, 10.
5. "From the War Zone," *Chicago Daily News*, July 16, 1915, 10.
6. "Shells Rain on City in Christmas Salute," *Chicago Daily News*, January 2, 1915, 4.
7. "Says US City Would Rebel at Army Rule," *Chicago Daily News*, February 10, 1915, 15.
8. "Bombard Exact Spot Shelled in August," *Chicago Daily News*, January 13, 1915, 4.
9. "Battle More Hotly for Bois Le Pretre," *Chicago Daily News*, January 28, 1915, 4.
10. "Old People's Home Is Razed by Shells," *Chicago Daily News*, January 23, 1915, 4.
11. "Cleft Head to Foot by Arrow from Air," *Chicago Daily News*, February 3, 1915, 4.
12. "War's Calmer Periods," *Chicago Daily News*, February 5, 1915, 10.
13. "German Shell Kills Tot in Mother's Lap," *Chicago Daily News*, February 10, 1915, 4.
14. "Border City in Fear Under Aerial Fleets," *Chicago Daily News*, March 10, 1915, 9.
15. "Ring Bells to Tell of German Victory," *Chicago Daily News*, March 3, 1915, 4.
16. "Price of Food High in the Battle Zone," *Chicago Daily News*, April 24, 1915, 13.
17. "Underground Attack Blow to French," *Chicago Daily News*, March 23, 1915, 4.
18. "Allies in Big Drive to Regain Positions," *Chicago Daily News*, April 28, 1915, 3.
19. Jim McConnell to Marcelle Guerin, postcard dated April 19, 1915, UVA archives.
20. Jim McConnell to Julia Follensbee (?), April 20, 1915, UVA microfiche.
21. Jim McConnell to Marcelle Guerin, postcard dated April 21, 1915, UVA Archives.
22. Jim McConnell to Paul Rockwell, April 21, 1915, UVA Archives.
23. Jim McConnell to Lewis Crenshaw, April 21, 1915, UVA microfiche.
24. Jim McConnell to Marcelle Guerin, April 23, 1915, UVA Archives.
25. "While They Wait," *Chicago Daily News*, June 14, 1915 (datelined April 24). 10.
26. James R. McConnell, "With the American Ambulance in France," *The Outlook*, September 15, 1915, 125–132.
27. McConnell, "With the American Ambulance in France," *Outlook* Magazine, September 15, 1915, 127.
28. Jim McConnell to Marcelle Guerin, April 27, 1915, UVA Archives.
29. Jim McConnell to Julia Follensbee (?), April 26, 1915, UVA microfiche.
30. Jim McConnell to Samuel McConnell (?), April 26, 1915, UVA microfiche.
31. Bryan, *Ambulance 464: "Encore des Blessés,"* 13.
32. Jim McConnell to Paul Rockwell, April 27, 1915, UVA Archives.
33. "Says Teutons Kill Their Own Officers," *Chicago Daily News*, May 6, 1915 (datelined May 1), 4.
34. "French Cannon Take Coveted Trenches," *Chicago Daily News*, May 8, 1915 (datelined May 2), 6.
35. "French Make Gains at a Heavy Expense," *Chicago Daily News*, May, 10, 1915 (datelined May 3), 8.
36. Jim McConnell to Julia Follensbee (?), undated but obviously early May 1915, UVA microfiche.
37. Jim McConnell to Samuel McConnell (?), May 2 and 3, 1915, UVA microfiche.
38. Jim McConnell to Paul Rockwell, May 3, 1915, UVA Archives.
39. Jim McConnell to Marcelle Guerin, May 5, 1915, UVA Archives.
40. Jim McConnell to Paul Rockwell, May 8, 1915, UVA Archives.
41. Jim McConnell to unknown, May 12, 1915, UVA microfiche.
42. "Trenches Captured and Lost by French," *Chicago Daily News*, May 19, 1915, 4.
43. "This Battlefield Is Inferno of Death," *Chicago Daily News*, May 21. 1915 (datelined May 16), 4.
44. Jim McConnell to Paul Rockwell, May 14, 1915, UVA Archives.
45. "Shells Maul US Ambulance," *Chicago Daily News*, May 19, 1915, 4.
46. Jim McConnell to Marcelle Guerin, May 16, 1915, UVA Archives.

47. Jim McConnell to Sarah McConnell, May 15, 1915, UVA microfiche.
48. "Dodge Shells Flee to House Cellars," *Chicago Daily News*, May 22, 1915 (datelined May 14), 6.
49. "Women Flee Frontier Town," *Chicago Daily News*, May 26, 1915 (datelined May 21), 4.
50. Jim McConnell to Marcelle Guerin, May 21, 1915, UVA Archives.
51. Jim McConnell to Paul Rockwell, May 26, 1915, UVA Archives.
52. Jim McConnell to Marcelle Guerin, May 31, 1915, UVA Archives.
53. "Mow Down Civilians in City on Frontier," *Chicago Daily News*, June 1, 1915 (datelined May 27), 3.

Chapter 4: With the American Ambulance Service

1. "Flee Big Benzine Shells" *Chicago Daily News*, June 4, 1915, 3.
2. Jim McConnell to Paul Rockwell, undated postcard, early June on the basis of content, UVA Archives.
3. Jim McConnell to Julia Follansbee (?), June 2, 1915, UVA microfiche.
4. Victor 17959–A, recorded February 9, 1916, author's copy.
5. Hansen, *Gentlemen Volunteers*, 102.
6. Jim McConnell to Marcelle Guerin, June 7, 1915, UVA Archives.
7. Jim McConnell to Paul Rockwell, June 10, 1915, UVA Archives.
8. Jim McConnell to Marcelle Guerin, June 23, 1915, UVA Archives.
9. Buswell, *Ambulance No. 10*, 5.
10. Ibid., 10.
11. Ibid., 22.
12. Ibid., 27.
13. Ibid., 29.
14. Ibid., 37.
15. Jim McConnell to Marcelle Guerin, June 23, 1915, UVA Archives.
16. "Rescuers Win Praise," *Chicago Daily News*, July 19, 1915 (datelined June 21), 10.
17. "Hundreds Each Night Flee Pont-a-Moussoun," *Chicago Daily News*, July 21, 1915 (datelined June 23), 7.
18. Jim McConnell to Paul Rockwell, June 24, 1915, UVA Archives.
19. Various, *Diary of Section VIII: American Ambulance Field Service*, 13.
20. "Work Being Done by American Ambulances in France," *The Sun* (New York), June 27, 1915, 4.
21. Jim McConnell to Marcelle Guerin, July 1, 1915, UVA Archives.
22. Jim McConnell to Paul Rockwell, June 27, 1915, UVA Archives.
23. Jim McConnell to Paul Rockwell, July 1, 1915, UVA Archives.
24. Jim McConnell to Paul Rockwell, July 1, 1915, UVA Archives.
25. Buswell, *Ambulance No. 10*, 44–52.
26. Jim McConnell to Marcelle Guerin, July 8, 1915, UVA Archives.
27. Jim McConnell to Paul Rockwell, July 8, 1915, UVA Archives.
28. Jim McConnell to Sarah Rockwell, July 8, 1915, UVA microfiche.
29. Jim McConnell to Paul Rockwell, July 8, 1915, UVA Archives.
30. Jim McConnell to Paul Rockwell, July 16, 1915, UVA Archives.
31. Jim McConnell to Marcelle Guerin, July 18, 1915, UVA Archives.
32. Buswell, *Ambulance No. 10*, 59.
33. Jim McConnell to Marcelle Guerin, July 21, 1915, UVA Archives.
34. Jim McConnell to Paul Rockwell, July 22, 1915, UVA Archives.
35. Jim McConnell to Julia Follansbee (?), July 22 and 24, 1915, UVA microfiche.
36. Buswell, *Ambulance No. 10*, 77.
37. Jim McConnell to Julia Follansbee (?), July 22 and 24, 1915, UVA microfiche.
38. Jim McConnell to Paul Rockwell, July 29, 1915, UVA Archives.
39. Jim McConnell to Sarah Rockwell, July 30, 1915, UVA microfiche.
40. Buswell, *Ambulance No. 10*, 97.
41. Ibid., 90.
42. Ibid., 108.
43. "Shells Cut Strange Capers; Men Escape," *Chicago Daily News*, July 30, 1915, 4.
44. Jim McConnell to Paul Rockwell, August 3, 1915, UVA Archives.
45. Jim McConnell to Marcelle Guerin, undated, but early September 1915, UVA Archives.
46. Jim McConnell to Julia Follansbee (?), August 23, 1915, UVA microfiche.
47. "American Ambulance Wins High Army Honor," *The Sun* (New York), September 19, 1915, 3.

Chapter 5: Changing Gears

1. "With the American Ambulance in France," *The Outlook*, September 15, 1915, 125.
2. Ibid., 126.
3. Ibid., 129.
4. Ibid., 141.
5. Ibid.
6. Ibid.
7. Ibid., 142.
8. Ibid., 144.
9. Alice S. Weeks, *Greater Love Hath No Man* (Boston: Bruce Humphries, 1929), 68.
10. Jim McConnell to Marcelle Guerin, Sept 29, 1915, UVA Archives.
11. McConnell, *Flying for France*, 15.
12. "Teuton Shells Rain On Pont-à-Mousson," *Chicago Daily News*, September 21, 1915, 4.
13, "Cannon Fray Grows Havoc at St. Mihiel," *Chicago Daily News*, September 24, 1915, 4.
14. "Commonplace of War," *Chicago Daily News*, September 29, 1915, 10.
15. Buswell, *Ambulance No. 10*, 147.
16. Jim McConnell to Paul Rockwell, October 8, 1915, UVA Archives.
17. Jim McConnell to Marcelle Guerin, October 8, 1915, UVA Archives.
18. Charles Bernard Nordhoff and James Norman Hall, *The Lafayette Flying Corps* (Cambridge, MA: Houghton Mifflin, 1920), Google Books copy, 1:341.
19. Jim McConnell to Paul Rockwell, October 11, 1915, W&L Archives.
20. "High Above the Battle Zone in France," *Chicago Daily News*, July 1. 1916, 6.
21. "See Plane Shot Down in Thrilling Air Duel," *Chicago Daily News*, October 14, 1915, 4.
22. Jim McConnell to Sarah McConnell, October 12, 1915, UVA microfiche.
23. Jim McConnell to Marcelle Guerin, October 16, 1915, UVA Archives.
24. Jim McConnell to Frank Tupper, October 18, 1915, UVA microfiche.
25. Jim McConnell to Paul Rockwell, postcard, October 19, 1915, W&L Archives.
26. Jim McConnell to Paul Rockwell, October 23, 1915, W&L Archives.
27. Jim McConnell to Marcelle Guerin, October 23, 1915, UVA Archives.
28. Jim McConnell to Paul Rockwell, October 26, 1915, W&L Archives.
29. Jim McConnell to Marcelle Guerin, October 27, 1915, UVA Archives.
30. Jim McConnell to Paul Rockwell, October 28, 1915, W&L Archives.
31. "Trench Secrets Laid Bare as Leaves Fall," *Chicago Daily News*, November 1, 1915, 4.
32. Weeks, *Greater Love Hath No Man*, 86.
33. Joshua E. Kastenberg, "Field Marshall Douglas Haig: A Negative Leadership Lesson in Military History," *The Reporter* 32, no. 1 (2005): 24.
34. Jim McConnell to Paul Rockwell, November 7, 1915, W&L Archives.
35. Jim McConnell to Paul Rockwell, November 13, 1915, W&L Archives.
36. Jim McConnell to Marcelle Guerin, November 13, 1915, UVA Archives.
37. Jim McConnell to Paul Rockwell, November 16, 1918. W&L Archives.
38. "Shakes Hands of Americans," *Chicago Daily News*, November 17, 1915, 4.
39. Jim McConnell to Paul Rockwell, postcard, November 20, 1915, W&L Archives.
40. Jim McConnell to Paul Rockwell, November 21, 1915, W&L Archives.
41. Jim McConnell to Paul Rockwell, November 24, 1915, W&L Archives.
42. Jim McConnell to Paul Rockwell, November 28, 1915, W&L Archives.
43. Jim McConnell to Paul Rockwell, postcard, dated "Monday," probably November 29, 1915, W&L Archives.
44. Jim McConnell to A. Piatt Andrew, November 28, 1915, Ronald Poteat.
45. Jim McConnell to Paul Rockwell, December 2, 1915, W&L Archives

Chapter 6: Learning to Fly

1. Jim McConnell to Paul Rockwell, postcard, January 1, 1916, W&L Archives.
2. Jim McConnell to Paul Rockwell, letter dated "Sunday" but presumed to be January 2, 1916, on the basis of content, W&L Archives.
3. Balsley, *The Diary of H. Clyde Balsley*, 106.
4. Weeks, *Greater Love Hath No Man*, 103.
5. Clyde H. Balsley, "The Diary of H. Clyde Balsley," *Cross & Cockade: Journal of the Society of World War I Aero Historians* 18, no. 2 (Summer 1977): 102.

6. Kiffin Rockwell to Paul Rockwell, September 27, 1915, W&L Archives.
7. Hansen, *Gentlemen Volunteers*, 102.
8. Parsons, *I Flew with the Lafayette Escadrille*, 48.
9. Ibid., 47.
10. Balsley, "The Diary of H. Clyde Balsley," 106.
11. Jim McConnell to Marcelle Guerin, January 9, 1916, UVA Archives.
12. Jim McConnell to Paul Rockwell, January 11, 1916, W&L Archives.
13. Balsley, "The Diary of H. Clyde Balsley," 108.
14. Jim McConnell to Marcelle Guerin, January 13, 1916, UVA Archives.
15. Weeks, *Greater Love Hath No Man*, 105.
16. Jim McConnell to Paul Rockwell, January 15, 1916, W&L Archives.
17. Philip M. Flammer, *The Vivid Air* (Athens: University of Georgia Press, 1981), 6.
18. Weeks, *Greater Love Hath No Man*, 102.
19. Jim McConnell to Marcelle Guerin, January 24, 1916, UVA Archives.
20. Jim McConnell to Paul Rockwell, January 27, 1916, W&L Archives.
21. Jim McConnell to Marcelle Guerin, January 28, 1916, UVA Archives.
22. Kiffin Rockwell to Vicomte and Vicomtessa Peloux, September 19, 1915, W&L Archives.
23. Jim McConnell to Paul Rockwell, February 2, 1916, W&L Archives.
24. Jim McConnell to Paul Rockwell, February 4, 1916, W&L Archives.
25. Jim McConnell to Marcelle Guerin, postcard, February 3, 1916, UVA Archives.
26. Jim McConnell to Paul Rockwell, postcard, February 6, 1916, W&L Archives.
27. Jim McConnell to Marcelle Guerin, postcard, February 7, 1916, UVA Archives.
28. Jim McConnell to Paul Rockwell, February 18, 1916, W&L Archives.
29. Marcelle Guerin to Paul Rockwell, February 21, 1916, W&L Archives.
30. Jim McConnell to Julia Follansbee (?), February 20, 1916, UVA microfiche.

Chapter 7: Advanced Training

1. Jim McConnell to Paul Rockwell, February 22, 1916, W&L Archives.
2. Jim McConnell to Paul Rockwell, February 24, 1916, W&L Archives.
3. Jim McConnell to Sarah McConnell, February 22, 1916, UVA microfiche.
4. Jim McConnell to Marcelle Guerin, February 24, 1916, UVA Archives.
5. Jim McConnell to Marcelle Guerin, March 2, 1916, UVA Archives.
6. Jim McConnell to Paul Rockwell, February 28, 1916, W&L Archives.
7. Jim McConnell to Paul Rockwell, March 6, 1916, W&L Archives.
8. Jim McConnell to Paul Rockwell, March 9, 1916, W&L Archives.
9. Weeks, *Greater Love Hath No Man*, 115.
10. Balsley, "The Diary of H. Clyde Balsley," 113.
11. Jim McConnell to Marcelle Guerin, March 17, 1916, UVA Archives.
12. Jim McConnell to Julia Follansbee (?), March 21, 1916, UVA microfiche.
13. Jim McConnell to Paul Rockwell, March 21, 1916, W&L Archives.
14. Jim McConnell to Frank B. Tupper, March 22, 1916, UVA microfiche.
15. Jim McConnell to Julia Follansbee (?), March 21, 1916, UVA microfiche.
16. Jim McConnell to Frank B. Tupper, March 22, 1916, UVA microfiche.
17. Balsley, "The Diary of H. Clyde Balsley," 113.
18. Jim McConnell to Marcelle Guerin, March 26, 1916, UVA Archives.
19. "Americans Learn to Be War Pilots in French School of Aviation at Pau," *The Sun* (New York), March 26, 2016, 2.
20. Lyn Macdonald, *The Roses of No Man's Land* (New York: Atheneum, 1989), 139–43.
21. Peter Hart, *The Great War: A Combat History of the First World War* (New York: Oxford, 2015), 364.
22. Jim McConnell to Paul Rockwell, March 27, 1916, W&L Archives.
23. Jim McConnell to Marcelle Guerin, March 28, 1916, UVA Archives.
24. Jim McConnell to Marcelle Guerin, March 29, 1916, UVA Archives.
25. Jim McConnell to Paul Rockwell, March 30, 1916, W&L Archives.
26. Jim McConnell to Paul Rockwell, April 4, 1916, W&L Archives.
27. Jim McConnell to Marcelle Guerin, April 4, 1916, UVA Archives.
28. Jim McConnell to Marcelle Guerin, April 10, 1916, UVA Archives.

29. Paul Ayres Rockwell, *War Letters of Kiffin Yates Rockwell* (Garden City, NY: Country Life Press, 1925), 115.

30. Steven A. Ruffin, *The Lafayette Escadrille: A Photo History of the First American Fighter Squadron* (Havertown, PA: Casemate, 2016), photos following 64.

31. Jim McConnell to Paul Rockwell, April 11, 1916, W&L Archives (letter is dated "Tuesday" but on the basis of context it was written on Tuesday, April 11, 1916).

32. Saint-Sauveur to Kiffin Rockwell, April 12, 1916, W&L Archives.

33. Jim McConnell to Ward McLanahan, April 13, 1916, UVA microfiche.

34. Jon Guttman, *SPA124 Lafayette Escadrille: American Volunteer Airmen in World War I* (Wellingborough, UK: Osprey, 2004), 16.

35. Flammer, *The Vivid Air*, 26.

36. Captain George Thénault, *The Story of the Lafayette Escadrille* (unpublished draft, published ca. 1932; W&L Archives), iii.

37. Herbert Molloy Mason Jr., *Lafayette Escadrille* (New York: Smithmark, 1964), 71.

38. Victor Chapman, *Victor Chapman's Letters from France* (New York: Macmillan, 1917), Google Books copy, 169 and 165.

39. Thénault, *The Story of the Lafayette Escadrille*, 32.

Chapter 8: Lounging at Luxeuil

1. Chapman, *Victor Chapman's Letters from France*, 170.

2. Jim McConnell to Paul Rockwell, undated postcard but from April 18, 1916, on the basis content, W&L Archives.

3. Jim McConnell to Marcelle Guerin, April 20, 1916, UVA Archives.

4. McConnell, *Flying for France*, 23.

5. Ibid., 31.

6. Kiffin Rockwell to Jim McConnell, Sept. 21, 1916, W&L Archives.

7. Jim McConnell to Marcelle Guerin, April 20, 1916, UVA Archives.

8. Carroll Dana Winslow, *With the French Flying Corps* (New York: Scribner's, 1917), Google Books copy), 167.

9. Thénault, *The Story of the Lafayette Escadrille*, 41.

10. Ibid., 30; and Chapman, *Victor Chapman's Letters from France*, 171.

11. Weeks, *Greater Love Hath No Man*, 128.

12. McConnell, *Flying for France*, 25.

13. Thénault, *The Story of the Lafayette Escadrille*, 30.

14. Jim McConnell to Marcelle Guerin, April 20, 1916, UVA Archives.

15. Thénault, *The Story of the Lafayette Escadrille*, 36.

16. Ibid., 39.

17. Jim McConnell to Paul Rockwell, April 30, 1916, W&L Archives.

18. Jim McConnell to Paul Rockwell, April 26, 1916 (incorrectly dated April 25), W&L Archives.

19. Jim McConnell to Marcelle Guerin, April 26, 1916, UVA Archives.

20. Ibid.

21. Kiffin Rockwell to Paul Rockwell, April 29, 1916, W&L Archives.

22. Jim McConnell to Paul Rockwell, April 30, 1916, W&L Archives.

23. Jim McConnell to Lewis Crenshaw, May 1, 1916, UVA microfiche.

24. Jim McConnell to Paul Rockwell, postcard, April 21, 1916, W&L Archives.

25. Jim McConnell to Julia Follansbee (?), August 23, 1915, UVA microfiche.

26. Jim McConnell to Marcelle Guerin, April 26, 1916, UVA Archives.

27. Flammer, *The Vivid Air*, 57.

28. Jim McConnell to Sarah McConnell, May 3, 1916, UVA microfiche.

29. Jim McConnell to Paul Rockwell, May 9, 1916, W&L Archives.

30. Thénault, *The Story of the Lafayette Escadrille*, 50.

31. McConnell, *Flying for France*, 128. Presumably this was a letter that Jim wrote to Frank Page on April 14, 1916.

32. Thénault, *The Story of the Lafayette Escadrille*, 47.

33. Hansen, *Gentlemen Volunteers*, 79.

34. Thénault, *The Story of the Lafayette Escadrille*, 50.

35. McConnell, *Flying for France*, 28–29.

36. Chapman, *Victor Chapman's Letters from France*, 178.

37. Lieutenant Bert Hall and Lieutenant John J. Niles, *One Man's War: The Story of the Lafayette Escadrille* (New York: Henry Holt, 1929), 131.

38. Jim McConnell telegram to Paul Rockwell, May 18, 1916, W&L Archives.

39. Paul Rockwell to Kiffin Rockwell, May 20, 1916, W&L Archives.

40. McConnell, *Flying for France*, 34

41. Jim McConnell to Marcelle Guerin, May 19, 1916, UVA Archives.

42. Kiffin Rockwell to Paul Rockwell, May 22, 1916, W&L Archives.

43. Jim McConnell to Frank (Tupper?), May 23, 1916, UVA microfiche.

44. Jim McConnell to Paul Rockwell, May 20, 1916, UVA Archives.

Chapter 9: Verdun

1. Jon Guttman, *The Origin of the Fighter Aircraft* (Yardley, PA: Westholme, 2009), 43.

2. Jonathan Olley, "The Forbidden Forest," *Orion*, undated but probably March 2011, https://orionmagazine.org/article/the-forbidden-forest/.

3. Alistair Horne, *The Price of Glory* (Harmondsworth, UK: Penguin, 1962; 1978 reprint), 328.

4. Thénault, *The Story of the Lafayette Escadrille*, 58.

5. Guttman, *The Origin of the Fighter Aircraft*, 48.

6. Thénault, *The Story of the Lafayette Escadrille*, 57.

7. Ibid.

8. Hall, *One Man's War*, 139.

9. Kiffin Rockwell to Paul Rockwell, May 22, 1916, W&L Archives.

10. Thénault, *The Story of the Lafayette Escadrille*, 59.

11. Ibid., 60.

12. Ibid., 61–62.

13. Harold B. Willis with Jeffrey S. Williams, *Through a Cloud of Bullets* (St. Paul, MN: Antietam Creek, 2019), 11.

14. "Arch" Whitehouse, *Legion of the Lafayette* (New York: Doubleday, 1962), 115.

15. Jim McConnell to Paul Rockwell, May 25, 1916, UVA Archives.

16. Jim McConnell to Marcelle Guerin, May 30, 1916, UVA Archives.

17. Jim McConnell to Marcelle Guerin, May 28, 1916, UVA Archives.

18. Jim McConnell to Paul Rockwell, May 28, 1916, UVA Archives.

19. Ibid.

20. Jim McConnell to Marcelle Guerin, June 4, 1916, UVA Archives.

21. Jim McConnell to Paul Rockwell, June 3, 1916, UVA Archives.

22. Balsley, "The Diary of H. Clyde Balsley," 116.

23. Jim McConnell to Marcelle Guerin, June 4, 1916, UVA Archives.

24. Jim McConnell to Sarah McConnell, June 4, 1916, UVA microfiche.

25. Balsley, "The Diary of H. Clyde Balsley," 116.

26. Kiffin Rockwell to Paul Rockwell, June 2, 1916, W&L Archives.

27. Chapman, *Victor Chapman's Letters from France*, 184.

Chapter 10: Death Strikes

1. Paul Rockwell to Kiffin Rockwell, June 5, 1916, W&L Archives.

2. Jim McConnell to Paul Rockwell, June 8, 1916, UVA Archives.

3. Chapman, *Victor Chapman's Letters from France*, 187.

4. Hall, *One Man's War*, 139.

5. Balsley, "The Diary of H. Clyde Balsley," 117.

6. Jim McConnell to Marcelle Guerin, June 13, 1916, UVA Archives.

7. McConnell, *Flying for France*, 130–32. On the basis of context, this letter was sent to Frank Page in mid-June 1916.

8. Jim McConnell to Paul Rockwell, June 15, 1916, UVA Archives.

9. Paul Rockwell to Kiffin Rockwell, letter dated "Monday," probably June 12 or 19, 1916, W&L Archives.

10. Jim McConnell to Paul Rockwell, June 15, 1916, UVA Archives

11. Jim McConnell to Marcelle Guerin, June 18, 1916, UVA Archives.

12. Kiffin Rockwell to Paul Rockwell, June 17, 1916, W&L Archives.

13. Thénault, *The Story of the Lafayette Escadrille*, 69.

14. Kiffin Rockwell to Paul Rockwell, June 17, 1916, W&L Archives.

15. McConnell, *Flying for France*, 38.

16. Jim McConnell to Marcelle Guerin, June 18, 1916, UVA Archives.

17. Ibid.
18. Balsley, "The Diary of H. Clyde Balsley," 118.
19. McConnell, *Flying for France*, 41
20. Nordhoff and Hall, *The Lafayette Flying Corps*, 2:60.
21. Jim McConnell to Paul Rockwell, June 21, 1916, UVA Archives.
22. Gordon, *The Lafayette Flying Corps*, 320.
23. US Citizenship & Immigration Services History Office, email to the author, August 22, 2018.
24. Jim McConnell to Paul Rockwell, June 21, 1916, UVA Archives.
25. Jim McConnell to Marcelle Guerin, June 23, 1916, UVA Archives.
26. Rockwell, *War Letters of Kiffin Yates Rockwell*, 142.
27. Mason, *Lafayette Escadrille*, 80.
28. Kiffin Rockwell to Paul Rockwell, June 23, 1916, W&L Archives.
29. McConnell, *Flying for France*, 44.
30. Jim McConnell to Paul Rockwell, June 25, 1916, UVA Archives.
31. Thénault, *The Story of the Lafayette Escadrille*, 128.
32. Hall, *One Man's War*, 147.
33. Kiffin Rockwell to Paul Rockwell, June 23, 1916, W&L Archives.
34. Jim McConnell to Marcelle Guerin, June 23, 1916, UVA Archives.
35. McConnell, *Flying for France*, 52
36. Ruffin, *The Lafayette Escadrille*, 62.
37. Gordon, *The Lafayette Flying Corps*, 68.
38. Mason, *Lafayette Escadrille*, 83.
39. Undated typed newspaper article, probably by Paul Rockwell, in the UVA microfiche.
40. McConnell, *Flying for France*, 45
41. Jim McConnell to Paul Rockwell, June 26, 1916, UVA Archives.
42. Jim McConnell to "Henry" (probably Henry A. Johnson), June 28, 1916, UVA microfiche.
43. Weeks, *Greater Love Hath No Man*, 149.

Chapter 11: A Hard Job

1. Jim McConnell to Paul Rockwell, July 1, 1916, UVA Archives.
2. Jim McConnell to Lewis Crenshaw, July 2, 1916, UVA microfiche.
3. Weeks, *Greater Love Hath No Man*, 151.
4. Ruffin, *The Lafayette Escadrille*, 65.
5. Jim McConnell to Marcelle Guerin, July 25, 1916, UVA Archives.
6. Jim McConnell to Marcelle Guerin, July 12, 1916, UVA Archives.
7. "Baldwin, James Mark," https://www.encyclopedia.com/people/medicine/psychology-and-psychiatry-biographies/james-mark-baldwin.
8. Paul Pavelka to Mrs. Weeks, May 19, 1916, W&L Archives.
9. Paul Pavelka to Jim McConnell, July 11, 1916, W&L Archives.
10. Jim McConnell to Marcelle Guerin, July 16, 1916, UVA Archives.
11. Jim McConnell to Sarah McConnell, July 23, 1916, UVA microfiche.
12. Alan D. Toelle, "A White-Faced Cow and the Operational History of the Escadrille Americaine N.124 to September 1916," *Over the Front* 24, no. 4 (Winter 2009): 335.
13. Jim McConnell to Paul Rockwell, July 25, 1916, UVA Archives.
14. Hall, *One Man's War*, 162.
15. McConnell, *Flying for France*, 68.
16. Jim McConnell to Paul Rockwell, July 25, 1916, UVA Archives.
17. Kiffin Rockwell to Paul Rockwell, July 27, 1916, W&L Archives.
18. McConnell, *Flying for France*, 133.
19. Jim McConnell to Paul Rockwell, July 25, 1916, UVA Archives.
20. "American Eyes of French Army: Volunteer Aviators at Battle Front," *Chicago Daily News*, August 25, 1916, 1.
21. Jim McConnell to Marcelle Guerin, August 5, 1916, UVA Archives.
22. McConnell, *Flying for France*, 135.
23. Ibid., 63.
24. Toelle, "A White-Faced Cow," 325.
25. Mason, *Lafayette Escadrille*, 97.

26. *Every Week* 5, no. 23 (December 3, 1917): 21.
27. Jim McConnell to Paul Rockwell, August 25, 1916, UVA Archives.
28. Weeks, *Greater Love Hath No Man*, 162.
29. Jim McConnell to Marcelle Guerin, August 25, 1916, UVA Archives.

Chapter 12: Depot des Éclopés

1. Jim McConnell to Paul Rockwell, August 26, 1916, UVA Archives.
2. Jim McConnell to Marcelle Guerin, August 27, 1916, UVA Archives.
3. Jim McConnell to Julia Follansbee (?), August 28, 1916, UVA microfiche.
4. Jim McConnell to Marcelle Guerin, August 31, 1916, UVA Archives.
5. Jim McConnell to Paul Rockwell, August 31, 1916, UVA Archives.
6. Jim McConnell to Marcelle Guerin, August 3, 1916, UVA Archives.
7. Paul Pavelka to Jim McConnell, August 31, 1916, W&L Archives.
8. Guttman, *SPA124 Lafayette Escadrille*, 32.
9. Jim McConnell to Paul Rockwell, September 4, 1916, UVA Archives.
10. Jim McConnell to Marcelle Guerin, September 7, 1916, UVA Archives.
11. Jim McConnell to Paul Rockwell, September 7, 1916, UVA Archives.
12. Jim McConnell to Henry A. Johnson, September 7, 1916, UVA microfiche.
13. Gordon, *The Lafayette Flying Corps*, 45.
14. Toelle, "A White-Faced Cow," 331.
15. Ibid.
16. Charles E. Snyder with Lonnie Raidor, Noel Shirley, and Greg VanWyngarden, "One Man's Photo Album," *Over the Front* 5, no. 4 (1990): 319.
17. McConnell, *Flying for France*, 77.
18. Parsons, *I Flew with the Lafayette Escadrille*, 147.
19. Jim McConnell to Marcelle Guerin, September 12, 1916, UVA Archives.
20. Jim McConnell to Paul Rockwell, September 12, 1916, UVA Archives.
21. Jim McConnell to Paul Rockwell, September 16, 1916, UVA Archives.
22. Jim McConnell to Marcelle Guerin, September 17, 1916, UVA Archives.
23. Ruffin, *The Lafayette Escadrille*, 78.
24. McConnell, *Flying for France*, 84.
25. Hall, *One Man's War*, 182.
26. Weeks, *Greater Love Hath No Man*, 165.
27. Kiffin Rockwell to Jim McConnell, September 21, 1916, W&L Archives.
28. Thénault, *The Story of the Lafayette Escadrille*, 88.
29. Ibid., 90.
30. Rockwell, *War Letters of Kiffin Yates Rockwell*, 160.
31. McConnell, *Flying for France*, 96.
32. Robert B. House, *Addenda to Rockwell Material*, North Carolina State Archives.
33. Weeks, *Greater Love Hath No Man*, 169.
34. Ibid., 170.

Chapter 13: Writing for France

1. Jim McConnell to Littleton W. Tazewell, February 17, 1917, UVA microfiche.
2. Paul Pavelka to Jim McConnell, September 26, 1916, W&L Archives.
3. Paul Pavelka to Jim McConnell, September 27, 1916, W&L Archives.
4. Jim McConnell to Marcelle Guerin, September 29, 1916, UVA Archives.
5. Paul Pavelka to Jim McConnell, October 1, 1916, W&L Archives.
6. Jim McConnell to Marcelle Guerin, October 8, 1916, UVA Archives.
7. Paul Pavelka to Paul Rockwell, October 7, 1916, W&L Archives.
8. McConnell, *Flying for France*, 100.
9. Ibid., 102.
10. Paul Pavelka to Paul Rockwell, October 7, 1916, W&L Archives.
11. Thénault, *The Story of the Lafayette Escadrille*, 81.
12. Paul Pavelka to Paul Rockwell, October 14, 1916, W&L Archives.
13. Frank W. Bailey and Christophe Cony, *The French Air Service War Chronology, 1914–1918* (London: Grub Street, 2001), 77.

14. Guttman, *SPA124 Lafayette Escadrille*, 56.
15. McConnell, *Flying for France*, 110.
16. Mason, *Lafayette Escadrille*, 148.
17. Paul Pavelka to Jim McConnell, undated but estimated as October 20, 1916, W&L Archives.
18. Paul Pavelka to Jim McConnell, undated but estimated as October 28, 1916, W&L Archives.
19. Paul Pavelka to Paul Rockwell, October 28, 1916, W&L Archives.
20. Weeks, *Greater Love Hath No Man*, 175.
21. McConnell, *Flying for France*, 5.
22. Ibid., 11.
23. Ibid., 25.
24. Ibid., 50.
25. Ibid., 54.
26. Parsons, *I Flew With The Lafayette Escadrille*, 8
27. Weeks, *Greater Love Hath No Man*, 179.

Chapter 14: End of the De Luxe War

1. McConnell, *Flying for France*, 114.
2. Gordon, *The Lafayette Flying Corps*, 390.
3. Flammer, *The Vivid Air*, 100.
4. Gordon, *The Lafayette Flying Corps*, 418.
5. Ibid., 218.
6. Ibid., 362.
7. May 8, 2018, phone interview between the author and Mr. Churchill at Savage Arms.
8. Thénault, *The Story of the Lafayette Escadrille*, 115.
9. Whitehouse, *Legion of the Lafayette*, 172.
10. "American Fliers in Big Air Battle," *The Sun* (New York), November 13, 1916, 2.
11. Bailey and Cony, *The French Air Service War Chronology*, 83.
12. Jim McConnell to Paul Rockwell, November 15, 1916, UVA Archives.
13. Weeks, *Greater Love Hath No Man*, 182.
14. Jim McConnell to Marcelle Guerin, November 16, 1916, UVA Archives.
15. Thénault, *The Story of the Lafayette Escadrille*, 100.
16. Gordon, *The Lafayette Flying Corps*, 4.
17. Flammer, *The Vivid Air*, 106.
18. James R. McConnell, "The Day's Work of an American Airman on the Somme," National Service 1, no. 1 (March 1917): 110.
19. Weeks, *Greater Love Hath No Man*, 184.
20. Jim McConnell to Paul Rockwell, November 19, 1916, UVA Archives.
21. Thénault, *The Story of the Lafayette Escadrille*, 103.
22. Ibid., 106.
23. Ruffin, *The Lafayette Escadrille*, 90.
24. Gordon, *The Lafayette Flying Corps*, 404.
25. March 6, 2020, interview with Kenneth James Rockwell.
26. Jim McConnell to Marcelle Guerin, December 7, 1916, UVA Archives.
27. Weeks, *Greater Love Hath No Man*, 187.
28. Ibid.
29. Jim McConnell to Paul Rockwell, December 11, 1916, UVA Archives.
30. Jim McConnell to Marcelle Guerin, December 14, 1916, UVA Archives.
31. McConnell, "The Day's Work of an American Airman on the Somme," 109.
32. Jim McConnell to Marcelle Guerin, December 14, 1916, UVA Archives.
33. Jim McConnell to Marcelle Guerin, December 15, 1916, UVA Archives.
34. Jim McConnell to Mrs. Weeks, December 15, 1916, UVA Archives.
35. Jim McConnell to Marcelle Guerin, December 26, 1916, UVA Archives.
36. Thénault, *The Story of the Lafayette Escadrille*, 112.
37. Ibid., 114.
38. Jim McConnell to Marcelle Guerin, December 26, 1916, UVA Archives.
39. Jim McConnell to Paul Rockwell, December 29, 1916, W&L Archives.
40. McConnell, "The Day's Work of an American Airman on the Somme," 115.

Chapter 15: Cold Misery

1. Guttman, *SPA 124 Lafayette Escadrille*, 65.

2. Jim McConnell to Paul Rockwell, December 29, 1916, W&L Archives.

3. Ibid.

4. Jim McConnell to Paul Rockwell, January 6, 1917, W&L Archives.

5. Jim McConnell to Marcelle Guerin, January 2, 1917, UVA Archives.

6. Jim McConnell to Paul Rockwell, January 6, 1917, W&L Archives.

7. Gordon, *The Lafayette Flying Corps*, 476.

8. Jim McConnell to Marcelle Guerin, January 7, 1917, UVA Archives.

9. Floyd Gibbons, *The Red Knight of Germany: The Story of Baron von Richthofen* (Garden City, NY: Doubleday, Page, 1927), 105.

10. McConnell, "The Day's Work of an American Airman on the Somme," 111–13.

11. Gordon, *The Lafayette Flying Corps*, 476.

12. Ibid., 342.

13. Jim McConnell, postcard to Paul Rockwell, January 24, 1917, W&L Archives.

14. Thénault, *The Story of the Lafayette Escadrille*, 120.

15. Parsons, *I Flew with the Lafayette Escadrille*, 238.

16. Jim McConnell to Paul Rockwell, February 7, 1917, W&L Archives.

17. Weeks, *Greater Love Hath No Man*, 196.

18. Parsons, *I Flew with the Lafayette Escadrille*, 235.

19. Jim McConnell to Marcelle Guerin, February 10, 1917, UVA Archives.

20. Gordon, *The Lafayette Flying Corps*, 57.

21. "The Fight Against STIs," BBC News Channel (online), October 16, 2005.

22. Dr. Clare Makepeace, "WWI Brothels: Why Troops Ignored Calls to Resist 'Temptation,'" BBC News Channel (online), February 27, 2014.

23. Howie-Willis, "The Australian Army's Two 'Traditional' Diseases: Gonorrhea and Syphilis," *Journal of Military and Veteran's Health* (Australia), vol. 27, no. 1.

24. "The British Army's fight against Venereal Disease in the 'Heroic Age of Prostitution'," *World War I Centenary*, Oxford University.

25. Snow, Dr. William F. and Swanson, Dr. Wilbur A., "Venereal Disease Control in the Army," *Journal of the American Medical Association*, August 10, 1918, 458.

26. Howie-Willis, "The Australian Army's Two 'Traditional' Diseases: Gonorrhea and Syphilis," *Journal of Military and Veteran's Health* (Australia), vol. 27, no. 1.

27. Snow, Dr. William F. and Swanson, Dr. Wilbur A., "Venereal Disease Control in the Army," *Journal of the American Medical Association*, August 10, 1918, 460.

28. Ian Howie-Willis, "The Australian Army's Two 'Traditional' Diseases: Gonorrhea and Syphilis—a Military-Medical History During the Twentieth Century," *Journal of Military and Veteran's Health* (Australia) 27, no. 1 (2019).

29. Jim McConnell to Paul Rockwell, February 14, 1917, W&L Archives.

30. Jim McConnell to Marcelle Guerin, February 14, 1917, UVA Archives.

31. Jim McConnell to Littleton W. Tazewell Jr., February 17, 1917, UVA Archives.

32. Jim McConnell to Marcelle Guerin, February 20, 1917, UVA Archives.

33. Jim McConnell to Paul Rockwell, February 25, 1917, W&L Archives.

34. Jim McConnell to Marcelle Guerin, February 26th, 1917, UVA Archives.

35. Gordon, *The Lafayette Flying Corps*, 57.

36. Jim McConnell to Henry A. Johnson, February 27, 1917, UVA Archives.

37. Edmond C. Genet, *An American for Lafayette: The Diaries of E. C. C. Genet* (Charlottesville: University Press of Virginia, 1980), 150.

38. Flammer, *The Vivid Air*, 301.

39. Paul Ayres Rockwell, *American Fighters in the Foreign Legion, 1914–1918* (Cambridge, MA: Houghton Mifflin, 1930), 251.

40. Nordhoff and Hall, *The Lafayette Flying Corps*, 1:343.

41. Genet, *An American for Lafayette*, 157.

Chapter 16: *Vive la France!*

1. Jim McConnell to Paul Rockwell, March 13, 1917, W&L Archives.

2. "Books of the Week Seen in Review and Comment," *The Sun* (New York), March 31, 1917, 6.

3. Harrison, "Pilots of the Skies," 7.

4. Nordhoff and Hall, *The Lafayette Flying Corps*, 1:343.

5. Rockwell, "Writings of the American Pilots in the Escadrille Lafayette," 131.

6. Rockwell, *American Fighters in the Foreign Legion, 1914–1918*, 251.

7. Colonel Paul Rockwell, interviewed by Cross & Cockade Society, 1962, USAF Oral History Program Interview 550, IRIS no. 0090450, 8.

8. Nordhoff and Hall, *The Lafayette Flying Corps*, 1:344.

9. Various, *N.124 Journal de Marche* 1 (March 16, 1917, Smithsonian Library.

10. Jay Winter and Blain Baggett, *The Great War and the Shaping of the 20th Century* (New York: Penguin Studio, 1996), 210.

11. Jim McConnell to Marcelle Guerin, March 16, 1917, UVA Archive.

12. Genet, *An American for Lafayette*, 164.

13. Ibid., 168.

14. "Carthage Youth Killed in Battle," *Hickory (NC) Daily Record*, March 23, 1917, 1.

15. Weeks, *Greater Love Hath No Man*, 103.

16. Unknown (probably Paul Rockwell), "Jim McConnell of Escadrille No. 124," *Red Cross*, July 1918, 24.

17. Charles Walthall, "An Exciting Recent Disco*very*," *Over the Front* 38, no. 4 (Winter 2023): 374.

18. E. A. Marshall to Paul Rockwell, March 24, 1917, UVA microfiche.

19. Thénault, *The Story of the Lafayette Escadrille*, 129.

20. Chouteau Johnson to Lewis Crenshaw, March 28, 1917, UVA microfiche.

21. Guttman, *SPA124 Lafayette Escadrille*, 69.

22. Thénault, *The Story of the Lafayette Escadrille*, 128.

23. Capt. Thénault to Julia Follansbee, ca. March 25, 1917, UVA microfiche.

24. Paul Rockwell, "Chicago Flyer Died for Love of France," *Chicago Daily News*, March 28, 1917 (UVA microfiche).

25. Sarah McConnell to Paul Rockwell, April 4, 1917, UVA Archives.

26. Mason, *The Lafayette Escadrille*, 189.

27. Chouteau Johnson to Lewis Crenshaw, March 28, 1917, UVA microfiche.

28. Chouteau Johnson to Paul Rockwell, March 27, 1917, UVA microfiche.

29. Parsons, *I Flew with the Lafayette Escadrille*, 252.

30. Chouteau Johnson to Paul Rockwell, March 27, 1917, UVA microfiche.

Epilogue

1. Rockwell, "Jim McConnell for France," 8–11.

2. Lewis Crenshaw to Judge Samuel McConnell, July 13, 1918, UVA microfiche.

3. Britton, "The Aviator."

4. Ruffin, *The Lafayette Escadrille*, xix.

5. Guerin, handwritten autobiography, 12.

6. Paul Rockwell to Dr. Douglas Tanner, November 15, 1976, UVA Archives.

7. Tanner, "Soaring Like An Eagle," 4.

8. Gordon, *The Lafayette Flying Corps*, 288.

BIBLIOGRAPHY

Archives

For conciseness, the names of the following archives have been shortened when used in footnotes and photo attributions. In the following list, the short name is given first, followed by a more complete description of the archive.

National Museum of the USAF (NMUSAF)

National Museum of the US Air Force, Research Division / MUA, 1100 Spaatz Street, Wright-Patterson AFB, Ohio.

North Carolina State Archives

Kiffin Y. Rockwell Papers, WWI Papers, Military Collection, State Archives of North Carolina, Raleigh, North Carolina.

National Air and Space Museum (NASM) Archives

James Rogers McConnell Collection [Truitt]. NASM.XXXX.0232. This collection was donated to the NASM in 1963 by James M. Truitt, a descendant of Jim's younger sister, Eleanor McConnell Truitt. Due to COVID concerns at the time of my research, I was unable to visit the museum to view the collection in person; however, they had previously given a microfiche copy of their collection to the University of Virginia. That university graciously loaned the microfiche cards to me, so my research was based on those copies. The original source materials are at the NASM. The collection also includes a photo album, which is not copied in the UVA microfiche cards but is available online from the NASM.

University of Virginia (UVA) Archives

James R. McConnell Collection, Albert and Shirley Small Special Collections Library, University of Virginia. This collection includes many letters from Jim McConnell, primarily to Marcelle Guerin and to Paul Rockwell, as well as documents and photos relating to Jim McConnell.

UVA Microfiche

Also in the University of Virginia Archives, but not a part of the Albert and Shirley Small Special Collections Library. This is a microfiche copy of the NASM Truitt collection, as noted above. Thirteen microfiche cards containing letters, magazines, newspaper clippings, and other materials relating to Jim McConnell's life and legacy. The letters are almost all typed transcripts of the original letters. In some instances the addressee's name has been omitted or cut out, probably out of privacy concerns because the addressee was still living at the time of the donation. I was often able to make an educated guess as to whom the letter was originally written to, on the basis of the content of the letter. When I quoted from these letters, I noted the addressee's name with a question mark, "(?)," to indicate it is not known for certain.

Virginia Military Institute Archives

VMI Archives, Preston Library, Lexington, Virginia.

Washington and Lee (W&L) Archives

Paul Ayres Rockwell Collection*, WLU Coll. 0301, Special Collections Department, Washington and Lee University, Lexington, Virginia.

* Paul Rockwell's papers are split into two collections at Washington & Lee University. Mr. Walker is the author of a biography of Lafayette pilot Ted Parsons. Presumably he had borrowed some of Paul Rockwell's papers to write this biography and donated them separately. In any event, to see the complete collection of Paul Rockwell's papers, you need to look at both collections.

Dale I. Walker Research Collection*, WLU Coll. 0334, Special Collections Department, James G. Leyburn Library, Lexington, Virginia.

Wright State University (WSU) Archives
The Raoul Lufbery Collection, 1917–1985 (MS-502). Box 1, file 3. Special Collections and Archives, Wright State University Libraries, 3640 Colonel Glenn Highway, Dayton, Ohio.

Books

Bailey, Frank W., and Christophe Cony. *The French Air Service War Chronology, 1914–1918*. London: Grub Street, 2001.

Bryan, Julien H. *Ambulance 464: "Encore des Blessés."* New York: Macmillan, 1918 (Google Books copy).

Buswell, Leslie. *Ambulance No. 10: Personal Letters from the Front*. Boston and New York: Houghton Mifflin, 1916. (US National Library of Medicine digitized copy.)

Chapman, Victor. *Victor Chapman's Letters from France*. New York: Macmillan, 1917 (Google Books copy).

Flammer, Philip M. *The Vivid Air*. Athens: University of Georgia Press, 1981.

Genet, Edmond C. *An American for Lafayette: The Diaries of E. C. C. Genet*. Charlottesville: University Press of Virginia, 1980.

Gibbons, Floyd. *The Red Knight of Germany: The Story of Baron von Richthofen*. Garden City, NY: Doubleday, Page, 1927.

Gordon, Dennis. *The Lafayette Flying Corps: The American Volunteers in the French Air Service in World War I*. Atglen, PA: Schiffer, 2000.

Guerin, Marcelle. Handwritten autobiography. UVA Archives.

Guttman, Jon. *The Origin of the Fighter Aircraft*. Yardley, PA: Westholme, 2009.

Guttman, Jon. *SPA124 Lafayette Escadrille: American Volunteer Airmen in World War I*. Wellingborough, UK: Osprey, 2004.

Hall, Lieutenant Bert. *En l'air (In the Air): Three Years On and Above Three Fronts*. New York: New Library, 1918 (Google Books copy).

Hall, Lieutenant Bert, and Lieutenant John J. Niles. *One Man's War: The Story of the Lafayette Escadrille*. New York: Henry Holt, 1929.

Hansen, Arlen J. *Gentlemen Volunteers: The Story of the American Ambulance Drivers in the First World War*. New York: Arcade, 1996.

Hart, Peter. *The Great War: A Combat History of the First World War*. New York: Oxford, 2015.

Horne, Alistair. *The Price of Glory*. Harmondsworth, UK: Penguin, 1962 (1978 reprint).

King, David Wooster. *L. M. 8046: An Intimate Story of the French Foreign Legion*. New York: Duffield, 1927 (Internet Archive, 2014, https://archive.org/details/lm8046intimatest00davi).

Macdonald, Lyn. *The Roses of No Man's Land*. New York: Atheneum, 1989.

Mason, Herbert Molloy, Jr. *Lafayette Escadrille*. New York: Smithmark, 1964.

McConnell, James R. *Carthage, North Carolina*. Carthage Board of Trade (29-page booklet), 1914. UVA microfiche.

McConnell, James R. *Flying for France: With the American Escadrille at Verdun*. New York: Doubleday, Page, 1917.

McConnell, James R. *The Select Section of the South*. Randolph & Cumberland Railroad (22-page booklet), n.d., UVA microfiche.

Nordhoff, Charles Bernard, and James Norman Hall. *The Lafayette Flying Corps*. Cambridge, MA: Houghton Mifflin, 1920 (Google Books copy).

Pardoe, Blaine. *The Bad Boy: Bert Hall; Aviator and Mercenary of the Skies*. Stroud, UK: Fonthill, 2012 (Kindle edition).

Parsons, Edwin C. *I Flew with the Lafayette Escadrille*. Indianapolis, IN: E. C. Seale, 1963.

Rockwell, Paul Ayres. *American Fighters in the Foreign Legion, 1914–1918*. Cambridge, MA: Houghton Mifflin, 1930 (Internet Archive, 2014, https://archive.org/details/americanfightersOOpaul).

Rockwell, Paul Ayres. *War Letters of Kiffin Yates Rockwell*. Garden City, NY: Country Life Press, 1925.

Ruffin, Steven A. *The Lafayette Escadrille: A Photo History of the First American Fighter Squadron*. Havertown, PA: Casemate, 2016.

Seawell, Meade. *Tale of a Tarheel Town*. Raleigh, NC: Edgeworth & Broughton, 1970.

Thénault, Captain George. *The Story of the Lafayette Escadrille*. Boston: Small, Maynard, 1921 (Google Books copy).

Thénault, Captain George. *The Story of the Lafayette Escadrille* (typewritten draft, unpublished, ca. 1932). W&L Archives.

Various. *Friends of France / The Field Service of the American Ambulance: Described by Its Members*. Boston and New York: Houghton Mifflin, 1916 (Project Gutenberg ebook).

Various. *Diary of Section VIII: American Ambulance Field Service.* Printed only for private distribution, 1917 (US National Library of Medicine digitized copy, https://collections.nlm.nih.gov/catalog/nlm:nlmuid-14310010R-bk).

Various. *Escadrille N.124 Journal de Marche* 1 (August 14, 1916–September 9, 1917). Smithsonian Library, https://library.si.edu/digital-library/book/escadrillen124j00.

Various. *Escadrille N.124 Journal de Marche* 2 (September 10, 1917–February 25, 1918). Smithsonian Library, https://library.si.edu/digital-library/book/escadrillen124j00.

Various. *Official Automobile Blue Book 1901.* New York: Official Automobile Blue Book, 1901 (Google digitized copy, https://babel.hathitrust.org/cgi/pt?id=hvd.32044056217144&view=1up&seq=5).

Weeks, Alice S. *Greater Love Hath No Man.* Boston: Bruce Humphries, 1939.

White, E. B. *Essays of E. B. White.* New York: Harper Colophon, 1977.

Whitehouse, "Arch." *Legion of the Lafayette.* New York: Doubleday, 1962.

Willis, Harold B., with Jeffrey S. Williams. *Through a Cloud of Bullets.* St. Paul, MN: Antietam Creek, 2019 (Kindle edition).

Winslow, Carroll Dana. *With the French Flying Corps.* New York: Scribner's, 1917 (Google Books copy).

Winter, Jay, and Blain Baggett. *The Great War and the Shaping of the 20th Century.* New York: Penguin Studio, 1996.

Magazine Articles

Balsley, Clyde H. "The Diary of H. Clyde Balsley" *Cross & Cockade: Journal of the Society of World War I Aero Historians* 18, no. 2 (Summer 1977): 97–124.

Baur, John T. "The Official Automobile Blue Book, 1901–1929: Precursor to the American Road Map." *Cartographic Perspectives* 62 (Winter 2009). File:///D:/Asus%20WebStorage/StevenTTom@aol.com/MySyncFolder/Jim%20McConnell/Books%20&%20Articles/Official%20Automobile%20Blue%20Book%20-%20.pdf.

Britton, Rick. "The Aviator." *MHQ: The Quarterly Journal of Military History* 31, no. 3 (Spring 2019). Republished by HistoryNet as "From Ambulance Driver to Fighter Pilot," https://www.historynet.com/the-aviator.htm.

Harrison, Harry Sydnor. "Pilots of the Skies." *Colliers*, August 4, 1917, 7, 26–27, 29.

Mattox, Henry E. "Chariots of Wrath: North Carolinians Who Flew for France in World War I." *North Carolina Historical Review* 73, no. 3 (July 1996): 287–308.

McConnell, James R. "The Day's Work of an American Airman on the Somme." *National Service* 1, no. 1 (March 1917): 107–15.

McConnell, James R. "Flying for France." *World's Work*, November 1916, 41–53.

McConnell, James R. "Flying for France." *World's Work*, March 1917, 497–509.

McConnell, James R. "With the American Ambulance in France." *The Outlook*, September 15, 1915, 125–32.

McConnell, Samuel P. "The Chicago Bomb Case." *Harper's*, May 1934, 730–39.

Olley, Jonathan. "The Forbidden Forest." *Orion*, undated but probably March 2011. https://orionmagazine.org/article/the-forbidden-forest/.

Rockwell, Paul A. "Jim McConnell for France." *The State*, February 1979, 8–11 (now *Our State* magazine). https://digital.ncdcr.gov/digital/collection/p16062coll18/id/58312.

Rockwell, Paul A. "Kiffin Rockwell's Letters to His Brother." *Every Week* 5, no. 23 (December 3, 1917): 21.

Rockwell, Paul A. "Writings of the American Pilots in the Escadrille Lafayette." *Ex Libris* 1, no. 5 (November 1923).

Ruffin, Steven A. "Flying in the Great War: Rx for Misery." *Over the Front* 14, no. 2 (1999) and 17, no. 2 (2002). http://www.overthefront.com/over-the-front-journal/back-issues.

"Samuel Parsons McConnell." *Successful American: A Monthly Magazine for the Home Circle and the Business Office*, October 1902 (digitized by Google Books).

Snow, Dr. William F., and Dr. Wilbur A. Swanson. "Venereal Disease Control in the Army." *Journal of the American Medical Association*, August 10, 1918, 45–6. https://profiles.nlm.nih.gov/spotlight/lw/catalog/nlm:nlmuid-101584931X7-doc.

Snyder, Charles E., with Lonnie Raidor, Noel Shirley, and Greg VanWyngarden. "One Man's Photo Album." *Over the Front* 5, no. 4 (1990): 319.

Tanner, Douglas W. "Soaring Like an Eagle: James McConnell, American Aviator for France." Unpublished article, UVA Archives.

Toelle, Alan D. "A White-Faced Cow and the Operational History of the Escadrille Americaine N.124 to September 1916." *Over the Front* 24, no. 4 (Winter 2009): 292–337.

Unknown (probably Paul Rockwell). "Jim McConnell of Escadrille No. 124." *Red Cross*, July 1918.

Walthall, Charles, "An Exciting Recent Discovery," *Over the Front* 38, no. 4 (Winter 2023): 374.

Wynne, H. Hugh. "Escadrille Lafayette." *Cross and Cockade* 2, no. 1 (1961).

Newspaper Articles

"Altgeld Will Be Named." *Chicago Daily News*, June 23 1893, 2.
"American Ambulance Wins High Army Honor." *The Sun* (New York), September 19, 1915, 3.
"American Eyes of French Army: Volunteer Aviators at Battle Front." *Chicago Daily News*, August 25, 1916, 1.
"American Fliers in Big Air Battle." *The Sun* (New York), November 13, 1916, 2.
"Americans Learn to Be War Pilots in French School of Aviation at Pau." *The Sun* (New York), March 26, 2016, 2.
"Americans Meet on French Front for First Time in Seven Years." *The Sun* (New York), July 12, 1915, 3.
"Books of the Week Seen in Review and Comment." *The Sun* (New York), March 31, 1917, 6.
"Boy Autoist Here from East." *Chicago Daily News*, July 31, 1902, 1.
"Boys End Long Auto Trip." *Chicago Tribune*, August 1, 1902, 3.
"Boy Nears End of Long Trip on Auto." *Chicago Tribune*, July 29, 1902, 7.
"Carthage Youth Killed in Battle." *Hickory (NC) Daily Record*, March 23, 1917, 1.
"Cannon Fray Grows Havoc at St. Mihiel." *Chicago Daily News*, September, 24, 1915, 4.
"Colossal Construction Company." *The Sun* (New York), March 30, 1901, 1.
"Commonplace of War." *Chicago Daily News*, September 29, 1915, 10.
"Decker's Story of the Fighting." *Chicago Daily News*, April 16, 1915, 10.
"Dodge Shells Flee to House Cellars." *Chicago Daily News*, May 22, 1915, 6.
"Flee Big Benzine Shells." *Chicago Daily News*, June 4 1915, 3.
"From the War Zone," *Chicago Daily News*, July 16 1915, 10.
"Fuller Firm Is Neutral." *Chicago Daily News*, February 13, 1900, 1.
"George A. Fuller Is Dead." *Chicago Daily News*, December 14, 1900, 1.
"High Above the Battle Zone in France." *Chicago Daily News*, July 1, 1916, 6.
"Hot Fight over the Veto." *Chicago Daily News*, July 10, 1897, 1.
"Hundreds Each Night Flee Pont-a-Moussoun." *Chicago Daily News*, July 21, 1915, 7.
"Jefferson Statue Unveiled." *Free Lance* (Fredericksburg, VA), June 18, 1910, 1.
"Judge McConnell Is Out," *Chicago Daily News*, October 6, 1894, 1.
"Judge M'Connell Resigns." *The Sun* (New York), January 5, 1904, 9.
"Mayo Methot's Career Told." *Sunday Oregonian*, June 13, 1915, 11.
"May Vote Bonds to Build New Railroad." *State Dispatch* (Burlington, NC), March, 29, 1911, 1.
"McConnell at the Front." *Charlotte Daily Observer*, July 14, 1915, 4.
"Mow Down Civilians in City on Frontier." *Chicago Daily News*, June 1, 1915, 3.
"Now Owns Lake and Mountain." *New York Daily Tribune*, September 28, 1909, 11.
"Randolph and Cumberland Railway." *The Courier* (Asheboro, NC), November 30, 1911, 4.
"Rescuers Win Praise." *Chicago Daily News*, July 19, 1915, 10.
Rockwell, Paul. "Chicago Flyer Died for Love of France." *Chicago Daily News*, March 28, 1917.
"Sam Parks Is Found Guilty of Extortion." *New York World*, October 30, 1903, 1.
"Sea Plane Shot Down in Thrilling Air Duel." *Chicago Daily News*, October 14, 1915, 4.
"Shells Cut Strange Capers; Men Escape." *Chicago Daily News*, July 30, 1915, 4.
"Shells Maul US Ambulance." *Chicago Daily News*, May 19, 1915, 4.
"Teuton Shells Rain on Pont-à-Mousson." *Chicago Daily News*, September 21, 1915, 4.
"The Record Postal Vote." *Chicago Daily News*, October 15, 1896, 4.
"Throw over Parks Men." *New York Daily Tribune*, November 24, 1903, 4.
"Trench Secrets Laid Bare as Leaves Fall." *Chicago Daily News*, November 1, 1915, 4.
"Trenches Captured and Lost by French." *Chicago Daily News*, May 19, 1915, 4.
"US Realty Reformers Out." *The Sun* (New York), January 16, 1904, 9.
"Wedding of Miss Stein." *Chicago Daily News*, March 9, 1900, 3.
"While They Wait." *Chicago Daily News*, June 14, 1915, 10.
"Women Flee Frontier Town." *Chicago Daily News*, May 26, 1915, 4.
"Work Being Done by American Ambulances in France." *The Sun* (New York), June 27, 1915, 4.

Websites

"The Ambulance." *WWI Centennial News* (podcast), episode 82, September 7, 2018. https://www.podcast.worldwar1centennial.org/page/4/.

"Baldwin, James Mark." https://www.encyclopedia.com/people/medicine/psychology-and-psychiatry-biographies/james-mark-baldwin.

"The British Army's Fight Against Venereal Disease in the 'Heroic Age of Prostitution.'" *World War I Centenary*, Oxford University. https://portal.sds.ox.ac.uk/articles/online_resource/The_British_Army_Fight_Against_Venereal_Disease_In_The_Heroic_Age_Of_Prostitution/25837285/1?file=46374286.

"Ethics and the Unions, Part 1." Industrial Workers of the World. https://archive.iww.org/history/library/Dolgoff/newbeginning/1/.

"The Fight Against STIs." BBC News Channel (online), October 16, 2005. http://news.bbc.co.uk/2/hi/programmes/panorama/4347912.stm.

"History of US Army Medical Service Corps—the Ambulance Service." https://history.army.mil/Portals/143/Images/Publications/Publication%20By%20Title%20Images/H%20Pdf/CMH_Pub_30-19-1.pdf?ver=tx7lOc4F_dNL22gDVD9eLQ%3d%3d.

Howie-Willis, Ian. "The Australian Army's Two 'Traditional' Diseases: Gonorrhea and Syphilis—a Military-Medical History During the Twentieth Century," *Journal of Military and Veteran's Health* (Australia) 27, no. 1 (2019): 11–22

"IMP Society." Wikipedia. https://en.wikipedia.org/wiki/IMP_Society.

"The Imp Society at the University of Virginia." https://aig.alumni.virginia.edu/imp/about/history/.

Kastenberg, Joshua E. "Field Marshall Douglas Haig: A Negative Leadership Lesson in Military History." *The Reporter* 32, no. 1 (2005). https://digitalrepository.unm.edu/law_facultyscholarship/430.

Makepeace, Dr. Clare. "WWI Brothels: Why Troops Ignored Calls to Resist 'Temptation.'" BBC News Channel (online), February 27, 2014. https://www.bbc.com/news/uk-england-25762151.

"North Carolina Railroads—Randolph & Cumberland Railroad / Railway." https://www.carolana.com/NC/Transportation/railroads/nc_rrs_randolph_cumberland.html.

"Priest's Woods." https://www.lieux-insolites.fr/cicatrice/14-18/bois/bois.htm (French website). Translated by Google Translate.

"St. Mihiel Salient—Bois le Prêtre." https://www.pierreswesternfront.nl/st-mihiel-salient-bois-le-pretre-priesterwald-fey-en-haye-destroyed-village-kuehlewein-brunnen-vilcey-sur-trey (French website). Translated by Google Translate.

"Seven Society." Wikipedia. https://en.wikipedia.org/wiki/Seven_Society.

UVA Library website. https://explore.lib.virginia.edu/exhibits/show/mcconnell/introduction.

Interviews/Correspondence/Miscellaneous

Colonel Paul Rockwell, interviewed by the Cross & Cockade Society, 1962. USAF Oral History Program Interview 550, IRIS no. 0090450.

Email to the author, August 22, 2018, from Allison Finkelstein, historian at the US Citizenship & Immigration Services History Office and Library.

Email to the author, February 2, 2022, from Sheryl Kaufmann, associate director of advancement services, Haverford School, 450 Lancaster Avenue, Haverford, PA.

Email to the author, May 7, 2020, from Anna Tserelova, academic records coordinator, Office of the University Registrar, University of Virginia.

House, Robert B. (probably, after an interview with Loula Rockwell). *Addenda to Rockwell Material.* North Carolina State Archives.

Phone interview by the author, March 6, 2010, with Mr. William James Kenneth Rockwell (Colonel Paul Rockwell's son).

Phone interview by the author, May 8, 2018, with Mr. Richard Churchill, senior supervisor of technical services at Savage Arms Corporation. Mr. Churchill said that to his knowledge, the Savage "Screaming Indian" logo was never used on ammunition boxes or crates, but a black-and-white version of the image was used on the operating manual for the Lewis machine gun (which they manufactured), and they used that logo on their catalogs from 1900 to 1926.

Phone interview by the author, October 20, 2020, with Janeice McConnell, Jim McConnell's niece.

PHOTO CREDITS

Chapter 1: Son of a Judge

Jim McConnell (baby photo): Smithsonian National Air and Space Museum (NASM 9A14466-003).

Judge Samuel P. McConnell: Public domain image from *Successful American: A Monthly Magazine for the Home Circle and the Business Office*, October 1902, Writer's Press Association, Park Row Building, New York City, p. 623.

Jim, age 11: Smithsonian National Air and Space Museum (NASM 9A14466-009).

Jim's car: Smithsonian National Air and Space Museum (NASM 9A14466-013).

Jim McConnell at UVA: Public domain image from McConnell, James R, "Flying for France," *World's Work Magazine*, March 1917, 502.

Jim, with bagpipes: Smithsonian National Air and Space Museum (NASM 9A14466-019).

Chapter 2: The American Ambulance Field Service

A "wounded" Jim being comforted by Marcelle: Smithsonian National Air and Space Museum (NASM 9A14466-025).

Jim with Paul Rockwell: Albert and Shirley Small Special Collections Library, University of Virginia.

Jim McConnell in his ambulance: Smithsonian National Air and Space Museum (NASM 9A14466-026).

Chapter 3: Pont-a-Mousson

The St. Mihiel Salient: 1915 German map (public domain) from "St. Mihiel Salient – Bois le Prêtre, " French web site https://www.pierreswesternfront.nl/st-mihiel-salient-bois-le-pretre-priesterwald-fey-en-haye-destroyed-village-kuehlewein-brunnen-vilcey-sur-trey, with annotations by author.

Jim in his American Ambulance Service uniform: Smithsonian National Air and Space Museum (NASM 9A14466-026).

Chapter 4: With the American Ambulance Service

Jim with one of the large ambulances: Smithsonian National Air and Space Museum (NASM 9A14466-028).

Chapter 5: Changing Gears

Mrs. Alice Weeks: Courtesy of the State Archives of North Carolina.

Jim in his steel "fireman's helmet": Photo courtesy of the National Museum of the United States Air Force.

Chapter 6: Learning to Fly

A Bleriot "Penguin": Photo from *The Lafayette Flying Corps* by Charles Nordhoff and James Norman Hall (public domain).

Jim in a Bleriot trainer: Smithsonian National Air and Space Museum (NASM 9A14466-034).

Jim in his flight leathers and crash helmet: Smithsonian National Air and Space Museum (NASM 9A14466-034).

Jim in his French army uniform and kepi: Smithsonian National Air and Space Museum (NASM 9A14466-029).

Chapter 7: Advanced Training

A Nieuport 11 in flight: https://commons.wikimedia.org/wiki/File:Nieuport_11_flyover.jpg. Wikimedia Commons (public domain).

Morane-Saulnier Type L "Parasol": https://commons.wikimedia.org/wiki/File:Champ_d%27aviation_d%27Amiens._Monoplan_Morane-Saulnier_L_18-07-15_-_Fonds_Berthelé_-_49Fi1871-38.jpg, Wikimedia Commons (public domain).

The *Pittsburgh Press* headline: Author's photo, taken at the Heinz History Center, Pittsburgh, PA.

Jim next to a training Nieuport: Smithsonian National Air and Space Museum (NASM 9A14466-034).

Jim in his leather flight jacket: Smithsonian National Air and Space Museum (NASM 9A14466-034).

Kiffin Rockwell next to Elliot Cowdin's Nieuport 11: Paul Ayres Rockwell Collection, Special Collections Department, Washington & Lee University.

Chapter 8: Lounging at Luxeuil

Villa Chatigny Today: Author's photo, taken in 2014.

Jim McConnell playing pool: Courtesy of the Virginia Military Institute Archives.

The first American Escadrille pilots at Luxeuil: Paul Ayres Rockwell Collection, Special Collections Department, Washington & Lee University.

Touring in the Vosges Mountains: Paul Ayres Rockwell Collection, Special Collections Department, Washington & Lee University.

Kiffin Rockwell regulating his gun: Paul Ayres Rockwell Collection, Special Collections Department, Washington & Lee University.

Lewis gun tipped down for reloading: https://www.airdromeaeroplanes.com/PhotoGallery/Historical%20Images/slides/LewisNieuportBebe.html (public domain).

Jim with two unidentified mechanics and freshly painted "Hotfoot" motif: Albert and Shirley Small Special Collections Library, University of Virginia.

Jim McConnell posing for the cinematographer: Albert and Shirley Small Special Collections Library, University of Virginia.

Captain Thenault "briefing" his pilots: Albert and Shirley Small Special Collections Library, University of Virginia.

Chapter 9: Verdun!

Fort Douaumont before the Battle of Verdun: https://commons.wikimedia.org/wiki/File:Fort_Douaumont_Anfang_1916.jpg (public domain).

Fort Douamont after the bombardment: File: Fort Douaumont Ende 1916.jpg, Wikimedia Commons (public domain).

Fort Douaumont as it appeared to the soldiers who fought there: https://commons.wikimedia.org/wiki/File:Nach_der_Wiedererst%C3%BCrmung_des_Forts_Douaumont.jpg (public domain).

Kiffin Rockwell has what appears to be a difficult conversation with Capt. Thenault: Paul Ayres Rockwell Collection, Special Collections Department, Washington & Lee University.

Chapter 10: Death Strikes

Escadrille aircraft at Behonne: Paul Ayres Rockwell Collection, Special Collections Department, Washington & Lee University.

Victor Chapman next to his damaged Nieuport: Courtesy of the State Archives of North Carolina.

Clyde Balsley, in front of his Nieuport: Paul Ayres Rockwell Collection, Special Collections Department, Washington & Lee University.

Bert Hall with "Backwards BERT" Aircraft: Public domain image from "Flying for France" in *World's Work Magazine*, March 1917, 502.

Chapter 11: A Hard Job

Jim showing off the Hotfoot emblem: Smithsonian National Air and Space Museum (NASM 9A14466-032).

Charles Nungesser in front of his Nieuport 17: Paul Ayres Rockwell Collection, Special Collections Department, Washington & Lee University.

German Observation Balloon being launched: https://commons.wikimedia.org/wiki/File:Bundesarchiv_Bild_102-00321A,_Westfront,_Aufsteigender_Fesselballon.jpg (Creative Commons license).

Norman Prince examining his le Prieur Rockets: Paul Ayres Rockwell Collection, Special Collections Department, Washington & Lee University.

Raoul Lufbury in front of a Nieuport at Behonne: Paul Ayres Rockwell Collection, Special Collections Department, Washington & Lee University.

Paul Pavelka in front of the "Hoodooed" Nieuport: Courtesy of the State Archives of North Carolina.

Chapter 12: Depot des Éclopés

Whiskey: Paul Ayres Rockwell Collection, Special Collections Department, Washington & Lee University.

Kiffin Rockwell, Whiskey, Bill Thaw, Paul Pavelka: Courtesy of the State Archives of North Carolina.

Kiffin Rockwell in front of his Nieuport 17: Courtesy of the State Archives of North Carolina.

Chapter 14: End of the De Luxe War

1906 Savage Arms catalog: Public domain.

N.124 insignia: Photo courtesy of the Steve Ruffin collection.

Jim and his Nieuport, ready to fly from Cachy: Paul Ayres Rockwell Collection, Special Collections Department, Washington & Lee University.

Jim McConnell and Paul Rockwell at Paul's wedding: Albert and Shirley Small Special Collections Library, University of Virginia.

Christmas with British friends, 1916: Paul Ayres Rockwell Collection, Special Collections Department, Washington & Lee University.

Chapter 16: Vive la France!

Groupe de Combat 13 commandant Phillipe Féquant: Photo courtesy of the Jean-Marc Simon collection.

Leutnant Heinrich Kämmerer, seated on the wheel of his Albatros DIII: Photo courtesy of the Jean-Marc Simon collection.

Epilogue

The Aviator: Photo courtesy of Daniel Kieth Addison

INDEX